YANKEE POLITICS IN RURAL VERMONT

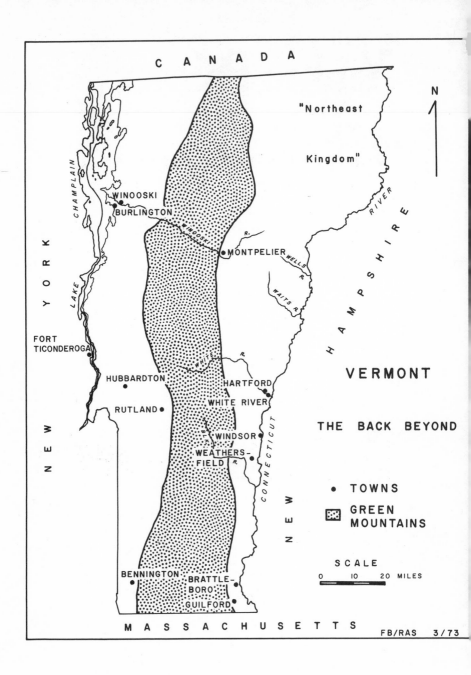

CANADA

"Northeast

Kingdom"

N

NEW YORK

LAKE CHAMPLAIN

WINOOSKI
BURLINGTON

WINOOSKI R.

MONTPELIER

WELLS R.

WAITS R.

RIVER

NEW HAMPSHIRE

FORT
TICONDEROGA

WHITE R.

HUBBARDTON

HARTFORD

RUTLAND

WHITE RIVER

WINDSOR

WEATHERS-
FIELD

R.

CONNECTICUT

NEW

VERMONT

THE BACK BEYOND

• TOWNS

GREEN
MOUNTAINS

SCALE
0   10   20 MILES

BENNINGTON

BRATTLE-
BORO
GUILFORD

MASSACHUSETTS

FB/RAS 3/73

Yankee Politics

in Rural Vermont

by Frank M. Bryan

The University Press of New England
Hanover, New Hampshire 1974

The University Press
Of New England

Member Institutions

Brandeis University
Clark University
Dartmouth College
The University of New Hampshire
The University of Rhode Island
The University of Vermont

Published with assistance from
the Andrew W. Mellon Foundation
Printed in the United States of America

To my mother, Jeanne Allen Bryan,
who aside from being a Democrat,
is one of the greatest Vermonters
who ever lived

Preface

At war with New York, shooting it out with the British, nego-
tiating with Canada, storming Congress to demand admittance
into the Union, playing Robin Hood with Albany sheriffs, capturing the largest British fort in America even before the Revolutionary War had begun, raiding Montreal with a handful of
irregulars and harassing Burgoyne's troops all the way to
Saratoga—that is Vermont as Vermonters see it. The exploits
continue into the War between the States and beyond—many
true, some myth, all of them feeding a healthy state ego.

There is a basis for self-congratulation. During the Great
Depression, Vermonters had the foresight to turn up their noses
at a grand federal project to pave the Green Mountains. The
nation lifted an eyebrow at this seemingly arrogant refusal to
accept an economic transfusion by building an asphalt highway
along the backbone of Vermont, but nobody laughs in this present age of environmental crisis. Vermonters have always shun-
ned centralism, and they voted Republican for a century after
their first vote for Lincoln in 1860. They believe in balanced
budgets and the Protestant Ethic. They joined Maine to reject
Roosevelt in 1936. Conservative? Yet in the 1950's they were
strongly against Joseph McCarthy; they have chosen to send the
liberal George Aiken to Washington for over thirty years running; and their rebuff to Barry Goldwater in 1964 was greater
than the national average.

Vermont ranks fourth nationally in expenditures for education. It has always helped its needy at rates surpassing national
averages, has maintained one of the finest highway systems in
America, and has faced up to the environmental crisis with
some of the toughest legislation anywhere in the United States.
Vermont really means it when it talks of democracy and "maximum feasible participation" and has proved it by preserving

town meetings into the age of technology. Finally, Vermonters are willing to back up their convictions where it counts most—in the pocketbook. Although fewer than half a million Vermonters are sprinkled over a wide expanse of forested and pastured granite, they consistently pay one of the highest per-capita tax bills in the nation.

Vermont, then, does not fit the usual patterns. It has combined ruralism with technology, fiscal conservatism with a social-welfare mentality, not much wealth with a lot of services, local democracy with an effective state government, and total one-party control with a degree of political responsiveness. And nowhere is it so unpredictable as in politics. In the face of the Eisenhower victory of 1952, the Democrats made their first great breakthrough in state politics. In the face of the Nixon landslide of 1972, Vermonters staged the biggest local upset in the history of the state, electing an out-of-state Catholic Democrat to the governorship on the theme that Vermont is for Vermonters. No wonder the attempts to make sense of its political system have been like milking a first-calf heifer: no matter how carefully one proceeds, the outcome remains in doubt.

This book is about politics in Vermont. I hope it will add to the literature of comparative state politics in at least two areas, the first of which is that it will increase the rather limited number of books dealing in depth with the political systems of individual states, and secondly, by using Vermont as a study base, that it will add some light to an array of concerns involving construction of theory. One of the more important of these concerns is the relationship between population density and politics; another is the role of one-party politics in the political system.

The book is also concerned with political change. The data base extends from the post World War II years through 1972, encompassing a quarter century that saw Vermont emerge from its limbo on the outskirts of the urban-industrial age into the age of technology. Politically, the state underwent a metamorphosis. I have attempted to measure and assess the new system as it unfolded, and to predict the direction of its future.

I thank Joe Wood and Richard Staab for their fine cartography. My former teacher Hope Kjellerup of Newbury helped with the editing of an earlier draft and has encouraged my work. My brother Dave critically read parts of the book and has my thanks for his perceptive comments. At Saint Michael's College, George Olgyay was supportive. My thanks go also to many of my students, in particular to Ken Bruno, whose senior thesis prompted me to write Chapter 5, and to Peter Hooper and Jim Gorski for their faith. Edward T. Rowe was an inspiration when I worked as his graduate teaching assistant at the University of Connecticut. His reading of the manuscript was thorough and of tremendous value. Most of all, a grateful acknowledgment is due Everett Ladd, who in the midst of a busy year took the time to help me through the many difficulties of book writing. His insightful judgment, hard work, professionalism, and support for my work over the last several years made the development of this book possible. Donna Crosby Bryan deserves much credit for any value the book may have. She spent so many of her nights behind a typewriter or over data sheets in the pursuit of a cause that must have seemed, to one who is concerned by nature with the beautiful things of life, utterly senseless. She did it anyway, and I will always be complimented.

Finally, there is Barbara, who wrote the computer programs, typed manuscript, did all the graphic work, made our cabin beside the pond sparkle with her flowers and her smiles, put up with my tantrums, and through it all maintained her sense of humor. Without her, quite simply if unoriginally, the book would never have been finished.

Winooski   F. M. B.
April 1973

Contents

List of Tables

List of Maps and Figures

YANKEE POLITICS IN RURAL VERMONT

Introduction

The most recent book on rural politics was published before the election of President Eisenhower.[1] Although there has been some direct attention to the subject since, mostly by sociologists, and tangential exposure has been provided by students of state and local government and (recently) comparative state politics, the fact remains that rural politics have been neglected.

We have witnessed for some time a pervading academic concentration on cities and their problems. Whatever the cause-effect relationship that spawned the flood of literature on the urban "crisis," it has been astonishing even in an age of scholastic opportunism. Urbanologists have appeared from everywhere to staff mushrooming urban affairs centers, programs, institutions, and departments across the country. But although these specialists have strained to include in their vision a complete panorama of urban-related phenomena, they have not taken account of the most urban-related factor of all—ruralism.

"Burn your cities and leave our farms," said William Jennings Bryan, "and your cities will spring up again as if by magic; but destroy our farms, and the grass will grow in the streets of every city in the country."[2] Bryan's biases are obvious, and certainly no one contends that American rural life can endure without the cities, yet the simplistic notion that American cities can endure without rural life underlies the failure to concentrate on the "hinges" (as Robert Redfield calls them) between the country and city.[3]

1. Lane W. Lancaster, *Government in Rural America* (New York: Van Nostrand, 1952).
2. Speech before the Democratic National Convention, 1898.
3. Redfield, *Peasant Society and Culture* (Chicago: University of Chicago Press, 1956), pp. 42-43. See also his *The Little Community* (Chicago: University of Chicago Press, 1955) and *The Primitive World and Its Transformations* (Ithaca, N.Y.: Cornell University Press, 1953).

Even a vigorous attempt to understand the relation between urban and rural politics will be doomed unless we solidify what we know about politics in rural places. That understanding is minuscule indeed, and has not provided the heuristic energy even to land us on "the first rung of theoretical thought."[4] Scholastically, this has had severe consequences, and nowhere are they as visible as in the literature addressing rural-urban linkages and their causal relationships.

Cities swirl in a universe of interacting forces, and their ties to the wide stretches of America which lie just beyond the last traffic lights become more complex, not less. Fully 70 percent of the people are now living in metropolitan areas, but they dwell on only one percent of the land space of the nation. The other 99 percent of America, containing fifty million people, must be dealt with if the cities are to sustain life. Rural areas are too crucial to be dismissed as a subject of study.

Another reason for studying rural politics involves a new research syndrome: "comparative state politics," the growth of which is primarily concerned with two post World War II developments in political science: the revolution in the field of comparative government—based on a belief in observable "laws" of political behavior, emphasis on functionalism as an analytical tool, and implicit faith in the utility of comparison.

There is a second development, which arose from research in the field of state politics itself and is divided along vertical and horizontal lines. *Vertically,* the new research focuses on a single or small number of systems; scholars seek to test broad-gauge generalizations by concentrating on limited environments; the focus is generally on either the legislature or on the party system, or on the relationship between the two. The *horizontal* approach grew from two distinct sources. The first came with the interest in party responsibility of the early 1950's, which lent added meaning to studies of party competition in the states. The attempt to measure party strength systematically on a cross-state basis is the first constant thread of horizontal research that can be identified in the myriad of studies dealing with state politics. The second came when the debate over reapportionment opened a new field of investigation. The two

4. David Easton, *The Political System* (New York: Alfred A. Knopf, 1953), p. 56.

steps in this process were studies proposing formulas for measuring the degree of malapportionment in state legislatures, and studies correlating policy outcomes in the states with degrees of malapportionment: these attempted to shed light on the theses of "invidious discrimination." It was a crucial development, for it injected the policy variable into cross-state research. Both these efforts have merged to promote new explorations that deal with the impact of party competition on public policy, the relation of economic inputs with political outputs, and, more generally, ecological development and political change.

The present book, a depth analysis of a single state, will contribute to the study of comparative state politics by way of the vertical approach. We hope to fill the void that exists to date in the many studies done on single-state systems. We also intend to explore the nature of rural politics as such by using the state of Vermont as a case study and by placing the results in the general perspective of state political systems.

Other factors have magnetized the rural setting as a focus for new and intensified research: (1) The tools of modern quantitative analysis were not available when ruralism was more widespread. (2) Americanists generally agree that demographic movements in the next decades will involve the repopulation of rural areas. People are increasingly seeking to live apart from one another. Urban areas are degenerating, and suburbia has lost its charm. Americans are looking with their hearts and pocketbooks into the back beyond. Their potential repopulation of rural areas demands that we learn more about the politics of modern ruralism. (3) Finally, most of what we know and say about rural politics and society is built upon the mythology surrounding men like Jefferson and Tocqueville, whose exaggerations have been enshrined while their good sense has been forgotten. "Those that labor in the earth," said Jefferson, "are the chosen people of God."

This book focuses in detail on what we believe are the two most important functional mechanisms in the political system— for inputs, the party system (Chapter 3) and for outputs, the legislature (Chapter 4). A brief historical overview (Chapter 1) and an analysis of the people who govern the system (Chapter 2) open the book. A case study in statewide decisionmaking (Chapter 5) and an assessment of how political life will develop in the modern rural technopolity (Chapter 6) conclude it.

One

The Back Beyond

It has been said that if one were to flatten Vermont, it would be as large as Texas. When the last glacier receded from northern New England 12,000 years ago, it had made Vermont the most mountainous area of any state now in the Union. The glaciers had given her no mountains of grandeur, high and massive, but thousands of hill-mountains, soft and round in contour and rarely higher than 4000 feet. Vermont is a land of ups and downs.

Where there is a valley, there is a stream; where there is a stream, there is bottom land; and bottom land attracts farmers. This separation by hill and valley is the nature of Vermont ruralism—people living apart from one another: on the sunset side of a mountain, in the shadows of a ridge, out of sight, out of hearing. It is not the ruralism of the flat Midwest. Vermont topography is naturally rural, providing no vast watersheds to urban places, no mountain-flatland junctures at which people might cluster, and no seaports in which to mass the paraphernalia of urbanism. Nearly everywhere a hill lies across the path of togetherness. This consistently hilly topography helps explain why, after two centuries of settlement, Vermont's largest city has only about 40,000 people. The growth of Vermont has been defined by the homestead and the hamlet.

Bounded on the east by the Connecticut River and on the west by Lake Champlain, this slice of hill country seemed foreboding to the Indians; they continually shied away, settling only momentarily on meadowlands along the rivers, such as the village at the Great Oxbow in Newbury on the Connecticut, but generally leaving Vermont a battleground, first for their own Indian nations and then for the nations of the white man.

Indeed the early history of Vermont reads like a chronicle of warring armies, the Long House of Hiawatha's Iroquois against the Algonquins of the St. Lawrence, the French against the British, and the British against the Colonials.[1] Vermont was born amid the sounds of the Revolutionary War in summer and the freezing winds of the lower Canadian plain in winter. It was the impact of these two variables, the fury of nature and of man, that was to shape its character, first as an independent republic and then as the first state to join the Union after the Revolution.

Frenchmen came to Vermont originally following Samuel de Champlain, who named Vermont in 1609. French settlement was transitory and generally military in nature as the Canadians sought to seal off the St. Lawrence River Valley from Iroquois raids by building forts on the shores of the huge lake that forms the northern half of her western border. The French had a profound if negative impact on the early settlement of Vermont; they and their Indian allies effectively blocked English migration into the hill country north of Massachusetts. At the turn of the seventeenth century the pressure for new land in lower New England grew, and cautious English probes began up the Connecticut River Valley toward Vermont. But the French and Algonquins, unwilling to antagonize the Iroquois further, directed their raids away from the tribes of the Long House of eastern New York and the Champlain Valley toward the English along the Connecticut River. Their raids across the Green Mountains followed the river valleys that today form the major east-west highway arteries of the state.

For over half a century the struggle between the English and the French held back colonial settlement of Vermont and provided the historical underpinnings for some of the most important literary works in colonial folklore, including Cooper's *Last of the Mohicans* and Roberts' *Northwest Passage*. The first permanent settlement therefore did not come until 1724, when a fort was built at a location on the Connecticut River which later was included in the town of Brattleboro. Early colonial settlement of other parts of Vermont was also military and was designed to buffer territory in northern Massachusetts from foreign attack. It was not until 1763, when the Treaty of Paris

1. Comments are drawn from a wide range of historical material which is listed in the bibliographical essay that completes this book.

ended the Anglo-French contest for the northern hemisphere of the New World, that peace came to the land of the upper Connecticut, the valley of Lake Champlain, and the Green Mountains between them. From this point on, migration into Vermont began in earnest.

The settlement of the "New Hampshire Grants" after the victories of Amherst and Wolfe pulsed from two distinct areas. The first pulse was the transfer of established political communities from Connecticut and Massachusetts into the northern Connecticut River Valley. These migrations came from places generally east of Hartford, Connecticut, more specifically from Tolland and Windham counties. For instance, the towns of Hartford, Wethersfield, and Windsor, Vermont, are adjacent to each other along the western bank of the Connecticut River, while the towns forming the "Fundamental Orders of Connecticut" were also named Hartford, Wethersfield, and Windsor and existed side by side near the Connecticut River in the Nutmeg State. The people who came to these settlements along the river on the eastern flank of the Green Mountains were more conservative than those who settled the lands to the west of the mountains. Historian Newton has pointed out that of the twenty-one Congregational churches in Vermont in 1780, nineteen were on the eastern side of the mountains.[2]

The second wave of settlement came from western Connecticut and Massachusetts and that part of New York on the eastern side of the Hudson. Those who followed the Housatonic River north from Connecticut to take up homesteads in western Vermont were far different from those who populated the river towns. Many were adventurers who remembered the fertile lands of Vermont from their travels through the state during the French and Indian War; others were escapees from New England Congregationalism, and a large number were land speculators. These people were joined by the freer souls of the eastern river towns who followed the Connecticut's tributary pathways into and through the mountains to the valley of Lake Champlain. Foremost among the settlers of the West were such liberals as the Allen family, of which more will be said shortly. Thus the

2. Earle Newton, *The Vermont Story* (Montpelier: Vermont Historical Society, 1949), p. 39.

early settlement of Vermont, patterned after its geography, was dichotomous: the river towns were almost direct reproductions of established political communities, stable and basically conservative, and the people to the west of the mountains, more radical and warlike, were more apt to be land speculators, adventurers, or religious outcasts than ministers and landed gentry.

In 1771, eight years after the Treaty of Paris, there were 7000 pioneers in Vermont, located for the most part in the south. During the next decade population began to flow in a pincer movement—first up both valleys and then squeezing into the central hills and mountains. In 1781 there were some 30,000 settlers in Vermont; by 1790 the figure had risen to 85,000, and nearly all her present 246 towns and cities were settled, with the exception of the Northeast Kingdom counties of Orleans and Essex and towns located deep in the Green Mountains. There was a continuing frontier in Vermont. The people did not cluster and then disperse, they moved up the valley a bit from their neighbors and settled; when the valleys were filled, they drifted up the smaller streams into the back beyond.

Vermont's early settlers did a number of things that have colored the character of the state ever since. They battled the land claims of New York (see below) in a bloodless guerilla conflict for nearly a decade and played a relatively large role in the war against the British, thereby creating a folklore and folk heroes. They patched up the east-west political division of the state which settlement patterns on either side of the Green Mountain ridge had created. They manned an independent republic for fourteen years, matching wits with both the Crown and the Continental Congress. Finally, they enacted a framework of government that has endured intact as one of the most liberal in the nation.

No sooner had the people settled in Vermont than they became embroiled in an intense land controversy that involved the colonies of New York and New Hampshire and the Crown itself. The rights and wrongs, legalities and documentaries of this quarrel have no crucial bearing on the development of Vermont's political structures; what is important is the profound impact the myths that surround the struggle have had on the business of building a consensual political system.

The great bulk of Vermont's frontier families had settled on lands known as the New Hampshire Grants. A decision by the King in 1764, however, placed Vermont territories under the control of New York. Amid the chaos caused by land speculators from lower New England and New York, a natural New England aversion to the New York county system of local government, and the anxieties of the homesteaders themselves appeared an electrifying leader: Ethan Allen.

Allen is to Vermont what Sam Houston is to Texas. He is probably more to Vermont than Francis Marion is to the Carolinas or Daniel Boone to Kentucky, since he was not a wanderer and his activities were sparked by an intense radical nationalism. Whatever his intentions (was he more interested in his family's land speculations than in the welfare of the Vermont freeman?) or the authenticity of his deeds (did he really demand the surrender of Fort Ticonderoga in "the name of the Great Jehovah and the Continental Congress"?), the fact remains that beginning in 1764 he led a band of "shock troops" (as his biographer calls them) up and down western Vermont in a continuing harassment of the "Yorkers," and ultimately blocked their designs on Vermont land. He did capture Fort Ticonderoga in 1775, a year before the Declaration of Independence was written. He provided Vermont with a folk hero, and the political socialization of Vermont youth has traditionally begun with tales of Ethan Allen and his Green Mountain Boys.

Opposition to New York also provided a focus of common concern for the new settlers, helped jell an early spirit of togetherness, and even soothed east-west tensions when the leaders of the river town read the new and highly aristocratic New York Constitution of 1777. Even Jacob Bailey, the vociferous anti-Allen, pro-New York river-town leader from Newbury, was appalled by the New York document.

But Vermont had a more important enemy in those days—the British Empire, the threat from which helped to produce harmony from the discord inherent in a frontier land beset with sociocultural divisions. This point is graphically made by Vermont's leaders, who were in the process of writing a constitution for their New Republic at Windsor when news of the fall of Fort Ticonderoga reached them. After a hasty final reading of this document, the leaders from the western part of the state immediately left to defend their homesteads from Burgoyne's Indians. Although there was some apathy to the war in the state, there is little doubt that Vermont played a role in the hostilities out of proportion to her numbers—a role catalyzed by the rampages of Ethan Allen early in the war.

First, Allen and his Green Mountain Boys (accompanied by Benedict Arnold) captured Fort Ticonderoga, the first major British property to be taken by the rebels, and caused the Continental Congress, still reluctant to antagonize the British, no little embarrassment. Vermont thus took the first giant step in the escalation of anti-Crown hostilities. Cheered by success and ample stores of rum in the fort, the Vermonters soon cleared Lake Champlain for the Colonialists. The cannons from the fort were dragged across country in the dead of winter to Dorchester Heights to drive Gage from Boston the following year.

Secondly, Vermont played a major role in the harassment of General Burgoyne's expedition down the lake to his ultimate defeat at Saratoga—the most important American victory in the war, for it prompted French entry against the British. At Hubbardton and then at Bennington, Vermont's regiment helped thwart Burgoyne's plans—although at Bennington, New Hampshire's General John Stark and his troops deserve most of the credit for the victory. Burgoyne himself said Vermont was "a country which abounds in the most active and rebellious race on the continent and hangs like a gathering storm on my left."

Vermont, like Texas, existed as an independent republic before joining the Union. The Republic of Vermont was formed at the Windsor Convention in 1777. For a decade and a half the republic carried on the business of an independent political state, making diplomatic maneuvers, coining money, putting down internal insurrections, and fashioning a body of law through a functioning legislature. When its people were rebuffed in their early attempts to join the Colonies, leaders of the state supposedly negotiated with Canada for a place in the British Empire.

The talks with Canada, called the "Haldimand Negotiations," also deepened momentarily the rift between east and west in Vermont as the leaders of the conservative river towns vociferously opposed what they considered to be treason on the part of the negotiators. Yet it was not long before the division be-

tween the settlements on either side of the mountains was
healed, and the people of both sections settled down to live
under the Vermont Constitution. This was not accomplished
without the use of some force, however. Ethan Allen, in the
services of Governor Chittenden, ransacked the town of Guilford when the latter petitioned to rejoin New York. In 1786
riots broke out in Rutland and Windsor over economic matters,
and the legislature called out the militia to deal with the rioters.
    When Vermonters met first to consider the prospects for
political union, they seem to have listened intently to advice
sent to them by Thomas Young of Connecticut. Young, a radical of the Thomas Paine sort, appears to have been one of the
important guiding lights behind the formation of the Republic
of Vermont and more specifically of its constitution. The Vermont document is a near replica of the new Pennsylvania constitution and reflects the thinking of radicals such as Benjamin
Franklin, Paine, and Young. All of which means that Vermont
accepted and has preserved one of the most liberal constitutional documents of the country. It was the first to outlaw slavery. It was also the first to allow universal manhood suffrage.
The constitution was short and to the point, providing for a
unicameral legislature to meet annually and for a Council of
Censors to propose amendments every seven years. Like so
many constitutions of this period, Vermont's gave little power
to the executive, even denying the governor a veto. At the same
time, Vermonters preserved their tradition of local town government by providing that the one-house legislature be filled by
representatives elected one from a town. Time has brought
changes to the original plan—a bicameral legislature, the end of
"one town—one vote," biennial sessions (although now the legislature meets annually through the use of "adjourned" sessions)
and a veto and two-year term for the governor, to name the
most important. But the brevity of the constitution, one of its
strengths, has remained. The institution of a time-lock clause,
which allows the constitution to be amended only in decennial
years, has protected it from the proliferation of amendments
that have ruined so many other state documents. Moreover, the
inability to amend, the brevity of the document, and the emphasis placed on legislative dominance have meant that social
change in Vermont has been able to travel the relatively easy

route of legislative enactment, avoiding the entanglements of constitutional revision.

Thus the early years of the Vermont political system were marked by a profound spirit of independence, the development of a voluminous folklore based on the exploits of a folk hero and chronicled by a growing folk literature, the repair of a clear sociocultural split in the state's settlement patterns that had manifested itself in intrastate political wars, and the institution of a frame of government that exemplified an intensely liberal state of mind. If political systems, like human beings, form basic character traits in their early years, the importance of Vermont's eighteenth-century experiences cannot be underestimated.

The threads of Vermont's history after the eighteenth century are woven in and about the twin predispositions to small-town life and government and legislative dominance at the state level. In the division of political power, however, the towns assumed and maintained the dominant role in fact, if not in theory.[3] Socially and economically the state preserved its rural-agricultural pattern, although there were twists in the fabric from time to time, the most important of which were the vast emigration from Vermont that began after the first surge of population growth in the early 1800's; the coming of the railroads, which established magnetic centers in the depot towns and drew many of the hill people back to the valleys and transportation centers; the failure of manufacturing to take hold, and the development of agriculture as the state's prime source of income—more specifically, the growth of dairying and the decline of sheep raising in the mid-nineteenth century; the development of the recreation industry; and the penetration of technocratic culture without urbanism.

Socioeconomic Development

Vermont's population grew very rapidly after she was admitted to the Union. If this trend had continued, she would no doubt

3. Frank M. Bryan, "Reapportionment and the Vermont Town," *Rural Vermonter* (Spring 1964), pp. 6-10.

by this time have joined her southern New England sisters in the great eastern megalopolis. But for various reasons it did not. In the first place, immigration slowed to a near halt. Secondly, emigration in great numbers siphoned off Vermont's large indigenous growth into the new lands of the West. The War of 1812, which alarmed prospective settlers with the threat of British and Indian invasion; the opening of new lands beyond the Appalachians, which called many potential Vermont settlers elsewhere; and the occupation of most of the good valley tillage, which discouraged continued agricultural immigration—all contributed to a sharp decline in the attractiveness of Vermont to outsiders.

Growing misuse of the soil, which impoverished many homesteaders; a scarcity of new land, which made nomads of farmer's sons after the first born; and the use of the state's lands for pasturage, which does not support people the way crop farming does—these also were forces prompting an exodus from the state. And the list continues: the failure of manufacturing to employ the large families of the farmers; the high price of land in Vermont compared to the cheap lands of the West; the intense economic difficulties that accompanied the crop failures of 1816, when there was almost no summer; an educational system which, unlike those in the mountains of the South, kept pace with the times and did not allow young people to live in blissful ignorance of the world without; and, perhaps most important, a population that was by nature migratory. All were factors helping to create the cultural-psychological forces that were to catch up large portions of Vermont's population and fling them westward into New York, the Ohio River Valley, Iowa, and on to California.[4] How to keep them down on the farm has been a crucial question in Vermont for well over a century.

Grafted to the latter stages of the vast emigration movement came an explosion of railroad building within the state. T. D. Seymour Bassett, the dean of Vermont historians, has said that "no other technological change had as much effect on Vermont society as the railroad." It was the vehicle, says Bassett, that

4. The credit for an in-depth analysis of this movement, from which much of the above was taken, goes to Lewis D. Stilwell, *Migration from Vermont* (Montpelier: Vermont Historical Society, 1948).

brought an early urban influence to Vermont. However, he is not talking of urbanism in our terms (large numbers of people living close to one another) but rather in economic terms. The railroads brought the end to self-sufficiency on the farms, emphasized the economic influence of the towns that became depots, and served as a magnet to draw many of the hill farmers from the back beyond to the new growth around the railroad centers. By the 1870's Vermont had passed from a homestead culture to a village-town culture. This early change is why today's hunter will often find a stone wall buried in timber a hundred years on the stump. The contemporary Vermont countryside is a graveyard of abandoned homesteads.

After the great sheep-raising boom of the mid-nineteenth century had passed, Vermont developed a dairying industry to make use of her farmlands, dabbled in manufacturing (especially in products demanding skilled labor, such as that required for the machine-tool industry), established a name for quarrying granite and marble, fostered a lucrative tourist industry, and became familiar with the civilization of the technocrat. Today the economy still depends on dairying; quarrying; tourism; small, skilled industry; and, increasingly, service establishments.

Since World War II the character of Vermont has changed in several ways, chief among which is the disappearance of the hill farm. The land on which these old homesteads were situated is being taken up swiftly by out-of-state summer people (as distinguished from tourists) and by land speculators. Of importance also is the impact of new communications and transportation systems. Television has opened the rest of the world to the people of the back beyond, all the way from downtown Burbank to Vietnam. The new interstate highway network has tied Vermont more closely to Montreal in the north and the East Coast megalopolis in the south. Despite this potential for communication and interaction, however, the essence of Vermont's sociological landscape, her profound ruralism, has remained intact.

Political Development

In the early years Vermont politics were marked by the mountain division described above. In the election of 1800, Jefferson won every county west of the mountains and lost every county east of the mountains. Locally the Federalists were unable to make much headway until the second war with England threatened to cut off Vermont's lucrative trade with Canada. Still, the struggle between Federalists and Republicans was defined by the mountains. With the end of the war Federalist power steadily decreased, as it did throughout New England.

The Whig-Democrat struggle that dominated American politics after the "Virginia Dynasty" fell was postponed in Vermont while a powerful anti-Mason party played havoc with the second-party system.[5] Anti-Masonry provided the opposition when the sectional appeal of John Quincy Adams provided a majority for the National Republicans in Vermont during the Jacksonian era. By 1830 the anti-Masons were commanding a majority of the votes. In 1832 Vermont was the only state in the Union that voted for the anti-Mason presidential candidate. When the Whigs and anti-Masons joined in 1836, Democratic fortunes in Vermont were dealt a serious blow. In the election of 1840 Harrison received nearly a two-to-one plurality, while across the river in New Hampshire Van Buren rolled up a landslide three-to-one vote.[6] The Democrats were hurt in Vermont by more than the anti-Masons, however. In 1839 many Democrats left the party to fight slavery under the auspices of the Liberty Party, while the Whigs suffered no serious defections. Adding to their troubles was the fact that they found themselves on the wrong side of the issue concerning the annexation of Texas.[7]

In 1844 Vermont's Whigs were strongly anti-Texas but managed to live with the candidacy of Henry Clay. Although the Taylor-Cass contest hurt both parties in Vermont in 1848, Cass hurt the Democrats more than Taylor hurt the Whigs. Again the Whig party held ranks while the Democrats were hurt by "Barn Burner" Van Buren. This was because the Whigs, with their lin-

5. Richard P. McCormick, *The Second American Party System: Party Formation in the Jacksonian Era* (Chapel Hill, N.C.: University of North Carolina Press, 1966).

6. Ibid., p. 102. McCormick calls this state of affairs a "conundrum for political analysts."

7. Neil A. McNall, "Anti-Slavery Sentiment in Vermont" (M.A. thesis, University of Vermont, 1938), pp. 83-95.

gering dislike for the Jacksonian era, remembered Van Buren as the enemy. Even in 1852, when a neighbor from New Hampshire ran as a Democrat, Vermont Whigdom refused to budge, and the state became one of only four to vote against Franklin Pierce.

For years the Whigs had withstood the pressures of internal antislavery sentiment—ignited first by the Liberty Party and then by the Free Soilers. But now abolitionist fever in Vermont was at white heat, and as the Nebraska issue began to boil, the luck of the Whigs ran out. When the Kansas-Nebraska bill passed the Senate, political bonds in Vermont began to snap. Bassett describes the period as "a time when a state which was overwhelmingly anti-slavery but 75 percent in favor of subordinating the issue to matters nearer home became 75 percent in favor of subordinating matters nearer home to the slavery issue."[8] Amid the political chaos that followed, Vermont's Republican Party was born. In 1858 Hiland Hall, a Republican, was elected governor with a plurality of 16,000 votes. In 1859 he increased his margin. Republicans did not relinquish their hold on that office for over a century.

Once established, the message of the Republican Party was quickly driven home by the war against the Confederacy. It is difficult to overestimate the impact the Civil War had on Vermont's political system. Vermont lost relatively more troops to the Union cause than any other northern state. Half of her able-bodied men joined the service. She contributed more than 10 percent of the state's total wealth in property to the war. It was the only state to have a brigade named after it, and elements of this unit contributed to the war with their effective flanking action against Pickett's troops charging Cemetery Ridge at the Battle of Gettysburg. The second Vermont Brigade sustained a 40 percent casualty loss during the war. In a single half day during the Battle of the Wilderness, Vermont suffered over 1000 casualties. Some indication of the strength of the antislavery appeal in Vermont can be gained by observing that in the Presidential election of 1860, Stephen Douglas, a native Vermonter

8. T. D. Seymour Bassett, "Urban Penetration in Rural Vermont, 1840-1880" (diss., Harvard University, 1952), pp. 433-34. Bassett's work contains the best account of Vermont politics for this period.

who had recently completed a tour of his home state, was defeated by a relatively unknown but antislavery Republican from Illinois by a four-to-one margin.

Vermont had a long antislavery tradition: Captain Ebenezer Allen of the famous Allen family and member of the Green Mountain Boys made a point of freeing the slave of a fleeing British officer eighty-three years before guns fired on Fort Sumter. A Vermont Supreme Court Justice demanded "a bill of sale from the Almighty" before he would return a fugitive slave. William Lloyd Garrison, himself a native son, began his antislavery tirades in his *Journal of the Issues* at Bennington. Thaddeus Stevens, a leading radical from Saint Johnsbury, demanded harsh treatment for the defeated South after the war from his seat in the U.S. Congress. The Vermont legislature began to issue tough antislavery statements when they opposed admitting Texas to the Union as a slave state: in 1849 the legislature condemned slavery as a "crime against humanity"; in 1856 it appropriated $20,000 for the free-state forces in Kansas.[9] Finally, Vermont's constitution, as has been noted, was the first state document of its kind to outlaw slavery. This strong antislavery tradition plus a vociferous military response to the War embedded Republicanism deep in the rock-ribbed backbone of Vermont, where it was to remain untouched for a century.

This Republicanism seems to have maintained a relatively high level of responsiveness to the people despite the party's complete domination of the state's politics. Few interpreters of the Vermont political system are willing to type it with the one-party tendencies of the South. A powerful tradition of localism, a very large and fluid legislature that defied enduring extralegislative manipulation, and the weakness of the governor's office itself were institutional factors that stood in the way of one-party myopia.

A dominant party machine would have had to control over 200 local governmental units—there was no effective county-level government to minimize political stratification. It would have had to influence 276 legislators, most of them amateurs without obvious levers of economic persuasion. It would have needed more executive control over both legislature and bureau-

9. Newton, *The Vermont Story*, pp. 125-26.

cracy—which simply did not exist. That is why the governor-ship, though controlled in part first by the railroads and then by industry (especially quarrying), was in no real sense any more than a statewide symbol of Republicanism. Prominent Vermonters occupied the governorship with regularity, insulating it from the rank and file until well into the twentieth century. Yet though these governors could no doubt further their business interests from Montpelier, the executive chair was for the most part a prestigious institution only, and the true focus of politics centered on the legislature.

Moreover, the Republican Party was capable of bending with the times, anticipating and then promoting innovations at the elite level (albeit with somewhat watered-down versions of minority proposals), and generally reacting in a positive manner to pressures for social change. The response of the party to demands for reform during the first two decades of the century bears witness to its ability to innovate on its own when cornered, boxing its way clear by supporting its own versions of proposed reforms. This was the tactic in regard to the direct primary, workman's compensation, and labor reform generally. Joseph Schlesinger reports that it was this kind of "mild progressivism" that allowed the old guard to maintain control of the state's politics.[10] During both the Progressive Era and the New Deal, Vermont underwent waves of innovative sentiments which were assimilated into the state's political structure by the dominant Republican Party. Though such assimilations were branded with Vermont's peculiar stamp of caution—a mixture of skepticism, individualism, and states rights—it seems clear that they were authentic expressions of sociopolitical change generated by legitimate public demand.

As we approach the central concerns of this study, which involve certain aspects of Vermont's rural political system since World War II, it may be well to outline several characteristics of the polity to be discussed:

1. It is a polity whose topography has helped to perpetuate ruralism as the essential social condition. For people to live apart from one another among Vermont's never-ending hills is

10. *How They Became Governor* (East Lansing, Mich.: Government Research Bureau, Michigan State University, 1957), p. 35.

as natural as people living close to one another around New York's harbor, at St. Louis' midwest prairie divide, or on Denver's plateau.

2. It is a polity the size of whose population has remained remarkably stable over the last century. A large indigenous yearly increase with limited immigration has been matched by a continuing emigration.

3. It is a polity whose economic structure is dominated by dairy farming, extractive industry, specialized manufacturing, tourism, and growing tertiary concerns. Since World War II the end of the hill farm, the coming of television, and the development of new transportation facilities have not been accompanied by increasing urbanization. Ruralism remains the dominant feature of Vermont's sociocultural map.

4. It is a polity whose politics have been marked from the beginning, as Lockard says, by a "curious mixture" of radicalism, populism, and conservatism. When John Adams imprisoned a Vermont Congressional Representative, Matthew Lyon , for sedition, Vermonters reelected him to Congress while he served his prison term in Vergennes. During New Deal days, however, Vermonters rejected the Federal Government's proposal to build a "smoky-mountain parkway" down the backbone of the Green Mountains, a move that some said would have brought much treasure to the state. Two decades later Vermont, the most Republican state in the Union, would have no part of the McCarthy scare, and attempts to have the Communist Party restricted from the ballot were stopped cold by the legislature. Though ruralism has meant localism in Vermont, it has not been overpowered by conservatism.

5. It is a polity whose politics have been dominated by a single party to a greater degree than in any other northern state. Yet one-partyism has not created a government marked by irresponsiveness. The state's dominant Republicans have seemed willing, when the need arose, to incorporate enough change to quiet the opposition.

6. Finally, it is a polity where history has invoked a special community ethic. To be a "Vermonter" still means to possess certain traits of character, whether actual or assumed, which create bonds of communal spirit that are very likely matched by few other states.

Two

The Rural Elite

When the variables of politics have been isolated, when the relationships have been measured and the causal sequences defined, one returns to the individuals, the core of the political system. Important political questions nearly always boil down to assessments of the political behavior of those who rule. The great American political crisis of the sixties sprang from a breakdown of the socialization function of the political system. Somehow we seem to have lost the ability to infuse the rules of the game into a broad spectrum of alienated citizenry: disadvantaged blacks in the ghetto to advantaged whites in suburbia. Who makes the decisions and why? Who governs? The blacks say that the white power structure rules; the Left says the military-industrial complex; the kids say the establishment. So it goes. As a matter of fact it went all the way to the Democratic National Convention of 1972, where the quota system was designed to alter in dramatic fashion the answer.

The question of who governs is not new. All basic texts in American politics grapple with it, usually citing scholars like Hunter and Mills[1] as proponents of the "power-elite" explanation and Truman and Dahl[2] as supporters of the "pluralistic" model of political recruitment. Despite a voluminous literature concerned with this debate, social scientists have yet to come

1. Floyd Hunter, *Top Leadership, U.S.A.* (Chapel Hill, N.C.: University of North Carolina Press, 1959). C. Wright Mills, *The Power Elite* (New York: Oxford University Press, 1956).

2. Robert A. Dahl, *Who Governs? Democracy and Power in an American City* (New Haven: Yale University Press, 1961). David B. Truman, *The Governmental Process* (New York: Alfred A. Knopf, 1951).

up with anything approaching a unanimous answer.[3] What about the pluralist-elitist question in the rural polity? What will be the character of the political rulers who Americans will encounter as they make their trek back to the rural areas over the next hundred years? The first problem to deal with is of political elites in Vermont. In this analysis no attempt will be made to determine if there is in rural society a clique of power wielders that does not reside in public officialdom. Our intention is to show the nature of the elected and appointed elite in a precise and complete manner in order to probe the character of the visible recruitment system. There is every reason to believe, however, that the data camouflage no hidden power centers.

What kinds of people are drawn from the local communities to hold the reins of government in a state where geography and history have scattered a few people over miles of farm land, hill country, and near wilderness? How do they compare with the ruling elites of the more urbanized states? Are the recruitment patterns in Vermont similar to those of New York, Ohio, or California? Is the stereotype of the "cornstalk brigades" that have been said to dominate rural politics valid? Does the ruling class mirror the population it serves, or is it a delegation not at all representative of the common man? Has the rural elite changed to match alterations in society at large?

To paint an accurate picture of the governing hierarchy of Vermont, biographical sketches of 2617 individuals were consulted, coded, and analyzed. The components of this elite cluster are (1) all state legislators elected over a twenty-five-year period, 1947–1971, including 1696 legislators, 1531 representatives, and 165 senators, who worked a total of over 3300 legislative years; (2) the 691 high-level nonelective state administrators serving over the same twenty-five years; department heads, their deputies and assistants, division directors and their immediate subordinates, and members of administrative boards and councils make up this category; (3) the eighty-five members of the judicial branch—judges of the State Supreme Court, supe-

3. Charles M. Bonjean and David Olson, "Community Leadership: Directions of Research," *Administrative Science Quarterly*, 9 (1964), 278-300.

rior judges, and district court judges; (4) the elected state officials chosen between 1946 and 1970 and their appointed subordinates (145 of these). In Vermont, the secretary of state, the auditor of accounts, the attorney general, and the state treasurer are elected along with the governor and the lieutenant governor every two years.[4]

A cluster of 2617 individuals seems broad enough to allow us to comment on the political leadership of a state with a population of about 420,000 persons, especially since the sample includes all elected state executive officers, all legislators, and all members of the upper echelon of the state's administrative branch. Secondly, a large number of the group have held numerous local offices as well. This participation in local government means that the statewide elite reflects the nature of local rulership, especially in the House of Representatives. As Table 1 indicates, a large percentage of the representatives have held local offices. Finally, the 691 nonelected members of the state's administrative hierarchy include a large number of nongovernmental elite. Members of the professional, business, and agricultural communities are recruited to serve on advisory boards of state government, such as the State Highway Board, the State Soil Conservation Council, or the Dairy Industry Council. These individuals are hired on a per-diem basis and are not regular fixtures of the governmental structure. They provide our cross section with extragovernmental local figures who hold positions of prestige and influence in the state. Moreover, the confidence we place in these data grows when it is realized that the 2617 individuals make up over half of one percent of the state's entire population. As complete a cross section of the New York ruling corps, for instance, would include over 100,000 people.

Overview

Table 2 summarizes ten categories of biographical data outlining the nature of the rural elite. The age-level figures show that only 16 percent of the entire 2617 members were forty years old or

4. State of Vermont, Secretary of State, *Vermont Legislative Directory and State Manual* (Montpelier, 1947-1971).

Table 1
Local Offices Held by State Governmental Personnel,
1947-1967 (percentages)

Governmental Branch	Town Clerk	Selectman	School Board Member
Legislature			
House	4	28	22
Senate	6	22	23
Executive	3	5	10
Judiciary	3	8	17
Administration	5	14	17

Source: State of Vermont, Secretary of State, *Vermont Legislative Directory and State Manual* (Montpelier, Vermont, 1947-67).

younger, and 35 percent were over sixty. It should be remembered, however, that these aggregate percentages are heavily biased by the legislative component—especially the House of Representatives, whose members comprise well over half of the total sample. Elsewhere, in the other three branches of state government, the executives appear to be the youngest, followed by the judges and the administrators. It would seem, therefore, that the observation that rural lawmakers tend to be older than their urban counterparts may have substance as far as the legislature is concerned but might well need qualification for the broader ranges of state governmental personnel.

By combining categories 2, 3, and 6 (Birthplace, Years in Town, and Military Service) we create a broader dimension to our elite cross section, namely parochialism. Nearly 67 percent of the lawmakers were native Vermonters, and only eleven of the other 33 percent were born outside the Northeast. Fully 44 percent had lived in the town they represented for over forty years. While military service has traditionally served as a prerequisite to political life in this country, only 36 percent of Vermont's ruling elite have had experience in the military. Once more, the legislature defines to a large extent the nature of the parochialism dimension. However, in this case the judiciary is similar to the legislature in that it contains largely local person-

Table 2
Biographical Data for the Governing Hierarchy, 1947–1971 (percentages)

Category		Branch of government					
		Legislature		Adminis-			
		House N=1531	Senate N=165	tration N=691	Executive N=145	Judiciary N=85	Totals N=2617
Age	21–40	11.5	18.0	20.9	41.4	20.0	16.3
	41–60	44.8	48.0	58.1	46.2	58.8	49.1
	61 or older	43.7	33.0	21.0	12.4	21.2	34.6
Birthplace	Vermont	72.6	64.4	56.3	53.1	72.6	66.7
	Northeast	18.8	18.4	30.4	34.5	19.0	22.7
	Other	8.7	17.2	13.3	12.2	8.3	10.6
Education	No high school	15.5	6.1	3.4	0.7	0.0	10.4
	Some high school	44.2	27.3	18.5	14.5	9.5	33.6
	Some college	6.1	5.5	8.8	7.6	3.6	6.8
	College graduate	25.5	37.0	34.1	24.1	10.7	27.9
	Post graduate	8.6	24.2	35.1	53.1	76.2	21.2
Years in town	1–20	25.3	23.4	37.6	55.1	26.2	30.0
	21–40	24.7	24.1	33.2	12.5	20.2	26.1
	41 or more	50.0	52.5	29.1	32.4	53.6	43.8
Occupation	Farmers	36.8	26.1	13.6	3.4	0.0	27.0
	Businessmen	17.7	30.3	13.6	4.8	1.2	16.2
	Lawyers	5.0	14.5	10.0	45.5	80.0	11.6

White collar workers	6.3	2.4	8.1	7.6	1.2	6.5
Public employees	2.6	3.0	27.1[a]	13.8	12.9	10.0
Other professionals	9.8	13.9	20.7	16.6	1.2	13.1
Laborers	12.2	0.6	0.4	0.7	0.0	7.3
Others	9.6	8.5	6.5	6.9	3.5	8.4
Military service Yes	26.1	61.8	47.6	53.8	44.7	36.2
No	73.9	38.2	52.4	46.2	55.3	63.8
Military officer[b] Yes	5.9	15.2	18.8	30.3	24.7	11.9
No	94.1	84.8	81.2	69.7	75.3	88.1
Party Democrats	18.9	23.2	17.8	14.5	18.8	18.6
Republicans	78.2	75.6	56.6	69.0	72.9	71.6
Independents	2.2	1.2	9.0	4.1	2.4	4.1
No answer	0.7	0.6	16.6	12.4	5.9	5.7
Sex Men	84.2	88.5	91.9	89.0	98.8	87.2
Women	15.8	11.5	8.1	11.0	1.2	12.8
Religion Catholics	14.9	23.0	18.5	17.9	28.2	17.0
Congregationalists	24.6	29.7	20.1	24.8	23.5	23.7
Episcopalians	5.4	4.2	9.1	11.7	12.9	6.9
Baptists	7.1	4.8	2.2	2.1	1.2	5.2
Methodists	17.3	6.1	9.1	5.5	7.1	13.5
Others	30.7	32.1	41.0	37.9	27.1	33.7

[a]This figure represents the many individuals in the bureaucracy who listed their occupation as the position they were holding in the administrative branch.

[b]This figure represents the percentage of the total members of each branch of government who were officers in the military.

Source: State of Vermont, Secretary of State, *Vermont Legislative Directory and State Manual* (Montpelier, Vermont, 1947–71).

nel. In fact, there are relatively more Vermonters within the judicial branch than in the legislature. They also match the legislators in length of residence in the town in which they live.

The executive hierarchy and the administrative core bear similar birthplace statistics and are not significantly dissimilar in terms of the percentages of those having lived long periods of time in their places of residence or in terms of military service. Once again, these two groups provide a contrast with the legislature, since there are substantially fewer native Vermonters in their ranks.[5]

The data on military service provide an additional observation of interest as they uncover a basic difference in the two houses of the legislature. Sixty-one percent of the senators served in the military as compared to only 26 percent of the representatives. The facts that senators are elected at large by county and representatives were chosen (before reapportionment) one to a town, and that the office of senator carries with it more prestige, offer some degree of explanation for this phenomenon—the service providing a measure of cosmopolitanism necessary for countywide ambitions, and the increased prestige of the office invoking a political advantage in veteran status. This latter point is strengthened when we note that the branch of government containing statewide elected officials (the executive) has the largest percentage (54) of former servicemen. We will say more on the political character of the legislature in a future chapter. Let the record show at this point, however, that military service can in no way be termed a prerequisite for election to the House. It was not a weight on the political scales of success or failure in the minds of rural people when they selected local representatives.

A look at educational levels reveals a further difference between the House and the Senate. A significantly higher proportion of the senators completed a college education. Moreover, a

5. Bruce M. Hackett, *Higher Civil Servants in California* (Berkeley: Institute of Government Affairs, University of California, 1967), p. 129. In contrast to the Vermont bureaucracy, the California system had fewer home-grown Californians in the administrative hierarchy. In the early 1960's, for instance, only 25 percent of California's higher civil servants had been born in the state. In Vermont the figure was 60 percent.

large number of senators had postgraduate training, a statistic the representatives could not match. Twice as many House members as Senate members had no high school training at all. Of the other three branches of state government, the judicial is the most extensively educated, as one would expect. The executive and administrative branches are once more quite similar, although the executive branch has more members with postgraduate training.[6] These figures on education follow the pattern in evidence throughout this analysis, which is, simply, a dichotomy between the House of Representatives and the rest of the government.

The data on occupations also conform to the pattern. In the House a majority of the membership consisted of farmers, businessmen, and laborers, in that order. In the Senate, the largest occupational groups were businessmen first, farmers second, and lawyers third, with "other professionals" running a close fourth. In the administrative branch, of those individuals who listed an occupation other than government service, the most popular categories were "other professionals," farmers, and businessmen. Lawyers dominated the judiciary and were by far the largest single group in the executive branch (80 percent in the former; 45 percent in the latter). The lawyers in the attorney general's office contributed heavily to the 45 percent. In summary, the rural elite included a substantial number of farmers and businessmen (a majority in both the House and Senate), but these were balanced by the professionals in the administrative hierarchy and the lawyers in the executive and judiciary. Only in the House were farmers the largest occupational group, and even there they did not dominate, as the lawyers did in the judiciary and executive.

Our picture of the rural elite is completed by painting in religion, political party, and sex categories. The three most popular religious groups were Catholics, Congregationalists, and Methodists. The last were included because of their large percentage in the House. In the Senate the Methodists were replaced by increased numbers of Catholics and Congregationalists. Generally speaking, the Senate exhibited more intense concentration in

6. Ibid., p. 48. The figures for the Vermont administrative branch for the early 1960's compare well with those of California.

the two most popular groups, Catholics and Congregationalists, while the rest of the membership is more diffuse. The administrators showed slightly more religious heterogeneity, with over 40 percent outside the five major groups listed. The judges had the least, with 68 percent concentrated in three major groups. Again, the executive branch looks similiar to the bureaucracy.

The low Catholic percentage in the executive branch is striking in view of their substantial percentage of the statewide population. Evidently Catholics have been held out of the executive decision-making apparatus in Vermont. In the Senate, however, the one man—one vote formula and constituency structure based on the county combined to give Catholics strength more in tune with their numbers. A final note points to strong Episcopalian representation in the judicial, executive, and administrative branches. These seem to reflect findings at the national level, where large numbers of Episcopalians are in nonelective government employment.

Closer inspection of the statistics for the religious background of Vermont's lawmakers underscores another pattern linked to political recruitment. It was suggested in our historical introduction that Vermont was settled in two geographical sectors, with the Green Mountain chain separating the western from the eastern regions of the state. Evidence of the sociocultural differences separating the two halves of Vermont was noted by the fact that in 1780, nineteen of the twenty-one Congregational churches in Vermont were located on the eastern side of the mountains.[7] Well over a century and a half later, in 1949, this pattern had maintained life enough to result in Congregational representation in the House being predominantly eastern in origin. Thirty-nine Congregational lawmakers came from Vermont's six eastern counties, while fourteen came from the state's western counties. Ten years later the relationship was stronger. Forty came from the East and only ten from the West. Given another decade and the reapportionment revolution, however, this highly visible geographic alignment had radically altered. In 1969 the number of Congregationalists in the House was greatly reduced. Of those who remained, eighteen came from the western six counties and only thirteen lived in the East.

7. Earle Newton, *The Vermont Story*, p. 39.

The Congregationalists in the legislature from the east hailed from the smaller towns and were swept aside by reapportionment. In the West, however, they were as likely to be located in the larger communities as the smaller ones, and this served to protect them. Moreover, the West gained seats on the East through reapportionment. This relative gain actually served to increase the absolute Congregational representation from that part of Vermont. This seems to be an important, if subtle result of reapportionment, indicating the powerful effect structural changes may have on recruitment patterns of more than a century's duration.

More will be said concerning political parties. It is clear at this point, however, that the rural elite in Vermont did effectively hold back minority-party representation. Nowhere did the Democrats make up even one quarter of the personnel analyzed, although their percentages in statewide elections during this period far exceeded 25. In the administrative branch, however, only 56 percent of the membership would admit to a Republican Party preference. This seems to indicate that those who administered the laws were less politically minded than the lawmakers, the higher executives, and the judges.

Vermont government was controlled by men. Only in the House did women achieve significant representation (15 percent). It is ironic to note that even here female representation has waned since the House was reapportioned in the act of 1965—which was vociferously supported by the Vermont League of Women Voters.

A Weberian "ideal type" of rural lawmaker would show that he is a male over sixty years old; he is parochial—a native, a localite, with no military service to broaden his horizons; he attended the local schools, which do not include a college; he is a member of the dominant political party (Republican), the dominant occupational group (farmers), and the dominant religion (Congregational).

Figure I outlines the nature of the rural elite viewed in this manner. Assuming for purposes of summary that each category listed (we have left out "officers in the military") contributes an equal value to the construction of our typical rural lawmaker, it is possible to rank the five areas of governmental service according to how greatly they contribute to the model. This may be

Figure I
Cross Section of the Rural Elite, 1947-1971

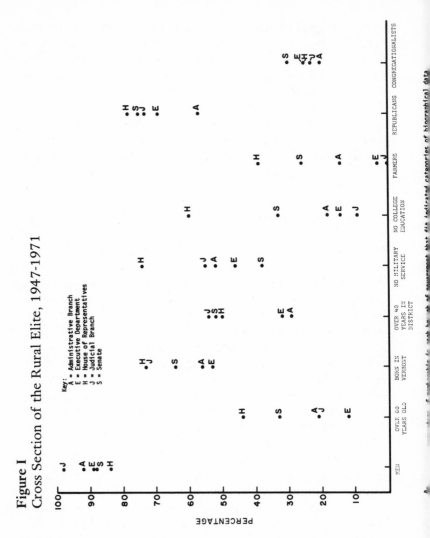

Key:
A = Administrative Branch
E = Executive Department
H = House of Representatives
J = Judicial Branch
S = Senate

done by totaling the percentage figures for each branch on one subdivision of each of the nine categories used. In other words, if the total membership of the House were over sixty years old, the score for that category would be 100. Since only 44 percent of the membership is over sixty, however, the score is actually 44. The scale runs from zero to 900, zero, if on each of the categories none of the members fit the criterion, 900 if all the members fit the criterion in all nine categories used. Figured this way, the relative positions of the five branches are as follows:

Branch	Score
House	527
Senate	438
Judiciary	406
Administration	359
Executive	343

It appears certain from these figures that the Vermont House of Representatives goes far in the direction of the purely rural model. Members were neither young nor well educated. They were parochial. Many were farmers and laborers. In their politics and in their religion, they were members of homogeneous and majority groups. Of equal significance, however, is the distance between the biographical character of the House of Representatives and the other four rule-making institutions. The Senate, which holds a legislative veto over the House, is as much akin to the executive, administrative, and judicial branches as it is to the House. The rural polity seems to have produced a balanced elite corps, in which the intense rural character of the state is reflected in the lower house of the Legislature, while the executive, administrative, and judicial branches exhibit something quite different, with the Senate occupying the center.

Elites, it is well known, produce elites. The "iron law of oligarchy" holds that within groups of leaders there is a center-seeking force that draws power from the many to the few. It would be silly to retest this hypothesis in Vermont, since there is no reason to believe that the state is immune to Michael's "iron law." But it does seem useful to ask the question: Was Vermont's inner circle colored differently from the rank and file?

The best environment in which to search for the answer is in the House of Representatives, where the committee chairmanships provide a convenient handle with which to identify elite within elite. There were approximately 170 different committee chairmen in the House between the years 1947 and 1972. Did they bear any markings that would distinguish them from the membership as a whole? The statistics show very few. Committee chairmen were better educated, with substantial graduate training. They were also more apt to be lawyers, out-of-staters, and military veterans, and less apt to be farmers, women, and Democrats.

Yet most of the percentage differences were not great. The variables of lawyer and postgraduate education show the most outstanding fluctuations, but they are, of course, tightly interdependent. The most meaningful tag we have with which to identify class differentiations—religious affiliation—shows that there were more Congregationalists and Episcopalians in the legislative elite cadre and fewer Methodists and Catholics. The strength of these associations was not great, although several were statistically significant. The associations involving more education, lawyers, and military service, and fewer Democrats and Methodists all produced coefficients of correlation between .40 and .60. Membership in fraternal organizations did not show great variation between the group of committee chairmen and the rest of the legislators, although there were more Masons and fewer Grangers in the leadership segment than one would expect given the composition of the entire House.

What seems most interesting about these findings is that the tendency to oligarchy did not move in the direction of the major biographical characteristics in evidence. In other words the core of the system did not exhibit significant maximization of the prominent qualities of the whole body, except in the case of Republicanism and Congregationalism. While none of the matches between the two groups revealed profound differences, the only movement that was visible pointed to a leadership cluster that was more cosmopolitan than the rank and file.

Comparison

A central theme of this analysis is that we are dealing with a polity where the people live apart from one another—so far apart that this circumstance leads to the question whether they might govern themselves differently from people who live in cities. If democratic systems are conditioned by the socio-cultural milieu that spawned them, one would expect the manner of governing in Vermont to be somewhat different from the manner of governing in California, Ohio, Missouri, or any state where the ratio of people to space is different. Pursuing this kind of speculation leads inevitably to comparison—an exercise we must now consider in regard to state elite structures.

Research on the character of state political elites is immediately limited by a scarcity of data with which to make comparisons. Difficulties in obtaining consistent data have held this analysis to a small number of variables and limited us to state legislators. Nevertheless, the four categories that have yielded sufficient data (Education, Occupation, Duration of Residency in Districts, and Religion) represent four of the most important elements of personnel structure and provide enough evidence to make judgments about the nature of political recruitment on a cross-state basis.

Occupation

To begin, a pair of simple and straightforward relationships are proposed: farmer legislators live, for the most part, in the rural states. Lawyers are a product of the urban milieu, and accordingly will be found predominantly in the legislatures of the more urban states.

Figure II shows the workings of the farmer-ruralism and lawyer-urbanism relationships. Here twenty-five states are arrayed along the horizontal axis according to their degree of metro-urbanism.[8] The measure of metro-urbanism used here doubles the percentage of a state's population living within a

8. John Crittenden, "Dimensions of Modernization in the American States," *American Political Science Review*, 61 (1967), 989-1001.

Figure II
Farmers and Lawyers in Various State Legislatures by Metro-Urbanis

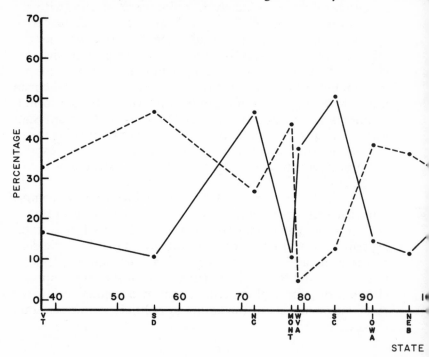

STATE

[a]Sources for the biographical data contained in this and other figures and tables utilizing s
and Kenneth N. Vines, eds., Politics in the American States (Boston: Little, Brown and Compa
Midwest Legislative Politics (The University of Iowa: Institute of Public Affairs, 1957); Ken
Indiana (Indiana University: Bureau of Government Research, 1961); Malcolm E. Jewell and Samu
in the United States (New York: Random House, 1966); Gilbert Y. Steiner and Samuel K. Gove, L
The University of Illinois Press, 1960). Legislative manuals, yearbooks and blue books were
Maryland, Michigan, Minnesota, Nebraska, New Jersey, New York, North Carolina, Rhode Island,
West Virginia.

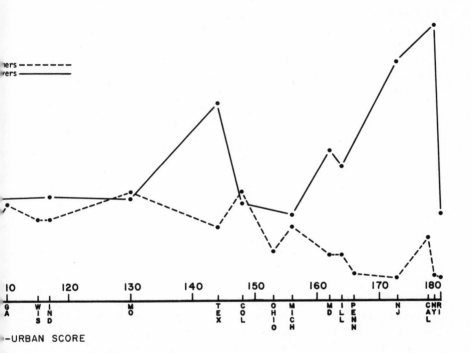

ers ------
ers ————

10   120   130   140   150   160   170   180

G   W   M   T C   O M   M I P   N   CNR
A   I   O   E O   H I   D L E   J   AYI
      S   X L   I C   L N   L
      D   O H   N

-URBAN SCORE

tion are: Herbert Jacob
uel C. Patterson, ed.,
gislative Politics in
n, The Legislative Process
itics in Illinois (Urbana:
the following states:
, South Dakota, Texas, and

standard metropolitan statistical area and adds the percentage of the population living outside the SMSA classified "urban" by the census. The effect of such a measure is to place states like North Carolina low on the scale (lower, for instance, than Iowa or Montana) and states like Colorado high on the scale—higher than Indiana or Texas. However, there is little difference between this measure and the one used by the U.S. Census (percentage living in SMSA's). The two correlate at .93 (Kendall tau).

Certainly the relationship between ruralism and farmer legislators seems to hold, although the pattern is not a smooth one. South Dakota is high with 47 percent of legislators involved in agriculture, and New Jersey and Rhode Island are low with about 2 percent. Vermont is substantially more rural than any of the other states and ranks fifth in farmer representation.

The same cannot be said for the hypothesized relationship between lawyers and urbanism. Though a cluster of rural states (Vermont, South Dakota, Montana, Iowa, and Nebraska) rank low in lawyer representation, and a group of urban states rank high (Texas, New Jersey, and New York), there are significant variations. On the rural end, North Carolina, West Virginia, and South Carolina all have a substantial number of lawyers in the legislative elite. On the urban end, Michigan and Rhode Island lack the percentages that one would expect in urban states. For instance, in Rhode Island, the most urban state studied, only 19 percent of the legislators are lawyers, while Vermont has nearly as many with 17 percent. These data undercut the generally held notion that lawyers in state legislatures are a product of urban environments.[9]

The discussion to this point has centered around the simple logic that ruralism means farming, urbanism means lawyers, and legislatures reflect socioeconomic environments. We need to explain the variations in the logic—variations that shake but do not destroy the ruralism and farmer-legislator connection and severely question the urbanism and lawyer-legislator connection.

Table 3 ranks the states used in this analysis by the percent-

9. William J. Keefe and Morris S. Ogul, *The American Legislative Process: Congress and the States* (Englewood Cliffs, N.J.: Prentice Hall, 1964), p. 125.

Table 3
Farmer Representation and Other Socioeconomic
and Structural Variables in Twenty-Five States[a]

State by % of farmers in state Legislature	State rank by ruralism	State rank by % farmers in the work force	State rank by farm income as a % of state income	State rank by degree of fair apportionment[b]
South Dakota	2	1	1	8
Montana	4	4	4	16
Iowa	7	3	2	23
Nebraska	8	3	3	2
Vermont	1	10	6	15
Minnesota	9	5	5	24
North Carolina	3	6	8	11
Missouri	14	11	12	17
Colorado	16	15	7	13
Georgia	11	12	11	25
Wisconsin	12	9	10	10
Indiana	13	14	14	5
Michigan	18	17	20	18
Texas	15	13	9	20
South Carolina	6	8	13	12
Tennessee	10	6	15	3
California	23	22	17	22
Ohio	17	19	18	1
Maryland	19	19	19	21
Illinois	20	19	16	14
West Virginia	5	16	21	7
Pennsylvania	21	22	22	4
New York	24	22	24	6
Rhode Island	25	25	25	19
New Jersey	22	24	23	9
	$\rho = .76$	$\rho = .88$	$\rho = .95$	$\rho = -.21$
	$p = .001$	$p = .001$	$p = .001$	$p = .158$

[a]The source for the socioeconomic rankings is *The Statistical Abstract of the United States* (U. S. Department of Commerce, 1960).

[b]The Schubert-Press measure is used here. Glendon Schubert and Charles Press, "Measuring Malapportionment," *American Political Science Review*, LVIII (1964), 302-27.

age of their legislators that are farmers, and compares this ranking with the states's degree of metro-urbanism and three other variables that might account for the fluctuations in the dependent variable, farmers in state legislatures. In the first place, since there is no assurance that rural areas are populated by farmers, perhaps farmer representation would correlate more soundly with the number of farmers in the community and not ruralism as such. Or, farmers in the legislature may be a function of the economic impact that farming has in the state. A prosperous farming community might be more apt to seek legislative power than a poor one. Finally, variations in political structure can be important. Malapportioned systems that give rural districts disproportionate strength in the legislature can be expected to contribute to heavier farmer representation.

By applying simple rank-order correlational techniques to the data, it is possible to compare the coincidence of farmer representation with these other variables. The data show that farmer representation and ruralism (the relationship plotted in Figure II) correlates with a coefficient of .76, farmer representation and farmers in the work force at .88, and farmer representation and farm income as a percentage of total state income at .95. All three relationships are statistically significant. If malapportionment did, indeed, promote farmer representation, we would expect a strong negative relationship between fairly apportioned systems and farmer representation. Our data indicate no such correlation. The −.21 coefficent is in the right direction, but too weak to be statistically significant.

It would be easy to infer too much from Table 3. The figures do suggest, however, that the incidence of farmers as an occupational group is not so much a function of ruralism as it is a function of the numbers of farmers in the state and the impact of agriculture on the economy. That is to say, it is not the condition of people living apart from one another which produces farmer representation but more a condition of what they are doing and how important that is to the state's economy. North and South Carolina underline this distinction. Both are rural. Each has a large number of farmers in the state's economy. Each has a similar system of apportionment. Yet South Carolina's agricultural impact on the state's economy was less than that of North Carolina. North Carolina, where farmers were economically more secure, had a much larger farmer corps in the legislature. West Virginia, although very rural, has a small agricultural force whose economic significance is small. Her legislature has relatively few farmers. Colorado, a state with significant metro-urbanism and not many farmers, nevertheless elects a sizable farmer force, and her farmers account for a relatively large percentage of the state's income. Vermont, the most rural state, has an agricultural sector that plays a disproportionate role in the state's economy—coincidental with a lack of farmers and a somewhat malapportioned electoral system. Which variable played the leading part in this relationship (economic or structural) cannot be inferred with certainty from these limited data; nevertheless, the very strong .95 correlation between farmer representatives and farm income is suggestive and provokes speculation concerning economic systems and political recruitment.

Although there is no strong relationship between malapportionment and farmer representation as such, there may be a relationship between the degree of farmer overrepresentation and malapportionment. In other words, it is evident from Table 3 that some states have substantial farmer representation despite a lack of farmers in the state. Vermont, Colorado, Michigan, and California rank higher in farmer legislators than they do in percentage of farmers in the work force. Why is this so? What operates to give farmers overrepresentation in some states and not in others? Table 4 ranks the states according to their degree of farmer overrepresentation and then compares this ranking with the degree to which their legislatures are fairly apportioned. It is evident that malapportionment is connected with farmer overrepresentation. Rhode Island deviated the farthest from a perfect one-to-one ratio between farmer citizens and farmer lawmakers. California was next, followed by Michigan, Colorado, Maryland, Vermont, and Montana. Ohio differs sharply; the most fairly apportioned legislature is coincidental with a high degree of farmer overrepresentation. South Carolina, Tennessee, and West Virginia all had a negative farmer-citizen to farmer-legislator ratio—there were relatively more farmers in the state than in the legislature. In none of these states were rural areas protected by grossly malapportioned systems.

Table 4
Farmer Overrepresentation and Apportionment
in Twenty-five States[a]

State by farmer over-representa-tion[b]	Rank	Rank by fair ap-portion-ment	State by farmer over-representa-tion	Rank	Rank by fair ap-portion-ment
Rhode Island	1	19	Minnesota	14	24
California	2	22	Iowa	15	23
Michigan	3	18	N. Carolina	16	11
Colorado	4	13	Nebraska	17	2
Maryland	5	21	S. Dakota	18	8
Vermont	6	15	Texas	19	20
Montana	7	16	Pennsylvania	20	4
Ohio	8	1	New Jersey	21	9
Missouri	9	17	Wisconsin	22	10
Indiana	10	5	S. Carolina	23	12
Illinois	11	14	Tennessee	24	3
Georgia	12	25	W. Virginia	25	7
New York	13	6			

$\rho = -.45$

$p = .013$

[a]The source for the rankings is *The Statistical Abstract of the United States* (U.S. Department of Commerce). See also Glendon Schubert and Charles Press, "Measuring Malapportionment," *American Political Science Review*, LVIII (1964), 302-27.

[b]The ranking for farmer overrepresentation is based on a ratio of farmer citizens to farmer legislators figured as percentages.

The observable relationship between farmer legislators and other socioeconomic variables fails to materialize for lawyer representation. Although there was a strong relationship between the number of farmers in a state and the number of farmers in the legislature, no such connection occurs for lawyers. Moreover, there is no strong correlation between urbanism and lawyer representation, although the coefficient is somewhat larger. The correlation between nonagricultural income and lawyer representation, however, is significant even though it lacks the statistical authority of measurements taken for farmers. (See Table 5.)

It is important to be aware of the magnitude of the gap between lawyer representatives and lawyer citizens. In New York

Table 5
Lawyer Representation and Other Socioeconomic
Variables in Nineteen States

State by percentage of legislators who are lawyers	State rank by lawyers in the work force	State rank by metrourbanism	State rank by nonagricultural income as a % of total income	State rank by fair apportionment
New York	1	2	2	3
New Jersey	4	3	3	6
So. Carolina	18	14	9	8
No. Carolina	19	17	12	7
Texas	8.5	8	11	16
West Virginia	14	15	4	4
Maryland	7	5	6	17
Illinois	3	4	7	10
Indiana	17	11	8	2
Missouri	8.5	9	10	13
Minnesota	12	11	15	19
Colorado	2	7	13	9
Michigan	16	6	5	14
Rhode Island	10	1	1	15
Vermont	13	19	14	11
Iowa	11	13	18	18
Nebraska	6	12	17	1
Montana	5	16	16	12
So. Dakota	15	18	19	5
	$\rho = .05$	$\rho = .38$	$\rho = .65$	$\rho = .19$
	$p = .419$	$p = .053$	$p = .001$	$p = .219$

Source: U.S. Department of Commerce, *The Statistical Abstract of the United States 1957-1962,* and Schubert and Press, *American Political Science Review,* pp. 302-27.

State, for instance, fully 69 percent of the state legislators were lawyers, while less than one percent of the work force was employed in the legal profession. The gap was even greater in all the other states that have been measured, especially North and South Carolina and West Virginia in the South and Indiana and Michigan in the Midwest. These data add to the already well-established observation that lawyers have been the largest single occupational group in American government.

Again, North and South Carolina, West Virginia, and Indiana add variety to the table. While all are somewhat rural and score relatively low in terms of nonagricultural income as a percentage of total state income, the Carolinas recruit a large number of lawyers into state government. The contrasts between New York and New Jersey on the one hand and the Carolinas on the other are sharp. All four states have lawyer legislatures. Yet somehow, lawyer government in New York and New Jersey seems more appropriate environmentally than lawyer government in North Carolina and South Carolina. In Illinois, Colorado, Nebraska, and Montana the recruitment patterns are different and the ratio of lawyer representative to lawyer citizen is much lower. Once more it is instructive to see if this tendency to recruit fewer lawyers is a product of malapportionment. One would expect that it would not be, since there is no relationship at all between metro-urbanism and lawyer legislators. Tables 5 and 6 verify this expectation by showing correlations of only .19 between lawyer representation and fair apportionment and .14 between lawyer overrepresentation and fair apportionment.

Education

Rural areas have long been the subject of dog-patch humor. In them, it has been suggested, the only wisdom is that of the Shakespearian fool, the country simpleton whose sage observations are the product of the unfettered life, a mind free from formalization—so the myth goes. But the difference between myth and reality is considerable. A rank-order correlation between ruralism and the percentage of the population over twenty-five years of age that have college degrees, using twenty states, shows a negative correlation of only $\rho = -.34$. This figure

Table 6
Lawyer Overrepresentation and Apportionment in Nineteen States[a]

State by lawyer overrepresentation	Rank	Rank by fair apportionment	State by lawyer overrepresentation	Rank	Rank by fair apportionment
No. Carolina	1	7	Michigan	11	14
So. Carolina	2	8	Missouri	12	13
New Jersey	3	6	Rhode Island	13	15
Texas	4	16	Vermont	14	11
W. Virginia	5	4	Colorado	15	9
Indiana	6	2	Iowa	16	18
New York	7	3	So. Dakota	17	5
Maryland	8	17	Nebraska	18	1
Illinois	9	10	Montana	19	12
Minnesota	10	19			

$\rho = .15$

$p = .266$

[a]Same sources as for Table 3.

does not reach a level of acceptable statistical significance ($z = 1.48$). We would therefore expect no significant relationship to exist between urbanism and educational levels of state lawmakers—as long as recruitment patterns are essentially similar in rural and urban milieus. And indeed the data on metro-urbanism and college graduates in state legislatures indicate that there *is* no connection between rural states and legislative bodies with lower levels of formal education. Whatever differentiates the results of political recruitment in these states in terms of educational levels cannot be directly tied to the rural condition.

No connection between state educational levels and ruralism does not rule out a positive correlation between state educational levels and legislative educational levels. Is it not reasonable to assume that the educational levels of the body politic will have an impact on the educational levels of the legislature? Put another way, states with more college graduates in the soci-

ety at large will have more college graduates in the legislature—
the degree of metro-urbanism notwithstanding. Data gathered
on twenty states, however, disprove this hypothesis. The degree
to which the population is educated has no consistent impact
on the educational levels of the legislature. The Spearman rank
correlation was – .21. North Carolina and West Virginia, for instance, rank high in terms of college graduates in the legislature
but very low in terms of state educational levels. Vermont and
Rhode Island select fewer college graduates for the legislature
from many more graduates in the state at large. Here are two
states that represent the extremes on the metro-urbanism scale
with essentially the same kind of recruitment process in regard
to the selection of college graduates for the state legislatures.
Both have a considerable number of college graduates from
which to choose, yet both select relatively fewer than nearly all
other states—Vermont from an intensely rural environment and
Rhode Island from an intensely urban environment. Correlating
ruralism and the overrepresentation of lawmakers with a college
diploma produces a weak coefficient (.11). The gap between the
people and the elites is no greater or smaller than in the urban
states.

Another way of considering these educational levels is simply
to conclude that large numbers of college degrees in a legislature
indicate a large number of lawyers in the legislature—the law
being a profession that nearly always requires a B.A. and usually
advanced postgraduate study. The data support this thinking.
The relationship between lawyers and educational levels is very
strong (.91). Few states with a scarcity of lawyers in the legislature also have a large percentage of college graduates.

Religion

Students of American politics have concluded, as we have here,
that legislatures seldom reflect the population in regard to such
things as occupation, education, and social status. Along these
dimensions the gap between the population and the elite is
large. On the other hand, members of elective hierarchies are
seldom dissimilar from their constituents in "birthright" characteristics, such as race, religion, and ethnic background.[10] Our

10. Herbert Jacob and Kenneth Vines, eds., *Politics in the American
States* (Boston: Little, Brown, 1965), p. 166.

task is to determine if there are any variations within the hypothesis that might be explained in terms of degrees of metro-urbanism. Ranking fifteen states by metro-urbanism and the percentage of Catholics in the legislature reveals that Catholics have generally stronger representation in the more urbanized states. However, there are significant variations. Vermont and California, states with extreme positions on the metro-urbanism axis, have equal percentages of their legislative seats occupied by Catholics. This may be explained by noting that rural Vermont has relatively more Catholics than intensely urban California. Perhaps what we really mean when we say Catholics are found more in the legislatures of urban states is that Catholics are found in the legislatures of states where there are many Catholics, most of which states happen to be urban. But rural states will have Catholics represented if Catholics live in that state. Rank-order correlations between Catholics in the legislature, metro-urbanism, and Catholics in the state verify this point. Metro-urbanism and Catholic legislators correlate with a coefficient of ρ - .63, while Catholics in the state correlate with Catholic legislators with a coefficient of ρ = .84.

This sample of fifteen state legislatures also seems to validate the point that the gap between legislative elites and the citizenry on such birthright characteristics as religion is considerably less than it is for characteristics such as occupation and education. Table 7 shows median ratios of citizens to legislators on four dimensions of personal data and indicates that the figures for religion are the closest to a perfect one-to-one-relationship, although farmers are not far off the mark.

Table 7
Median Ratios of Legislators to
Citizenry: Four Characteristics
in Selected States

Personal characteristics	Ratios
Farmers	1.5 - 1
Lawyers	67.3 - 1
College graduates	7.8 - 1
Catholics	0.9 - 1

Length of Residency in District

Although the data are limited, they suggest that there is no relationship between length of residency in the district a legislator represents and ruralism. The standard assumption that the rural legislature is made up of home-grown boys is sorely tried by these data. Ohio, New Jersey, and Rhode Island have more legislators that have lived in their districts all their lives than have South Dakota, West Virginia, and Nebraska. Vermont, the most rural state, has fewer than all six. California has by far the lowest percentage, a fact coincidental with intense metrourbanism. One suspects that this is a product of California's dynamic sociocultural environment rather than urbanism as such. Whatever the reasons for the California statistic, there is no evidence to suggest that urban states will produce legislators who are more mobile than those of rural states.

When we pull together some of our observations concerning the Vermont elite in comparison with the ruling bodies in the more urban states, we find few consistent patterns that can be tied directly to a rural-urban dichotomy. Farmer legislators seem to be a product of the rural condition, but lawyers do not always disappear from state legislatures as ruralism increases. Rural states do not produce a lawmaker of inferior educational background—rather, educational levels appear to be tied to the number of lawyers in the legislature. Homegrown legislators are not peculiar to a rural environment; they are just as likely to be found in urban areas. These conclusions all   seem to suggest that fluctuations in legislative elites do not match fluctuations in the rural-urban continuum. Simply stated, traditional rural-urban distinctions may have little bearing on political recruitment patterns in the states.

Under the Rural Microscope

To this point, efforts directed at a better understanding of the effect of ruralism on legislative elites have proceeded on a cross-state basis. Continuing the effort introspectively, we will discuss the impact of intrastate variations in ruralism. Before reapportionment the Vermont House of Representatives provides an excellent laboratory for such an experiment. Each of the state's 246 towns sent a legislator to Montpelier, producing a legislative body where 150 members resided in towns with fewer than 1000 inhabitants. Another 26 percent of the legislators came from towns with a population of fewer than 2500. Only 13 percent came from constituencies of more than 2500 people. We emphasize that the Vermont legislature is populated by rural people.

Table 8 presents data designed to answer the question: Do variations of district size (when all districts have fewer than 50,000 inhabitants and a great majority are only small towns and villages) affect recruitment patterns? Is it, in other words, possible to talk about degrees of ruralism after population totals have dropped below a certain point?

It would appear that district size has played an important role even in such a rural state as Vermont, although the record is mixed and time plus reapportionment have provided sharp changes in certain areas. In three categories, town size has shown a consistent and positive relationship to biographical factors. Catholics, lawyers, and Democrats all are associated with the larger towns in each of the three House sessions reviewed over a thirty-year timespan.

There are also areas in which town size seems inapplicable as a causal variable. Little evidence suggests that the smaller towns sent older delegations to the legislature, nor is there any consistent evidence that the smaller towns elected more native Vermonters, more men, or less experienced legislators. Finally, there are areas in which a pattern linked to ruralism in 1949 and 1959 changed in 1969 after reapportionment. In 1949 and 1959 it was clear that the larger towns were sending fewer legislators with no college education than were the smaller towns. In 1949, 77 percent of the legislators from the towns of fewer than 1000 people elected representatives that did not indicate attendance at a college in their biographical sketches. Only 48 percent of the towns with a population of 2500 or more, however, elected legislators with no college education. A decade later, this relationship was still the same, although educational levels had increased in all three classes of towns. With the passing of ten more years and the coming of reapportionment, we find that of the twenty-seven small-town legislators only ten

Table 8
Biographical Data for Vermont House Members, by Year and Town Size[a] (percentages)

Categories	1949			1959			1969		
	Rural towns N=152	Small towns N=64	Large towns N=29	Rural towns N=149	Small towns N=66	Large towns N=30	Rural towns N=27	Small towns N=45	Large towns N=78
Over 60 years old	39.5	37.5	34.5	53.0	47.0	56.7	51.8	51.1	50.0
Born in Vermont	75.7	82.8	81.7	69.1	72.7	80.0	59.3	73.3	65.4
Lived in town over forty years	56.6	65.6	62.1	45.0	51.5	60.0	55.6	50.0	43.8
No college education	77.0	60.9	48.3	58.4	56.1	30.0	37.0	55.6	42.3
Occupation									
Farmers	50.7	40.6	17.2	39.6	30.3	16.7	3.7	20.0	3.8
Lawyers	0.7	4.7	24.1	1.3	1.5	23.3	0.0	2.2	14.1
Businessmen	11.8	26.6	44.8	16.8	24.2	26.6	40.7	28.9	23.1
Religion									
Catholics	10.9	10.7	27.6	10.7	21.9	43.0	0.0	20.0	43.6
Congregationalists	23.8	34.4	20.7	24.2	19.7	26.7	37.0	24.4	16.7
Men	84.2	96.9	96.4	77.9	86.4	93.3	81.5	95.6	85.9
Republicans	87.5	79.7	58.6	89.3	71.2	50.0	96.3	71.1	51.3
Freshmen	54.6	50.0	51.7	38.3	48.5	60.0	14.8	42.2	21.8

[a] Rural towns have less than 1000 population. Small towns have from 1000 to 2500 population. Large towns have over 2500 population.

(37.0 percent) did not attend college. The relationship between size of town and educational levels has broken down.

Another example of the changes in the relationship between measures of ruralism and biographical characteristics of legislators is that now the representatives from towns of fewer than 1000 people are no more apt to be farmers than representatives from the towns of more than 1000. Now most of the farmer legislators in Vermont live in the middle-sized towns. Although the empirical record has not been drawn together, this trend may very well be a result of the circumstance that Vermont's smallest towns have generally been hill towns, and farmers have been steadily disappearing from the sides of Vermont's hills over the past several decades. It may also be caused by reapportionment, since so many of the smallest towns have been swallowed up in larger districts, which probably do not lend themselves to the kind of campaign farmers most appreciate, the "reputational" friends-and-neighbors approach. We must remember, however, that the sample of farmers we are talking about after reapportionment is small. There is also a definitional problem in coding occupations described as "farming," since Vermont politicians have a propensity for inflating their connections with what has been regarded by some as a sacred vocation in Vermont—dairy farming.

Nevertheless, for whatever reasons, the relationship between size of town and farmer representation has weakened. Another occupational category, businessmen, also provides evidence of a change from patterns prevalent in the old legislature. In 1949, the relationship between size of town and the selection of businessmen was strong: 12 percent of the smallest towns, 27 percent of the medium-sized towns, and 45 percent of the largest towns elected businessmen. By 1959 the relationship had deteriorated, and by 1969 it had been completely reversed. In that year the tendency was for businessmen to be elected from the smaller towns.

Finally, there are instances of individual sessions revealing relationships between town size and type of representative. In 1949 there was a weak positive relationship between bigger towns and younger representatives. In 1959 Vermonters are more apt to be in the delegations from the larger towns, as are legislators who have lived all their lives in the town they represent. Women were more often from the smaller towns than the larger ones. Increasing town size also seemed to be associated with freshmen legislators in that year.

It is instructive to focus on the first two years of our analysis (1949 and 1959) in order to evaluate the impact of rural-urban distinctions within Vermont in comparison to rural-urban distinctions across the country. To discard the 1969 session is not to suggest that the reapportioned legislature somehow reflects an environment that has substantially changed. It is to say, however, that the old legislature, since it was based on the one town—one vote principle, was an excellent laboratory for observing causal forces between size of place and biographical quality of representation. The N is much larger, 246 rather than 150, and each lawmaker was elected from an integral community rather than an artificially contrived "constituency," as is the case in many districts in Vermont today.

The observation (in 1959) that larger-town representatives are more closely tied to their districts than rural ones coincides with our cross-state findings. There it was shown that legislative elites of the urban states are generally anchored to their districts to a greater degree than are their counterparts in the more rural states. So do the findings that Catholics are associated with larger towns and farmers with the smaller ones. Yet while our interstate analysis failed to turn up any other substantial relationships between degrees of ruralism and different quality of rulership, our intrastate analysis seems to have done so. The educational levels of legislators were tied to rural-urban distinctions in Vermont—they were not in the nation at large. Lawyer legislators in Vermont came from the urban places—lawyer legislators across the country were not necessarily found only in the urban states.

Dynamics

The overview of Vermont's rural elite included members of the state's hierarchy that served over a twenty-four year period, from 1947 to 1971. Our comparative analysis focused on legislative personnel serving in the years 1957 and 1959. These two sessions were chosen because they provided a view of the legis-

lature midway between 1947 and 1969 and because nearly all
the other data available from other states was drawn from these
years. The intrastate analysis used data from the 1949, 1959,
and 1969 decennials in order to reveal changes in the hypothetical relationship between district size and type of legislator.

Our next consideration is the dynamics of the rural elite: the
changing nature of personnel types in rural government. Does
the character of the rural elite react to changes in the polity at
large? If so, how quickly? Has there been a decrease in the number of farmers in the community and in the legislature? As educational levels in rural society change, do the educational levels
of the ruling group change as well?

The two decades following World War II were dynamic ones
for Vermont. Symbolic of the changes was the fact that in the
early sixties the human population of the state finally surpassed
the cow population. For the first time in decades personal income soared to match national increases. Property prices skyrocketed as the hill farmer disappeared and outsiders snapped
up their homesteads for summer retreats. Schools were consolidated, the interstate highway system linked Vermont to lower
New England, television antennas sprouted suddenly from the
rooftops of farmhouses, and more and more ski resorts appeared on the shadowed side of the mountains. All this development was paralleled by vibrations in the world of politics. In
1959, the state shucked a hundred years of tradition and filled
its only Congressional seat with a Democrat. The heresy was
compounded in 1962 when, for the first time in 109 years, a
Democrat seized the governor's office. Philip Hoff stayed there
for three terms.

How did all this change affect the people of rural politics in
the legislature and the state administration? Changes in the
kinds of people elected to the House of Representatives were
probably linked in some fashion to reapportionment. Between
1947 and 1965, for instance, there was a steady increase in the
percentage of lawmakers over 60 years old (see Table 9). The
reapportioned legislatures demonstrated a reversal of this trend
by a sharp drop in older representatives. The strength of the
agricultural component in the House had been slowly eroding
since the war. With the demise of one town—one vote, however,
14 percentage points were quickly washed away, more than

Table 9
Biographical Data by Governmental
Branch and Time Periods
(percentages)[a]

Categories	House				
	1947 to 1949	1951 to 1955	1957 to 1959	1961 to 1965	1967 to 1971
Over 60 years old	41	47	51	58	49
Catholics	12	8	16	20	31
College graduates	23	38	38	38	41
Farmers	43	40	35	29	15
Women	12	17	19	19	12
Index of Parochialism[b]	250	232	233	236	199

[a]The percentage figures for the House and Senate are averages of yearly figures. The percentages for the bureaucracy are based on one total taken for the entire time period.

twice the loss of any previous timespan. Although the largest relative gain the Catholics had experienced occurred between the 1951 and 1955 sessions and the 1957 and 1959 sessions (the percentage doubled from 8 to 16), their largest absolute gain came in the sessions following reapportionment, when their strength increased from 20 percent to 31 percent. Only the education levels remained unmoved after reapportionment. The percentage of college graduates in the House has remained remarkably constant since the 1951–55 sessions. During these three years educational levels leaped dramatically upward, from 23 percent who were college graduates in the 1947–49 totals to 38 percent in the 1951–55 sessions.

Percentages of women in the House are an especially interesting case, for they show how the feminist movement has been hurt by reapportionment. In the sessions prior to reapportionment the number of women in the legislature had shown a substantial gain. Yet in the years following, only 12 percent of the

Table 9 (cont.)

	Senate					Bureaucracy			
1947 to 1949	1951 to 1955	1957 to 1959	1961 to 1965	1967 to 1971	1947 to 1950	1951 to 1956	1957 to 1962	1963 to 1968	1969 to 1972
35	50	45	49	50	30	29	30	21	18
10	18	33	29	38	10	13	17	32	22
48	48	68	76	66	63	64	70	74	72
28	34	20	13	18	21	18	14	12	7
7	7	10	10	9	6	6	8	9	11
246	215	211	179	181	203	194	197	163	140

bThe Index of Parochialism is the cumulative percentage scores for the following four categories: place of birth, years in district, military service, and place attended college. Individuals born in Vermont, having lived for many years in their towns of residence, having attended college in Vermont (if they attended college) and having no military service would rank high on parochialism.

House members have been women. It is not an exaggeration to suggest that *Baker v. Carr* set the women-in-politics movement in Vermont back twenty years. Evidently "one *man*—one vote" has been taken literally in the Green Mountain State.

The final dimension of elite character measured here, the Index of Parochialism (IP) combines several categories. This index is the cumulative percentage scores for the following four categories: place of birth, years in district, military service, and place attended college. If, for instance, all members of the House in a particular time period were born in Vermont, all had lived in their districts all their lives, all had no military service, and all of those who had attended college had done so in Vermont, the IP would be 400, the total of the four percentage figures of 100. If no House member matched any of these criteria, then the House would be completely cosmopolitan with a score of zero. It would be foolhardy to claim for this measure any scientific reliability. There is clearly no guarantee that the index, which does not discriminate among, or weight, the data sets included, is an accurate operational definition for parochialism. Yet it is a handy technique for purposes of summary and is linked securely enough to a unidimensional "parochial-cosmopolitan" field to allow comparative distinctions of some value. When applied to the membership of the House of Representatives over a twenty-four-year timespan, it reinforces our suspicions that reapportionment was operative in altering the nature of Vermont's elite corps. After a mild drop in the early 1950's, the IP had remained remarkably constant for a decade. But after 1965 (the last session before reapportionment), it fell markedly from 236 to 199. Though we have no precise evidence with which to tie the empirical record to the hypothesis, the coincidence of reapportionment and this major lowering of the IP is significant.

Vermont's upper chamber was not importantly restructured after *Baker v. Carr.* It may not be surprising, therefore, to discover that the major changes that occurred in the Senate's membership did not occur coincidently with reapportionment, as they did in the House. Catholics came in greater numbers to the 1957 and 1959 sessions. Farmers suffered their greatest losses before 1960. College graduates increased tremendously during the late 1950's. Age levels changed the most in the three sessions between 1951 and 1955, when the percentage of the senators over sixty increased from 35 to 50. These figures have remained substantially the same ever since. Although the data for women has not changed radically in twenty years, the only increase that did occur came well before the 1960's. The Senate's IP scores conform to this pattern. Parochialism in the upper body decreased in a two-step sequence, once in the early 1950's (31 points) and again a decade later in the sessions between 1961 and 1965 (32 points). After 1965, while the IP in the House was plunging rapidly, it remained constant in the Senate.

The data points used to measure the dynamics of recruitment in the legislature were structured to allow maximum assessment of the impact of reapportionment. In dealing with the bureaucracy they were redrawn to permit an accurate view of the impact of political change—in this case the first breakthrough of a Democrat to the governor's chair in a century. Philip Hoff won in 1962 and served as chief executive for six years. Did the color of the bureauracy shift during this period? The evidence is mixed. Clearly, age levels fell sharply during the Hoff era (1962-68), and the number of Catholics working in state government increased sharply. Parochialism in the bureaucracy dipped importantly as well (34 points) and continued its decline when the chief executive's post returned to the GOP. On the other hand, the percentage of college graduates did not fluctuate, the percentage of farmers continued its steady decrease, and the percentage of women continued its steady increase. All were seemingly unaffected by the dramatic happenings in Vermont's political world. It should also be noted that increases in the number of Catholics were no doubt a result of a new influx of Democrats brought into the Hoff administration and not evidence of the independent entrance of a new social class into rural government.

This influx brings up the question of strict political implantations on the part of the Democrats. It has long been known that Vermont's new Democratic governor was caught on the horns of a dilemma well known to chief executives occupying posts in hostile political territory: play ball with the opposition in terms of appointments, hope for reciprocal support in the legislature, but risk alienating one's own party, or ensure peace in the ranks by staying within the party for appointments, but risk the hostility of an opposition party with the power to lower the legislative boom on executive proposals. It is generally believed that Hoff alienated many rank-and-file Democrats through his refusal to pack his administration with party loyalists. However, the data in the file used here indicate that during the latter stages of the Hoff administration substantial numbers of Democrats were finding their way into state government. In the new listings during this time, Democrats were outnumbering Republicans nearly two to one. In the group that left state government with or soon after Hoff, there were twice as many Democrats as Republicans. Moreover, in the cluster of new arrivals that entered the bureaucracy of Republican Governor Deane Davis after 1967, the Republicans outnumbered the Democrats three to one. Evidently the spoils system is still operative.

Making comparisons between the two branches of Vermont's legislature produces a pair of interesting observations concerning the dynamics of recruitment. The first involves the reaction of the two bodies to the reapportionment revolution. We have seen that after reapportionment the percentage of the membership over sixty years old decreased in the House but failed to change in the Senate. The percentage of college graduates increased in the House but decreased in the Senate. Farmers decreased in the House but increased in the Senate. Finally, the House took on a more cosmopolitan coloring while the Senate became more parochial. Perhaps bicameralism contains a built-in mechanism that balances the defects of structural changes in the electoral system. This kind of thinking is not dissimilar to the assessment of the state's press, which has often indicated that the Senate's post-reapportionment behavior has been akin to that of the House before reapportionment. If this observation is valid, it may be because of the parade of key figures in the House that moved to the Senate in the years following reapportionment. In 1969 Ward Bedford, a talented and experienced legislator, Leo O'Brien, the minority leader during the dynamic Hoff years, Fred Westphal, a highly respected conservative spokesman for the antireapportionment forces; Richard Mallary, a competent speaker of the House for three important sessions between 1966 and 1968, and Sanborn Partridge, a principal architect of the new apportionment plan, all migrated to Vermont's upper chamber. By 1971 Mallary and O'Brien had left, but they were replaced by Arthur Gibb, Graham Newell, and John Alden, three important figures in the House of Representatives. Also returning to the Senate in 1971 after some years of absence were Fred Fayette and Russell N. Niquette, two influential Democrats from Chittenden County. Add to all this evidence the fact that John Burgess, the Lieutenant Governor and thereby President of the Senate, was himself Speaker of the House in 1969, and it is easy to understand why the Senate has appeared to reflect the past of the House. By 1971 the thirty Senate members had seventy sessions of experience in the House behind them, and the great portion of that experience came prior to reapportionment. They also had 100 sessions of previous service in the Senate. This means that the average legislative experience per member of the Senate was five sessions, an amazing statistic given the biennial elections each Senator must face.

This may help to explain the next point of comparison between the two Houses. Although the nature of the membership in both bodies has changed since the war, in the Senate these changes arrived many years before they did in the House. Evidence will be presented in later chapters to show that the breakthrough of the minority party in Vermont came in the early 50's. Possibly the Senate, based on a one man—one vote electoral system, reacted swiftly to these political vibrations, while changes in the House had to await reapportionment, since the one town—one vote principle isolated it from societal movements. The logic of this explanation is appealing and, given a lack of more satisfying evidence, should be accepted.

In comparison to the legislature, changes in the bureaucracy were generally less dramatic. Those sharp alterations that are in evidence took place during the years of the Hoff administration (1963-68) and were probably politically inspired. Concentrated analysis of the statistics of this period suggests no other explanation. In a future chapter we will suggest that changes in legislative politics in Vermont were the result of political forces riding on the shoulders of a breakthrough minority and adhering to the "innovative party" theory. Evidently Hoff was also able to affect the tone of the bureaucracy.

Quotas

Events at the two major party national conventions in 1972 threatened to create an oddity of American presidential politics—a confrontation between the parties on a question of democratic theory. For a brief moment it seemed as if the struggle might, at least in one dimension, rise above traditional campaign techniques and practices. The issue in question was the quota system of representation, and it cut to the core of the theory of representative democracy. It is a comment on the nature of American political debate to note that even a confrontation over such an elementary problem (no basic text in American government fails to discuss it, usually at some length) would have been a major breakthrough for those who hope to see campaigns some day rise above their present levels.

On the face of it, the question is simple. Is representative democracy working when major subgroups in the political system are not found within the elites that control the country? Can a black be represented by a white? Can a farmer be represented by a lawyer? Can a woman be represented by a man, the young by the old, the uneducated by the educated? These questions are not reserved for national politics. Recently, the newsletter of Vermont's third party, the Liberty Union, pointed to the Vermont legislature as a repository for lopsided ratios between those who rule and those who do not.

Given their premises, the Liberty Union is not wanting for evidence. Some groups in Vermont are overrepresented, some are underrepresented. The old are heavily overrepresented in the House and Senate. While those over 60 years old make up about 15 percent of the state's population, they hold one-half the seats in both Houses. The bureaucracy, however, approximates the state percentage. Fewer than 20 percent are over 60. In 1971 there were over seven men in the House for every woman. In the state the sexes were about evenly divided. In the Senate there were nine men for every woman. The administrative branch was similar to both the House and Senate, with about 12 percent of the total number recorded consisting of women. Native Vermonters were also underrepresented in the Senate and the bureaucracy, but in neither case were the ratios far off. In the House the percentage of native Vermonters matched almost perfectly the statewide figure. Overrepresented were college graduates and farmers. In the former case the discrepancies were huge, especially in the bureaucracy. In the latter they were reasonably close.

Figure III arrays the data for farmers in the work force of the state and in the three branches of government that concern us here. Farmer representation deserves special attention because a shrinking agricultural sector has been a most profound socioeconomic phenomenon in Vermont in recent decades. Farmers, who accounted for one-third of Vermont's workers in the years immediately following the war, made up only 11 percent of the work force in 1964 and only 6 percent in 1970. In the bureaucracy, appointive recruitment capability may have served to cushion the blow felt by the farmers in the legislature, where they suffered a continuing loss of representation. In the House

Figure III
Farmers in Vermont Government and the Labor Force, 1948-1970

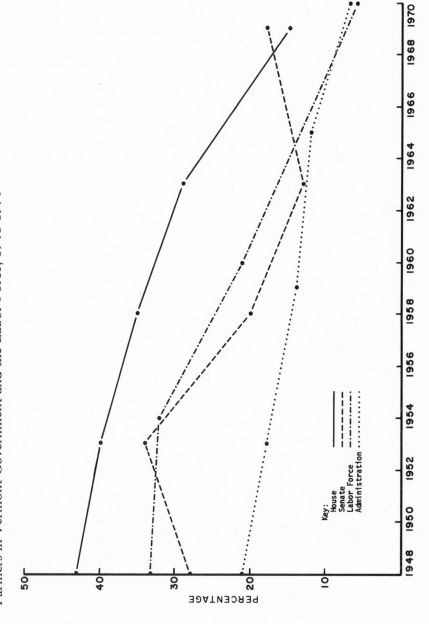

malapportionment seemed to preserve a degree of agricultural influence. But even with the electoral system stacked in their favor, representation dropped in the years before *Baker v. Carr.* The Senate's formula of one man–one vote lowered farmer strength from 34 percent in the 1951-55 sessions to 13 percent a decade later in the sessions immediately preceding reapportionment. However, although reapportionment in the House of Representatives cut the floor out from under the farmers (they lost 14 percentage points in four years), the Senate seemed to take up the slack; and farmer representation there has even increased since 1965.

If we view farmer representation as a test of the quota theory, we find that although the ratios were not perfect in Vermont, they were at least balanced. Farmers were underrepresented in the bureaucracy, overrepresented in the House, and fairly represented in the Senate. It does not seem reasonable to predict that the farmer work force will dip below 5 percent. Time will tell if the farmer delegation in the legislature will be adjusted downward to meet the 5 percent level. It also seems fair to suggest, given the remarkable parallel decrease in farmer strength in the state and the House of Representatives, that ratios, however unfair, do shift with time and react to structural changes in government (in our case, reapportionment).

Pathways to Power

Like the Indians who followed trails through the Green Mountains to raid English settlements, Vermont's leading politicians have taken identifiable pathways through political thickets to arrive at positions of influence and power. Schlesinger in his unique treatment of nearly one thousand state governors has singled out Vermont as the "best example of the state wide elective hierarchy."[11] What Schlesinger means is that in Vermont there was a clear prerequisite to the governorship: serving in a statewide elective office, specifically the lieutenant governorship. His evidence bears repetition. Between 1930 and 1950 six out of seven Vermont governors were lieutenant governors

11. Joseph Schlesinger, *How They Became Governor*, p. 32.

before they became governor. Many of these had held leadership posts in the legislature prior to their election as lieutenant governor. Moreover, of those who attained the governorship by side-stepping the lieutenant governor's post, several were speakers of the House of Representatives.[12] In Vermont before 1950, there was a system within which successful political careers (as evidenced by election to the governorship) did not just happen but were carefully constructed by apprenticeship through a hierarchy of clearly predictable elective offices.

Looking past Schlesinger's data into the last two decades of Vermont's political life reveals in the beginning a remarkably similar landscape. All of Vermont's chief executives in the 1950's held the lieutenant governorship before they were elected governor. Lee Emerson, from the Northeast Kingdom town of Barton, exemplifies very well the stepladder pattern. He served two terms in the House, was elected speaker during his third term, moved to the Senate, was elected lieutenant governor, and was then governor. Joseph Johnson and Robert Stafford each served an apprenticeship as lieutenant governor.

Since the beginning of the decade of the 1960's, however, there has been evidence that the pattern is dissolving: (1) Ray Keyser, who followed Stafford as governor, bypassed the lieutenant governorship and was elected directly from his post as speaker of the House. To do so it was necessary to defeat the incumbent lieutenant governor and heir apparent to the governorship, Robert Babcock. (2) Philip Hoff unexpectedly threw a wrench into the machinery by winning as a Democrat. (3) Deane Davis, the Republican who took over when Hoff left, was not an experienced legislator and had never held a statewide elective office. Davis was in strict violation of the apprenticeship rule, although he had held a myriad of important posts in local and state government in the state. (4) After Davis' two terms were over, in 1972, the lieutenant governor, John Burgess (a man clearly in line for the governorship under the old system, since he had been speaker of the House as well) refused to run for governor and chose instead to repeat as lieutenant governor. His action brought an editorial from the state's largest daily newspaper, the *Burlington Free Press*, suggesting that he either

12. Ibid., p. 30.

try for the governorship or move aside for upward-mobile politicians. The editorial reflected how deeply ingrained the apprentice pattern has been in Vermont. Finally, neither of the candidates to try for the governorship in 1972 was molded in the traditional cast. James Jeffords, who lost in the primary, had served only one term in the Senate and was then elected attorney general before running for governor. Luther Hackett, who won the 1972 Republican primary, had been majority leader in the House and had sought the governor's office from a somewhat obscure post in the administration of Governor Davis.

At the congressional level, Vermont's senators and representatives have likewise conformed to rigid modes of selection, and, unlike the patterns displayed in gubernatorial politics, these modes seem to be holding fast. Of Vermont's ten senators that have served since the introduction of the direct primary system, seven held statewide elective offices immediately preceding their move to the U.S. Senate (either governor or congressman), two were outside elective politics, another was a congressman holding one of the two House seats claimed by Vermont prior to the 1930 census. Six of the ten had been elected to the state legislature. Two of these had served in both chambers, and two were speaker of the House.

Vermont has elected a dozen congressmen since 1914. Seven of these were members of the Vermont legislature earlier in their careers. Three were speakers. Two governors moved on to Washington; four held positions in the state's bureaucracy prior to their election to Congress. In general, however, the apprentice system for the national House of Representatives has been more open than for the national Senate.

One of the most striking characteristics of rural Vermont's selection processes for the state's representatives at the national level has been the fact that the hinges on the door to the federal Senate swing inward, not outward. For changes to occur in Vermont's Senate delegation, one must usually await the death of an incumbent. One of Vermont's Senate seats has not been opened because of the retirement of an incumbent since the nineteenth century, and the other seat was released for this reason on only two occasions. Never in this century has an incumbent senator been denied his office in Washington. Moreover, this practice seems as healthy today (1972) as it was fifty years ago. Today as yesterday, when an incumbent senator dies in office, it causes reverberations all along the pathways to power. The incumbent congressman moves to the Senate, a leading Republican on the home front moves to the House, and re-assessment of career goals are made everywhere. In short, what seems to have happened in Vermont is that a selective procedure molded and preserved by the Republican Party is breaking apart from inside out. While the old statewide elective system is no longer operative at the gubernatorial level, the traditional patterns of selecting the state's congressional delegation still await the kind of jolt Democrat Philip Hoff provided when he moved into the governorship in 1962.

Another constraint on the open selection of Vermont's leaders grew out of a social-geographical dichotomy rooted in the original settlement and early political history of the state and defined by the Green Mountain crest line which splits the state in half, north to south. As noted in Chapter 1, the state was constructed from two different kinds of social timber: on the sunrise side of the mountains was the northern extension of the Puritan Commonwealth; on the sunset side were the radical adventurers of Connecticut. The friction between these two groups was pronounced during the Revolutionary War and led to attempts to separate the Connecticut River Valley from the rest of Vermont.[13] Out of this sociocultural tension grew the Mountain Rule—an attempt on the part of the state's elite to bridge the gap between the people on the two sides of the mountains by alternating political posts between the Connecticut River Valley counties and the Champlain Valley counties. The practice has been clearly visible and has not failed to catch the eye of nearly all observers of Vermont politics. Recently, it has undergone rigorous scrutiny by Gould and Hand at the University of Vermont,[14] who put teeth into the Mountain Rule

13. Frank M. Bryan, "The State That Might Have Been," *Vermonter* (December 1966), pp. 9-14.

14. Lyman Jay Gould and Samuel B. Hand, "The Geography of Political Recruitment in Vermont: A View from the Mountains," in *Growth and Development of Government in Vermont*, ed. Reginald L. Cook, The Vermont Academy of Arts and Sciences, Occasional Paper No. 5 (1970), 19-24.

hypothesis with their data on the selection of Vermont's senators. Since Vermont began sending its two senators to Washington, only four of thirty-nine pairings have not followed the Mountain Rule. There has been longitudinal consistency as well. George Aiken, Vermont's senior senator, occupies a seat that has forever been held by someone from his eastern side of the mountains. The western portfolio remained in the hands of a westerner from the beginning through World War II.

There is convincing evidence that this particular pathway in Vermont was etched in the consciousness of the state's decision-makers. Early congressional districts were drawn with the Mountain Rule in mind. At least one intravalley political showdown for the Republican nomination for the governorship had to be postponed when the rule dictated that the selection for that particular year must come from over the mountains. When their turn came again, the hostile camps were ready to continue the struggle. The legislature, in preparing potential districts for high office, drew up plans that mirrored traditional east-west selection patterns.[15] Hand and Gould note: "The Mountain Rule not only legitimized a sectional claim to office in the eyes of the general populace but also eliminated a host of otherwise candidates from the field. When it was the western turn only western candidates offered themselves. Likewise only easterners came forth when the turn for that section came due."[16]

Did the Mountain Rule penetrate the lower echelons of the elective office pyramid? The evidence is mixed. As far as the delegation to the U.S. House of Representatives is concerned, the effect of the rule was neutralized, for districts have been drawn coincidentally with the division caused by the mountains. The five men that have served since Vermont's delegation was reduced to a single congressman elected at large have not followed the pattern at all: four of the five have been from the eastern counties.

The selection of governors, however, has followed the Mountain Rule. In the twentieth century the electoral pendulum has swung evenly back and forth across the mountains. The situa-

15. Ibid., p. 20.
16. Ibid., p. 21.

tion lasted until 1944, when Mortimer Proctor followed William Wills to Montpelier. Since both represented southwestern Vermont, this may well have spelled the end of the Mountain Rule as far as the governor's chair is concerned. After Proctor there came three successive candidates from the Connecticut River Valley. Since then, governors have lived on opposite flanks of the mountains. One of these, Vermont's first Democratic chief executive in a century, was in no way selected by the logic of the Mountain Rule, which had been an intraparty Republican phenomenon. Deane Davis lived in the state capital, and while Washington County is clearly on the eastern side of the mountains, Montpelier's linkage with Burlington and the West via the Winooski River Valley is as strong as its connection with the East.

Professor Gould suggests that, although the data have not yet been drawn together, his findings for the judiciary followed the Mountain Rule.[17] A cursory look at the evidence indicates that Gould's conclusions are correct. For instance, eight of the ten chief justices of the State Supreme Court chosen since 1900 were picked from sides of the state opposite from their predecessors.[18] Data for speaker of the House, another very important post in Vermont, show that the legislature was not concerned with the Mountain Rule as it selected its leadership—at least not in this century. No clear pattern is visible in the selection of speakers, although the office has been a valuable crystal ball for predicting the careers of upward-mobile politicians. Evidently the Mountain Rule did not penetrate the walls of the legislature.

To summarize, pathways to power in Vermont have followed two important routes, the apprenticeship system and the Mountain Rule. Though both have been extremely accurate forecasters of political career patterns, both seem to have weakened in certain respects since World War II. There is some doubt that either pattern will survive the communication and transportation revolutions that have beset Vermont in the decades following the war.

17. Gould interview, September 10, 1972.
18. State of Vermont, Secretary of State, *Vermont Legislative Directory and State Manual* (Montpelier, 1947-1971).

Conclusions

We have analyzed the personal background of Vermont's 2500 leading political figures serving over the last quarter century. At long range the statistics show an elite cluster that varied substantially from one governmental branch to the next. The Vermont House of Representatives, the body that usually has served as the prime reference point for assessments of the kinds of people that rule Vermont, exhibited many of the qualities that we suggested fit the model of the rural politician. The other parts of Vermont's system were made up of men and women with different biographical backgrounds. Within the House, the leadership segment, though not remarkably different from the rank and file, seemed to have more cosmopolitan qualities than the rest of the membership. Clearly, they did not accent the parochial flavor that typified the House when it was compared with the Senate, the judiciary, the executive offices, or the bureauracy.

Matching Vermont's legislative elite with its counterparts in other states indicates that there are few differences between them which can be related strictly to the rural condition. When states are ranked on a scale of metro-urbanism, we find that home-town legislators and Catholics are apt to serve in the legislatures of urban states, and that farmers are apt to serve in rural states. Even these findings are subject to qualification. Yet the rural-urban continuum did cause variations in the background characteristics of the legislators within Vermont, especially in the years before reapportionment.

The nature of Vermont's governmental leadership over the last twenty-five years has not remained static. Changes in each branch of the system seemingly have been tied to particular political events in the state. In the Senate changes occurred in the 50's during the years of the Democratic breakthrough. In the House the changes came during the time of reapportionment. In the bureaucracy, new types of people filtered in during the later years of the term of Philip Hoff, Vermont's first Democratic governor in a century.

Holders of political power in Vermont were not typical of the population at large and fell short of satisfying the quota theory of representation. Only in certain areas did the legislators reflect the kinds of people in the state. Age levels in the bureaucracy were close to those of the state as a whole. Native Vermonters were found in equal numbers in the House of Representatives, and farmers were more accurately "represented" in the Senate. For the most part, however, rural politicians were different from the population outside government. Although the farmers' quota has generally been inflated, it is clear that it has been adjusted downward in recent decades to match decreases in the percentage of farmers in the work force. Vermont is as rural as ever, but it has not insulated its farmer politicians from changes in the composition of the state's socioeconomic character.

Finally, we sought to make sense of the maze of political patterns that have developed in Vermont in the twentieth century. The task was immensely simplified by the existence of two obvious pathways to power. The apprenticeship system for statewide elective office has traditionally been operative in the selective process for governors. Moreover, the governorship seems to be one step of a ladder used constantly by upward-mobile politicians. Built into the system are the speakership of the House, a seat in the Senate, the lieutenant governorship, and the national congressional offices. Another striking pattern of recruitment has been the Mountain Rule, which has dictated that Vermont's senators, governors, and members of the state judiciary be balanced to represent the valleys of the Connecticut River and Lake Champlain, which fall away, east and west, from the crest line of the Green Mountains. The Mountain Rule offers an exciting case study for political geographers and seems to have been a potent force in Vermont's recruitment processes.

Three

Party Politics in a Rural Setting

When the only one-party state north of the Mason-Dixon Line and the only one-party *Republican* state anywhere begins to shift gears politically, eyes are turned.

Without doubt, Vermont's recent history provides a special opportunity to view close up the phenomena accompanying political change. Though we cannot be certain at this point that the Democratic insurgence is permanent, we do know it happened and we do know that it ended an era that began over a century ago. When we add these facts to the fact that Vermont is the most rural state (except Alaska) and consider that dozens of scholars have said ruralism poisons party competition, we cannot help being intrigued by the possibilities.

The development of political parties has been one of the major contributions of the modern western democracies to the theory and practice of politics. The party has become the dominant functional component of the American political system, and students of politics in this country have reacted accordingly. The literature on parties is voluminous. Indeed, many analytical views of entire political systems have focused on the parties, heuristically—relying on this single component to direct and rationalize the myriad of concerns that touch the governmental process. It is not far off the mark to suggest that the study of comparative state politics has been more than anything else the study of political parties, both in the legislature and out. Our purpose here is to supplement this literature through a descriptive-analytical treatment of party politics within an intensely rural milieu.

Two phenomena stand immediately above the uncertainties surrounding Vermont party politics. These are ruralism and one-partyism. Their coincidence is so striking that we cannot move further without dealing with it. Ample evidence has already been presented to document Vermont's rural condition. With the exception of Alaska she occupies the cellar of our scale of metro-urbanism. At the same time, Vermont places near the bottom of various measures of two-party competition. In 1954 Ranney and Kendall typed Vermont as a "one-party state in which the second party has won less than 25 per cent of all elections and has also won over 30 per cent of the vote in less than 70 per cent of all elections and has won over 40 per cent of the vote in less than 30 per cent of the elections." Using Malcolm Jewell's measure, Vermont is classified as a one-party dominant state in which a single party controls both houses of the legislature but not always the governorship.

More recently, Pfeiffer has classified Vermont as the least competitive of the Republican-controlled states—a modified one-party Republican state. Richard Hofferbert's analysis ranks Vermont forty-first among forty-eight states according to party competition. John Fenton places Vermont thirty-fourth among forty-six states. Finally, Dawson and Robinson rank Vermont thirty-sixth among forty-six states. Though each of these measures defines party competition differently, they all show Vermont among the top dozen one-party states and the most completely Republican state in the nation.[1]

Much has been said about the relationship between urbanism and party competition. Unfortunately, a clear picture that speaks directly to the problem has yet to be drawn.[2] Notwithstanding the fact that many studies have uncovered a relation-

1. Malcolm E. Jewell, *The State Legislature* (New York: Random House, 1962), p. 10. Austin Ranney and Willmoore Kendall, "The American Party Systems," *American Political Science Review*, 48 (1954), 477-85. David G. Pfeiffer, "The Measurement of Interparty Competition and Systematic Stability," *American Political Science Review*, 61 (1967), 457-67. Richard I. Hofferbert, "A Classification of American State Party Systems," *Journal of Politics*, 26 (1964), 550-67. John H. Fenton, *People and Parties in Politics* (Glenview, Ill.: Scott Foresman, 1966), p. 34. Richard E. Dawson and James A. Robinson, "Inter-Party Competition, Economic Variables, and Welfare Policies in the American States," *Journal of Politics*, 25 (1963), 265-89.

2. Philip Coulter and Glen Gordon, "Urbanism and Party Competition: Critique and Redirection of Theoretical Research," *Western Political Quarterly*, 21 (1968), 274-88.

Table 10
Ruralism and Party Competition
in the American States

States by Ruralism	States by lack of party competition			
	Fenton's ranks	Hofferbert's ranks	Pfeiffer's ranks	Dawson's rank's[a]
Alaska	—	—	15	—
Vermont	11	8	12	36
Mississippi	1	1	2	46
Idaho	32	37	35	6
North Dakota	10	20	20	35
South Dakota	13	21	17	31
Wyoming	28	47	34	13
Arkansas	5	5	5	40
North Carolina	8	7	10	37
Maine	15	14	18	30
Montana	37	26	33	2
New Hampshire	18	17	26	19
West Virginia	24	22	27	21
Kentucky	17	25	29	24
South Carolina	1	3	3	45
Iowa	14	35	31	29
New Mexico	22	27	28	26
Nebraska	—	19	14	—
Kansas	16	13	22	23
Tennessee	7	12	11	32
Alabama	4	4	7	41
Georgia	2	2	1	43
Oklahoma	12	15	19	34
Virginia	9	10	9	38
Wisconsin	20	31	41	28
Indiana	26	38	37	13
Minnesota	—	33	43	—
Louisiana	2	6	4	44
Oregon	19	28	23	27
Missouri	29	23	25	22

Table 10 (cont.)

States by Ruralism	States by lack of party competition			
	Fenton's ranks	Hofferbert's ranks	Pfeiffer's ranks	Dawson's ranks[a]
Washington	37	30	40	9
Delaware	35	48	48	1
Texas	3	11	6	42
Colorado	33	45	44	15
Florida	6	9	8	39
Utah	34	29	49	5
Ohio	23	42	39	17
Arizona	14	18	21	33
Michigan	25	39	47	17
Nevada	35	24	24	16
Maryland	21	36	30	25
Illinois	31	44	46	4
Hawaii	—	—	13	—
Pennsylvania	32	46	42	7
Connecticut	29	43	45	9
New Jersey	30	41	38	20
New York	27	34	50	12
Massachusetts	36	40	36	3
California	31	32	32	11
Rhode Island	33	16	16	8
	$\rho = .49$	$\rho = .46$	$\rho = .44$	$\rho = -.46$
	$p = .001$	$p = .001$	$p = .001$	$p = .001$

[a]Dawson's ranks list competitiveness from most competitive to least competitive; thus the correlation is negative.

ship between urbanism and party competition, it has been impossible to relate competition to any strict definition of urbanism. What is usually meant by the statement that urban politics are more competitive than rural politics is simply that clustered in urban centers there are apt to be heterogeneous elements that define party conflict. Even this conclusion is subject to much qualification.

A rank-order analysis of the American states shows no overpowering relationship between party competition and ruralism. Kendall's tau correlations between our scale of metro-urbanism and four measures of party competition produce coefficients that are statistically significant but very weak. (See Table 10.) Rural states such as Idaho, Wyoming, and Montana with high levels of party competition and more urban states such as Arizona, Florida, Texas, and Louisiana with very low levels of competition leave the relationship somewhat uncertain. These data lend little credence to the hypothesis that ruralism by itself has any independent impact on the degree of interparty competition. Statements such as: "Rural Agriculture States with homogeneous populations do not provide enough social division to support well organized, disciplined, and competitive parties"[3] do not square with these examples of several rural western states and several southern and southwestern urban states.

In Vermont the relationship between competition and urbanism holds at about the same strength as nationally. During the Depression the farming towns were essentially noncompetitive, while towns with higher percentages of their population on relief rolls were more competitive. (See Table 11.) In recent times the larger towns are still apt to approach a two-party split in their voting habits for governor, but the farm population is no longer an important indicator of noncompetitive areas. Hidden in these measurements is the fact that competition in Vermont has simply meant that the Democrats were in the running. There is a clear lack of many noncompetitive Democratic towns in the state. In other words, since competition is strongly related to Democratic success (the correlation coefficient in 1968-70 was .82), there is no way to determine if in fact the larger towns spawn a competitive environment.

It may very well be that the big towns are simply near the midpoint of a purely Republican to purely Democratic continuum and thus appear to be a seedbed of competition. When

3. Thomas R. Dye, *Politics in States and Communities* (Englewood Cliffs, N.J.: Prentice Hall, 1969), p. 99.

Table 11
Relationship between Party Competition and Socioeconomic
Variables in Vermont Towns, 1934–1936 and
1968–1970: Simple Correlation Coefficients (N = 246)[a]

1934–1936		*1968–1970*	
Variables	*Correla-tions*	*Variables*	*Correla-tions*
Farm population	−.44	Population size	.30
Population on relief	.42	Sales and clerical	
Population size	.31	workers	.27
Population increase,		Native born popula-	
1920-1940	.24	tion	−.22
Per capita delinquent		Population under	
taxes	.09	21 years old	.17
Population density	.07	Median family in-	
Per capita town		come	.11
indebtedness	.05	Farm population	.06
		Population below	
		the poverty level	.01

[a]Party competition is measured as the percentage point deviation from 50% of the Democrats' share of the vote for governor. Coefficients ⩾.18 are significant at the .05 level.

the Democrats did crush the Republicans in Vermont in 1964 and 1966, town size actually correlated negatively with competition (−.31). Once again the point is not to refute the observation that urban places are more apt to show competition than rural places; rather, it is to discredit the all-too-often accepted corollary, that rural places cannot be competitive.

Scholars more concerned with the political end of the sociopolitical combination are closer to the root source of party competition when they identify certain historical watersheds as most important in shaping the contemporary political map.[4] Vermont's one-party system was not a result of her ruralism (a sociological variable); it was the result of her Whig sympathies

4. Austin Ranney, "Parties in State Politics," in Jacob and Vines, eds., *Politics in the American States*, pp. 68-69. Fenton, *People and Parties in Politics*, pp. 4-10.

in the beginning and her total commitment to and sympathy with the Union cause during the Civil War (a political variable)—a commitment, hardened by time, that withstood even the urgings of depression and the massive national switch of 1936. What ruralism has done in Vermont is to *shelter* a one-party system for over a century. Urbanism may well provide positive conditions for competition by bringing with it the raw material for feeding new political fires. But the blaze must be politically ignited and sustained by political fuel.

The following paragraphs, supporting this hypothesis, show that when new political fires began in Vermont, they sprang from essentially the same tinder that had existed for decades. Only the spark was unique. Competition did not emerge from a new urbanism in Vermont; it came from people seeking power.

One-Partyism, 1926-1950

To this point we have said that Vermont is intensely rural, that it has been a strict one-party state (and may still be, as we shall see), and that the connection between these two variables is more likely to be reinforcing than causal. We must still confront, however, the crucial questions that strike directly at the heart of representative democracy. Can a one-party state meet the essential criteria of representative democracy? What is the nature of citizen participation in the politics of a state where there is no effective opposition to the majority party? Does a single-party system operate to provide the electorate alternatives of political personnel and policy?

If the effect of one-partyism is to lower the temperature of political struggle to the point where activity at the polls is torpid, and if there is no opportunity for the people to select their own leaders from a choice of at least two, then little can be said to defend the rural one-party state as a functioning democratic polity. Our task in resolving these questions requires two considerations, the first of a hypothesis about the relationship between participation and party competition, and the second of the nature of factionalism within the Republican Party.

Participation and Party Competition

The first hypothesis seems logical enough. In one-party states, participation will be low in general elections. Milbrath points to a syndrome of causal variables centered around the thinking that people will not bother to vote when the result is wholly predictable.[5] Milbrath presents solid evidence. Using the Dawson and Robinson measure of party competition with the Spearman rank-order correlation technique, he finds a strong positive relationship (.807) between one-partyism and low turnout. Six other measures of party competition were also tested with many different measures of turnout, and all but one showed similar results. A close look at Milbrath's comparisons, however, reveals some puzzling distortions. Vermont, for instance, ranks much higher in participation than her competition would seem to warrant. New York, New Jersey, Maryland, and Missouri rank lower than one would presume, given Milbrath's strong positive correlation between competition and participation. In West Virginia we have a case study that suggests that turnout is conditioned primarily by "variables of political style and culture." This state in the Appalachian Mountains has constantly produced high turnout whether intrastate competition is high or low.[6] These considerations, coupled with the fact that the latter end of the participation scale is occupied exclusively by the states of the Old Confederacy, lends credence to the suspicion that sectional and/or political-cultural variables peculiar to the South color Milbrath's conclusion that participation is positively related to interparty competition. These observations demand another look at his work, first by holding the southern sectional variable constant and retesting for the other thirty-seven states that remain, and second, by placing the relationship under our rural microscope to determine whether it holds at the intrastate level in Vermont.

5. Lester W. Milbrath, "Political Participation in the States," in Jacob and Vines, *Politics*, p. 50.
6. Gerald W. Johnson, "Research Note on Political Correlates of Voter Participation: A Deviant Case Analysis," *American Political Science Review*, 65 (1971), 768-76.

In order to retest the "competition means participation" hypothesis, a Kendal tau rank-order correlation was applied to Milbrath's own measurements of participation and four ranks of intrastate party competition in the thirty-seven non-Confederate states. Whereas Milbrath found a correlation of .807 between his rankings for participation and the Dawson-Robinson ranking for competition, using all forty-eight states (Alaska and Hawaii are excluded), our correlation between the sets of data excluding the deep southern states reveals a tau coefficient of only .432. Furthermore, the other three correlations produced much lower coefficients.[7]

Election data from Vermont's fourteen counties lend limited support to the Milbrath thesis. Figure IV plots the relationship between party competition and participation in Vermont between 1926 and 1950 when one-partyism was dominant. The data correlate with a tau coefficient of .495. It seems clear that Vermont's more competitive counties were apt to have higher levels of voter participation.

By shifting our focus from counties to towns, thereby expanding the number of observations from 14 to 233, and by increasing our operational definitions of participation, it is possible to make more precise assessments of the nature of participation in a one-party environment. In the 1936 presidential election, for instance, Vermonters turned out in greater numbers in the more competitive towns. It is also true that the average percentage of registered voters to attend the polls in the election for governor in 1934 and 1936 correlated significantly with political competition. But the correlations in Table 12 indicate that the strongest relationship was between turnout in 1936 and F.D.R.'s percentage of the two-party vote. Since (as we have observed earlier) competition in Vermont simply meant that Democrats were receiving close to one half the vote—there were almost no noncompetitive Democratic towns—it is difficult to determine in any strict sense if it was the competitive situation that prompted more voting or simply the fact that Democratic candidates stimulated a second-party turnout. Nevertheless, on the face of it, there was a clear, although weak

7. Fenton's ranks produced a coefficient of .277; Hofferbert's, a coefficient of .218; and Pfeiffer's, a coefficient of .212.

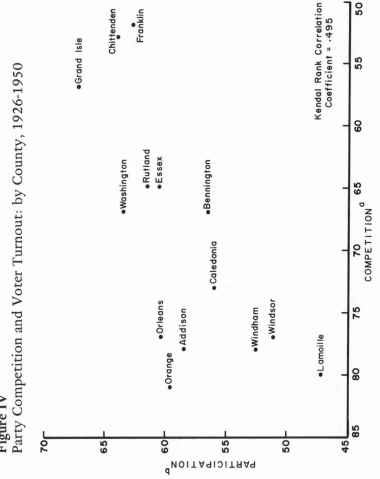

Figure IV
Party Competition and Voter Turnout: by County, 1926-1950

[a]Average percentage of Republican votes for governor, 1926-1950.
[b]Average percentage of registered voters that voted for governor, 1926-1950.

Table 12
Relationship between Socioeconomic and Political Variables,
and Political Participation in Vermont, 1934–1936:
Simple Correlation Coefficients[a] (N = 233)

		Political participation		
Socioeconomic variables	*Turnout on the Green Mountain Parkway issue*	*Presidential year turnout 1936*	*Off year turnout 1934*	*Average turnout, 1934–1936*
Population size	−.10	−.03	.00	−.01
Population density	.03	.06	.05	.06
Population increase 1920–1940	−.21	−.01	.00	.00
Farming population	.19	.01	−.01	.00
Population on relief	.03	−.08	−.14	−.13
Per capita town indebtedness	.04	.05	.08	.08
Per capita delinquent taxes	−.11	−.05	−.04	−.05

Political variables				
Democratic vote for governor, 1934–1936	−.08	.26	.15	.23
Increase in Democratic vote for Governor, 1934–1936 over Democratic vote for governor, 1928-1930	.05	−.14	−.03	−.08
Vote for Roosevelt, 1936	.02	.33	.20	.30
Party competition 1934–1936	.05	.26	.18	.25

[a]Coefficients ≥18 are significant at the .05 level.

relationship between competition and higher voting levels in rural one-party Vermont.

Other variables attached to socioeconomic factors proved to be weak predictors of voter activity. (See Table 12.) Turnout at the polls both in presidential and off years was not tied to town size, the percentage of the population engaged in farming, town population growth or density, economic conditions, or the percentage of the population on the relief rolls. Increased participation in the Green Mountain Parkway referendum was associated significantly with population growth. The percentage of the registered voters casting ballots on the Parkway issue decreased as town population increased between 1920 and 1940. But this relationship was not strong. It seems evident that voting levels in Vermont's one-party system were unaffected by socioeconomic conditions. In this posture Vermont reflects, once again, the situation in West Virginia, where scholarship reveals that degrees of participation are disoriented from socioeconomic conditions.[8]

Despite some inconsistencies, therefore, the evidence seems to suggest that one-partyism works to dampen the spirit of participatory democracy. Yet the exceptions are numerous. Certainly, as Milbrath himself emphasizes, there are other factors, principally constraints of a legal nature, that reinforce nonparticipation in the South.[9] Moreover, there is a very strong possibility that a state's political culture itself has an independent impact in determining turnout levels. It may be no coincidence that Vermont, whose political culture has been classified as a kind that encourages political participation, ranks twenty-sixth in off-year election turnout and eighteenth in turnout during presidential years—this while Vermont has placed near the bottom of the scale of party competitiveness.[10]

In sum, one-partyism probably does play a role in depressing political participation. Yet in Vermont, participation has been average to high despite the fact that Vermonters generally were aware of what the outcome of elections would be prior to voting. While Vermont's more competitive counties and towns had

8. Johnson, "Research Note," pp. 773-74.
9. Milbrath, p. 46.
10. Ibid., pp. 38-40.

higher participation scores than her noncompetitive counties and towns, neither ruralism nor the dominance of the Republican Party worked to drag participation below national levels. Vermont's voting percentage for governor for the years 1920–60 was exactly equal to the percentage voting for governor in Ranney's list of two-party states for the years 1956–60.[11]

In a one-party state we might expect that the primary election would be the focus of the struggle for power and that the election totals would be higher in these earlier intraparty contests. This condition prevailed in the South, where the winner of the primary was certain to be the statewide victor. In Vermont, however, the people evidently did not act as if they viewed the primary as the critical election. Turnout for the general election was about 23 percentage points higher than in the primary. Vermont's turnout in the primary (33.1 percent) generally approximated the turnout in the southern one-party Democratic states, but though the southern states lose 15 percentage points in their participation scores for the general election, Vermont gains 23. The relationship between competition and participation in the general elections holds at approximately the same intensity for the primary elections. In those years when the Republican nomination was hotly contested, there was a likelihood that voting would be heavier. The two variables correlated at .504. Participation in the primaries seems to lend support to our conclusion that ruralism, a high rate of activism by the citizenry, and one-partyism were coincidental in Vermont.

Factionalism

If one-partyism did not stifle voting activity and thus pull rural Vermont away from the model of the democratic polity, what about the question of alternatives? Since the majority party was the only winner in the general election, did struggles within the Republican Party function to present the citizenry real electoral alternatives? Or was the Republican Party a monolithic hier-

11. Ranney, in Jacob and Vines, *Politics*, p. 75.

archy that sterilized Vermont's high participation totals by offering no choices at the polls? What, in other words, was the nature of factionalism in Vermont?

Key has outlined several models of intraparty factionalism based on his analysis of the southern states.[12] First, there are the chaotic multifactional systems. Each candidate runs with a coalition which has jelled around him but will probably disperse when the elections are over. Localism or friends-and-neighbors politics is the only pattern that can be distilled from such a system. South Carolina, Alabama, Mississippi, Arkansas, Texas, and Florida fit this category. Secondly, there are the bifactional systems, in which primary politics are dominated by two power blocs and the voters usually divide their votes accordingly. Georgia and Louisiana are in this category. The Democratic Party in Kentucky has also been typed as bifactional.[13] Finally, there are the states in which one powerful majority faction predominates, usually spurred to unity by opposition Republicans. North Carolina, Tennessee, and Virginia are examples.[14]

What was the nature of Vermont's one-party system—a system that is northern, Republican, and rural while the states of the Key analysis are southern, Democratic, and generally a shade more urban than Vermont? There are several points which suggest that Vermont's one-party arrangement was conditioned by a dominant unifactionalism. In the first place, as Key suggested, the pressure of the minority can be an impetus toward unifactionalism; and, although there is evidence to the

12. V. O. Key, Jr., *Southern Politics in State and Nation* (New York: Alfred A. Knopf, 1949), pp. 298-314.

13. Malcolm E. Jewell and Everett W. Cunningham, *Kentucky Politics* (Lexington, Ky.: University of Kentucky Press, 1968), pp. 131-78, and Malcolm E. Jewell, *Legislative Representation in the Contemporary South* (Durham, N.C.: Duke University Press, 1967), pp. 56-76.

14. There is some evidence that does not square with Key's classification. In Tennessee, William Goodman observes, "While the Democratic cup seemed to be running over, its very preponderance created an amorphous grouping incapable of being manipulated or wielded as a single instrument." William Goodman, *Inherited Domain: Political Parties in Tennessee* (Knoxville: Bureau of Public Administration, University of Tennessee, 1954), p. 30.

contrary,[15] the logic certainly seems sound. Vermont, it will be remembered, always had a relatively strong minority party. It was the strength of a persistent Democratic Party that kept Vermont out of the fringe classifications of one-partyism which several southern states now occupy.

Secondly, Vermont's homogeneous environmental characteristics might well be considered conducive to the maintenance of a monolithic power structure within the Republican Party. We may wonder if a population of 400,000 is large enough to support a dichotomy in the electorate at the primary level. Moreover, the economic community, dominated as it was by agriculture, harbored no large islands of cohesive interests to serve as gravitational centers for political factions. Finally, the dominant ethnic-religious subgroup in Vermont, the French Canadian, was almost purely Democratic and did little to discolor the homogeneity of the Republican Party. Certainly this kind of environment was potentially open to control by a dominant Republican faction. There were simply few socioeconomic variations in Vermont's culture for opposition to cling to and grow.

A third point that underlines the potential for unifactionalism in Vermont is the nature of the electorate. As Figure V indicates, the electorate in rural Vermont responded sharply to the pull of national influences in the general election. In presidential years, Vermonters attended the polls at a consistent rate. In the off years, however, the electorate was fickle and turnout varied substantially. Generally, voting for governor was much lower in the off years. Compared to the general election, however, participation in the primary was remarkably stable from year to year. In other words, it appears that a small yet consistent electorate could be counted on to vote in the primary. The primary was apparently immune from the sharp deviations that typified the vote in the general election. There was, evidently, a large reservoir of Republican voters that always could be counted on to (1) vote in the general election in presidential years, (2) sometimes, as in 1934 and 1938, vote in the general elections in off years, and (3) stay away from the primary al-

15. Jewell and Cunningham, p. 131. The authors report that in Kentucky "The signs of growing Republican strength have not yet forced a truce in Democratic factional battles."

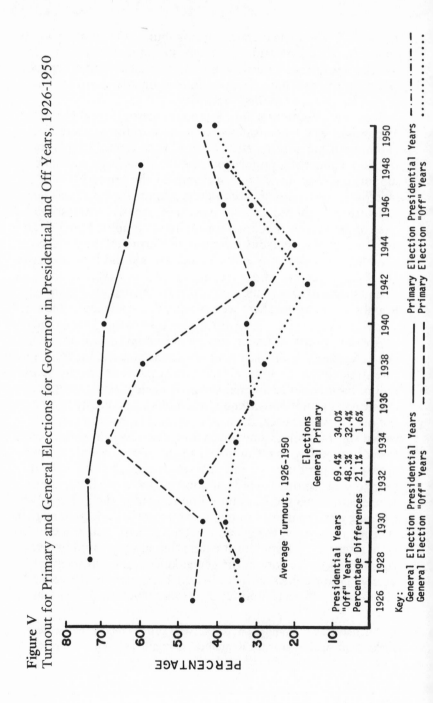

Figure V
Turnout for Primary and General Elections for Governor in Presidential and Off Years, 1926-1950

together. This kind of small, stable primary electorate is not of the kind that would rise up to threaten a dominant faction. It is a kind that would help maintain unifactional control.

Finally, there are two observations, discussed in a different context in Chapter 2, which point to the existence of some kind of absolute authority. The first of these was the Mountain Rule; the second was the remarkably stable apprenticeship system of political recruitment for the governor's office.

We have said that Vermont's sociocultural environment is essentially homogeneous. One exception is the French Canadian settlement in the northern tier of counties. Another is the remnant of a sociogeographical dichotomy rooted in the original settlement and early political history of the state and defined by the Green Mountains, which split the state in half, north to south.

This cultural dichotomy could have provided the soil for the growth of a bifactional system. Quite the contrary, however, is the case. The party seems to have been in complete control of this potentially disruptive phenomenon and was able to dole out the governorship to Republicans from first one side of the mountains and then the other. The lines of selection continually crisscross the mountains. The point is that no party beset by the chaos of multifactionalism or split bifactionally could engage in the luxury of a rational and consistent recruitment system designed to assuage intraparty squabbles that might arise from a natural geographical and historical cleavage in the state.

We have also indicated that Vermont's governors were subjected to a rigorous political apprenticeship. A party that can require its candidates to fulfill certain political prerequisites is not a party subjected to important factional pressures. Reasoning in this manner certainly lends support to the unifactionalism thesis—a majority faction based not on a traditional party machine, like Virginia's, but rather on a fraternity of office holders.

While all of these elements—a threatening minority, a homogeneous environment, a small and stable electorate in the primary, the Mountain Rule, and apprenticeship recruitment—point to some kind of control center within the Republican Party, considerable material has been published to the contrary. In fact, the most thorough analysis of Vermont's political sys-

tem we have to date, Duane Lockard's,[16] supports the thesis
that Vermont Republicanism can be defined in bifactional
terms. After noting a dichotomy of views over the nature of
Vermont's one-party system (Ranney and Kendall for multifactionalism, and Ransone for a Virginia-like bifactionalism pattern), Lockard sides with bifactionalism, although he does not
agree with Ransone's Virginia-Vermont equation.[17]

Both Ransone and Lockard point to Vermont's Proctor family as the conservative pole of a two-way split in the Republican
Party. The liberal wing is described as the "Gibson-Aiken" faction, after two prominant anti-Proctor figures. Lockard's analysis overstates the case, however, and exhibits a misuse of election statistics. In the first place, Lockard himself seems hesitant
and continually emphasizes the use of caution in his interpreta-
tions. Secondly, evidence shows that there was little deep meaning in the Proctor-Gibson rivalry even at the elite level.

Two instances indicating that Proctor and Gibson had buried
the hatchet during the time of Lockard's analysis are Proctor's
support of the Stassen-Gibson liberal faction of Vermont's delegation at the Republican national convention in 1948 in opposition to the conservatives, and his active support for Eisenhower
in 1952 when he went to the national convention as chairman
of a liberal delegation that included Preston Gibson.[18] A third
and most significant criticism of the placement of Vermont in
the bifactional category is that alleged bifactionalism in Vermont does not square with examples of bifactionalism in other
states. Take Kentucky, for example. Malcolm Jewell, using one
of V. O. Key's criteria for bifactionalism (the greater part of the
primary vote is divided between two persons, neither of which
receives a total far exceeding 50 percent), concludes that "the
Democratic party in Kentucky meets these criteria of a bifactional system almost perfectly." How well does Vermont fit the
Key-Jewell criterion? Very poorly, as Table 13 shows. Though
Kentucky's primaries cling to the bifactional model, Vermont's

16. Duane Lockard, *New England State Politics* (Princeton: Princeton
University Press, 1959), pp. 8-45.
17. Ibid., pp. 14-15.
18. Paul T. David, Malcolm Moos, and Ralph M. Goldman, *Presidential
Nominating Politics in 1952: The North East* (Baltimore: The Johns Hop-
kins Press, 1954), pp. 54-69.

strayed again and again. In five of the twenty-three primaries there was no contest at all. In five more elections, the winner failed to get a majority of the votes. Three of these were three-way contests, and in the other two, four candidates were listed. In almost one half the primaries, therefore, no bifactional alignments appeared. Half of these were unifactional and the other half were multifactional. Moreover, these contests were spread quite evenly over a forty-four year period. In Kentucky, however, bifactionalism was consistent and intense. At no time did multifactionalism occur, and at no time were elections left uncontested.

The evidence that lays the Proctor-Gibson myth to rest, however, is contained in Lockard's own data. Lockard outlines two areas of the state in which he claims that the strength of the opposing factions was clustered. The three north central counties of Orleans, Lamoille, and Washington were the Proctor counties, and the three southern counties of Bennington, Windsor, and Windham made up the anti-Proctor area. However, Lockard's analysis spans only an eight-year, six-election period. One would be hard put to conclude that one-partyism in any state was bifactional with such limited data unless the historical record were supportive, and it is not.

First, looking at the Aiken half of the Gibson-Aiken faction, there is no evidence to show that there was, as Lockard himself says, "any similarity between his areas of strength and the areas of greatest strength for more recent anti-Proctor candidates."[19] Of even greater significance is the fact that Aiken's strength did not match up negatively with Proctor's strength. Using towns and cities as observations and plotting the Aiken vote in 1940 against the Proctor vote in 1946 produces a positive gamma coefficient of .11. Although this coefficient is not statistically significant, its direction is opposite from what the hypothesis suggests—that the Proctor and Aiken voting power will be negatively associated. We must reject the idea that the Aiken vote was a predictor of opposition to Proctor.[20]

19. Lockard, p. 21.
20. John Arsenault, "Opposition to Aiken—1940 and 1968" (MS, Spring 1973, Special Collections Section, Bailey Library, University of Vermont, Burlington). My Pearson's r for the Aiken-Proctor relationship was $r = .01$.

Table 13

Factionalism in Vermont and Kentucky in Primary
Elections for Governor

Vermont

Year	Candidates		Percentage of the vote received	
	Total	Winning ⩾5%	Winning %	Top two %
1926	3	3	48.0	77.7
1928	2	2	65.8	100.0
1930	3	3	51.2	92.0
1932	2	2	54.0	100.0
1934	2	2	57.1	100.0
1936	4	3	42.2	76.5
1938	2	2	89.3	100.0
1940	1	1	100.0	—
1942	1	1	100.0	—
1944	2	2	63.0	100.0
1946	2	2	57.1	100.0
1948	2	2	54.4	100.0
1950	3	3	41.3	74.6
1952	2	2	51.9	100.0
1954	2	2	67.5	100.0
1956	1	1	100.0	—
1958	1	1	100.0	—
1960	4	4	29.6	58.0
1962	1	1	100.0	—
1964	3	3	42.3	79.4
1966	2	2	59.1	100.0
1968	2	2	62.3	100.0
1970	2	2	79.7	100.0

Secondly, a close look at primaries where there was a clear struggle between a Proctor and an anti-Proctor candidate reveals that Lockard's repositories of traditional[21] factional strength

21. Lockard, p. 24.

Table 13 (cont.)

| | | Kentucky[a] | | |
| Year | Candidates | | Percentage of the vote received | |
	Total	Winning ≥5%	Winning %	Top two %
1939	4	2	52.5	98.3
1943	4	3	53.6	85.6
1947	3	2	54.9	98.3
1951	3	2	75.1	97.1
1955	3	2	51.4	99.2
1959	4	2	52.3	98.6
1963	4	2	53.8	97.0

[a]Figures for Kentucky in Jewell, *Legislative*, pp. 56-57.

are simply nonexistent. In the 1934 clash between Benjamin Williams, Vice President of the Proctor Marble Company, and Charles Smith, his opponent in the primary, there was a clear test of the hypothesis. Smith, the eventual winner, charged that

Williams was the choice of a political ring.[22] Yet Williams, the
Proctor candidate, did better than Smith precisely in Lockard's
anti-Proctor counties. Smith, the anti-Proctor candidate, out-
scored Williams in the three counties that Lockard labeled Proctor territory. In 1944 Mortimer Proctor himself won the Republican primary and the governorship. Once again Lockard's
"traditional" pattern is nowhere to be found; and once again
the Proctor candidate made a remarkably poor showing in exactly those areas which Lockard claims were, only two years
later, the electoral anchor for the "Gibson-Aiken versus The
Proctor Machine" bifactional pattern. In short, examination of
two clear test elections for the Lockard thesis shows that
Proctor candidates continually received more support in the
anti-Proctor counties, while anti-Proctor candidates earned higher percentages in pro-Proctor areas. There was no evidence of a
geographically based Proctor versus Gibson-Aiken bifactional
pattern in Vermont at the primary level prior to 1946. The
1944 primary election underlines the strong pull of friends-and-
neighbors politics in Vermont. Simpson, Proctor's opponent,
received 100 percent more votes in his home county than he did
statewide. Proctor also received his highest percentage at home,
winning 80 percent of the votes in Rutland County.

There is no doubt that there was a Gibson-Proctor feud in
1946. Gibson came home from the war, challenged Proctor's
traditional second term, and defeated him in the primary. Lockard claims this exposed the tone of Republican politics in Vermont by revealing a bifactional pattern rooted in sectionalism.
A close look at his supporting evidence, however, shows that
the Proctor loss of 1946 was more likely a result of the friends-
and-neighbors phenomenon. In only *one* of the three so-called
anti-Proctor counties did Gibson run exceptionally well and
that was his home county, Windham, where he received 80 percent of the vote—29 percent above his statewide average. In the
other two counties of the Lockard-labeled anti-Proctor group,
Gibson averaged *below* his statewide percentage. Lockard's statistic for Gibson was in reality a function of his overwhelming
home-county support. On the other hand, Proctor ran better in

22. Richard Judd, "The History of the New Deal in Vermont" (diss.,
Harvard University, 1959), p. 94.

this so-called hostile country than he did at the state level. It was in Caledonia County, land of his old political enemy Arthur Simpson, that Proctor did most poorly. Here he received only 28.8 percent of the vote, his lowest showing by far except for Gibson's home county.

The 1946 election provides the best opportunity to observe Gibson-Proctor bifactionalism, as it pitted the two men directly against each other. It was sectional loyalty in the rural Vermont tradition that brought Ernest Gibson to power. If Proctor had received traditional Proctor support in Gibson's home county and traditional support in the Northeast Kingdom's Caledonia County in addition to a fair cut of the Democratic counties of Chittenden and Franklin, he would have won the election. In a very real sense we may conclude that, three times defeated at the hands of Proctor candidates, Arthur Simpson had the last laugh.

The election of 1948 reinforces the friends-and-neighbors thesis. Lee Emerson from Orleans received 85 percent of that county's votes. This was his best showing. Gibson, on the other hand, earned 78 percent of his home-county tallies, his highest figure. Moreover, his counties of greatest strength did not include, as Lockard claims,[23] the southern counties of Windsor and Bennington when Gibson's home county is omitted from the three-county total. As in 1946, his strongest counties, other than his home county, were the northwestern counties, Franklin and Chittenden.

In 1950 the Republicans ran three candidates in their primary. Voting conformed rigidly to the friends-and-neighbors pattern. All of the three candidates received their highest percentage in their home county and their second highest percentage in an adjacent county. Moreover, the Proctor candidate, Lee Emerson, who had lost to Ernest Gibson in 1948, did not win his largest totals in the Proctor counties, except for the county where he lived. Two years later Emerson ran again, this time against a single candidate from the south, Henry Vail. Once more the returns punched holes in Lockard's thesis. Washington County, a Proctor county, ranked ninth in Emerson's list, and Vail did better in Rutland County than he did in Windham County.

23. Lockard, p. 22.

In the final election of Lockard's era of bifactionalism Vail
ran once more. This time the establishment candidate, Joseph
Johnson, was from Vail's home county. Of all the elections
analyzed, the 1954 contest came closest to matching the Lockard alignment. Yet given Vail's exceptionally poor showing
statewide and the fact that his popularity was strictly limited to
the southern regions of the state as it had been in 1952, the
most appealing conclusion is that Vail's success in anti-Proctor
areas was a result of his local draw, and Johnson's higher ratios
in the northern Proctor counties was a result of Vail's complete
impotence in this area. Lockard claims that Johnson's poor
showing in 1954 in the southern counties where he lived is important because it negates the possibility of a friends-and-neighbors pull. This reasoning is fallacious, since a two-candidate race
where both candidates live in the same area is in the nature of a
zero-sum game. Obviously both candidates cannot do exceptionally well in the same territory. Johnson's vote in the South
was of necessity lower than his statewide percentage, since Vail
did so poorly outside his home grounds. It was the very fact of
Vail's friends-and-neighbors appeal (an appeal established two
years earlier) that eliminated Johnson's friends-and-neighbors
potential. It is also noteworthy that Vail's best county was not
any of the three hypothesized anti-Proctor counties; it was Rutland County, home of the Proctor family.

Knocking down the bifactional view of Vermont's one-party
system weakens the underpinning of an important thesis concerning the relationship between input mechanisms and policy
outputs in political systems. Put briefly, the location of a one-
party system lacking clear factional political camps within a
political system that habitually produces benevolent policies
concerning the "have nots" in society plays havoc with Key's
hypothesis that bifactional and/or two-party systems are necessary to ensure that the underprivileged classes get their share of
the political pie. In his study of Vermont elections, sociologist
Frederick Maher underscores Vermont's traditionally liberal tax
policies and her strong commitment to spend large amounts of
public money to serve the needy portions of the public sector.
Lockard, contends Maher, has colored Vermont's behavior to fit
the Key hypothesis:

If Vermont had had a regressive general sales tax and did not have a graduated personal income tax it is clear Lockard would have cited this as very clear support for the proposition that non-competitive party politics makes for a tax situation that bears down heavily on the have nots. Since in fact the reverse is the case Lockard ignores the non-existance of a general sales tax in Vermont and "explains" the presence of a personal income tax by describing it as a temporary triumph of Vermont bi-factionalism. . . . Considering that Vermont . . . is always noted as one of the least competitive states . . . the relative progressiveness of the tax structure, the extent to which the state makes a tax effort, and the level of the tax burden in Vermont are a challenge, to say the least, to any easy assumption that the "haves" in Vermont have been able to exploit the non-competiveness of the party system for their economic benefit.[24]

The findings here (that bifactionalism was not prevalent in Vermont) provide further evidence that the underprivileged need not depend on tight, competitive political environments with recognizable power centers to provide them with equalized policy commitments.

To summarize, one-party politics in Vermont were dominated by a coalition of elected officials in the Republican Party. It was, however, a benevolent unifactionalism, maintained by unwritten subtleties and a consensus concerning recruitment patterns and the Mountain Rule—not by a "machine" of the Byrd variety. The only patterns evident in electoral statistics were friends-and-neighbors gravitational centers that usually defined the nature of the opposition. (See Figure VIII.) When new forces confronted the system, they won quite easily—there was no powerfully organized machine to resist them. There was nothing in Vermont to approximate what we generally consider to be a bifactional system. The alleged Gibson-Aiken versus Proctor bifactional system is largely a myth.

24. Frederick J. Maher, Jr., "Vermont Elections" (diss., Columbia University, 1969), pp. 44, 94.

We return, then, to our original question: did the one-party system offer Vermonters a choice of candidates in a manner that would approximate the two-party model of representative democracy? It appears not to have done so. Although there were contests for the Republican nomination, and many of these were closely fought, there was no enduring faction around which to rally the opposition or from which to demand responsiveness. Opposition came and went, depending not on organization but rather on localistic and personalistic appeals. Under the umbrella of an elected-official consensus, opposition remained but never jelled within a single mold.

Breakthrough 1952-1960

While Vermont politics prior to 1952 operated under the auspices of a benevolent Republican aristocracy, the Democrats had not played dead. Unlike the one-party South, Vermont maintained a functioning minority party. It is generally believed that the most important source of inspiration for the persistent visibility of the Democrats was the desire to maintain an organizational apparatus for the dispensation of patronage. But it is also true that the Democrats continually held from 10 percent to 20 percent of the seats in the legislature and captured up to 40 percent of the vote for governor. In fact, during the Depression they earned as much as 42 percent of the vote. But their success was short lived and the party totals fell again during the war years and sharply in the early postwar period. (See Figure VI.) The Depression years also saw the Democrats come closer in other statewide elections. In the 1934 senatorial election, Democrat Fred A. Martin threatened vociferous anti–New Dealer Warren Austin when he polled over 48 percent of the vote. Despite this kind of spasmodic thrust at individual Republicans, however, the political system remained the exclusive domain of the GOP.

The Democrats drew their support from the state's principal ethnic-based subculture, the Roman Catholics. Frederick Maher, Jr. finds strong correlations between Catholics and Democrats in Vermont's counties. There is also, says Maher, evidence that religion is the prime causal factor, since the relationships are

Figure VI
Voter Turnout and the Democratic Vote for Governor, 1936-1972

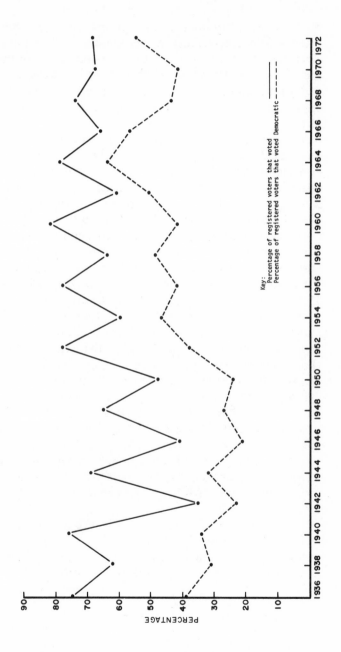

strengthened when other variables such as occupation are controlled.[25] Other correlations figured by town for the elections of 1934 and 1936 indicate that during the Depression years when Vermont's Democrats were doing very well in statewide elections, their vote was positively associated with the percentage of the population on relief, population increase, town size, and population density. It was negatively associated with farmers as a percentage of a town's population and with per-capita farms.

When we adjust for the pull of the New Deal, we find that the appeal of the Democrats had spilled over into Vermont's hinterland in the mid thirties, and their gains were not necessarily linked to their home territories. Those towns in which the Democrats had made their greatest increases in 1934 and 1936 over the base vote in the elections of 1928 and 1930 were negatively associated with population gains and town size and positively associated with the farming community. Since we also know that the Democratic gains were negatively associated with the Democratic vote, we can be certain that their upsurge in the 1930's was indeed a raid on Republican strongholds.

It is interesting to note, however, that both F.D.R. in 1936 and Fred Martin in 1934 received votes in relation to the percentage of the population on relief. Evidently political appeal of the New Deal was tied in part to the economic spin-offs of the Depression. But the intrastate New Deal Democratic vote (the average Democratic vote for governor 1934-36) did not correlate with the relief rolls. It also pays to bear in mind that the linkage between town size and the Democratic vote in Vermont has traditionally been overemphasized. The independent relationship seems to have been regional. Maher puts it this way: "The smaller towns in the Democratic areas were generally more Democratic than the larger towns in the Republican areas."[26]

A Democratic breakthrough with staying power at the state level came in the early fifties, more specifically in the election of 1952. At this time the Democrats, in the teeth of the Eisenhower gale, achieved their largest gain in the popular vote in

25. Ibid., p. 98.
26. Ibid., p. 184.

memory (over 14 percent), reversed a pronounced downward trend evident since the Depression, and, what is most important, established a continuing plateau in the electoral scoring at the 40 percent-plus level.[27]

The details of the Democratic breakthrough in 1952 are treated in two doctoral dissertations, each of which reaches different conclusions regarding the causal forces behind the new Democratic successes. One is Douglas Hodgkin's analysis of comparative breakthrough elections—from which we borrow heavily in the following paragraphs.[28]

Defining breakthroughs as elections for governor where the minority party gains twelve or more percentage points in the partisan division of the vote, reaches at least the 35 percent mark, and retains one-half or more of the gain in the next elec-

27. Douglas I. Hodgkin, "Breakthrough Elections: Elements of Large and Durable Minority Gains in Selected States Since 1944" (diss., Duke University, 1966), pp. 13-14.

28. Ibid., pp. 13-14. Some point to the Meyer victory for Congress and the Leddy near-victory for governor in 1958 as the breakthrough. In that year Vermont sent its first Democrat to Congress, and the Democratic candidate for governor lost by less than a percentage point; see Harris E. Thurber, "Vermont: The Stirrings of Change," in George Goodwin, Jr., and Victoria Schuck, eds., *Party Politics in the New England States* (Durham, N.H.: New England Center for Continuing Education, 1968), pp. 71-73. Robert Babcock sees the breakthrough as coming in 1954 when the woolen mills closed in Winooski and the Republicans ignored the situation. This helped win a group of senatorial seats for the Democrats from Chittenden County and give them an authentic power base: Babcock interview, December 10, 1968. Andrew E. Nuquist, a leading student of Vermont politics, agrees with Hodgkin that the breakthrough came in 1952: Nuquist interview, November 17, 1968. Samuel Miller, author of a study of the Democratic Party in Vermont ("The Vermont Democratic Party and the Development of Intra-Party Responsibility," M.A. thesis, University of Vermont, 1960), agrees with the 1952 assessment and ties the breakthrough to the appearance of second and third generation ethnic minorities in the power structure of the Party: Miller interview, December 19, 1968. A minority sees Republican failures in policy innovation and leadership at the base of a genuine electoral uprising against the Republican Party; see, for instance, Robert C. Spencer and James J. Best, "Vermont: A Case Study of the Transition from a One to a Two-Party State" (MS, University of Vermont, Bailey Library Special Collections, 1965).

tion, Hodgkin identifies the causal agents in the Vermont break-through as a bitter Republican primary struggle reinforced by a Democratic gubernatorial candidate who campaigned actively throughout the state.[29]   There can be little doubt that dissension within the Republican Party was heated to the extreme in the early 50's, and Democrat Robert Larrow was certainly a popular candidate who surprised the state with his energetic campaign.

The 1950 primary raised great havoc within the ranks of the Republican Party. The winner, Lee Emerson, received only 41 percent of the popular vote, the lowest plurality with which any Republican primary winner had entered the general election. Moreover, never before had the top two candidates received only 74.6 percent of the vote. The effect of the primary of 1950 was not felt in that year, however, since the Democratic percentage of the vote actually dropped to 25, the third lowest since 1926. The most divisive primary in the history of the party came coincidentally with one of their strongest victories in the general election.

The meaning of the 1950 primary manifested itself in the Emerson bid for reelection in 1952, when the Party again split sharply in the primary; and this time a distinct anti-Emerson mood was manifest in the southern counties. It should be remembered that this was the third time Emerson had involved the party in a divisive primary. He did it in 1948 against Gibson, when he held the latter to a smaller percentage of the primary vote than he had received against Mortimer Proctor two years earlier. He did it in 1950 against Peter A. Bove and J. Harold Stacy. He did it once more in 1952. At no point in the history of the Republican primary had one man caused such internal dissension.[30]

Another reason for the anti-Emerson feeling in 1952 was undoubtedly the bad feelings generated by Emerson's relations with the legislature. Governor Emerson fought the legislature

29. Hodgkin, p. 39.
30. When George Aiken ran for the governorship in the 1936 primary, the party split four ways. Aiken won with 42.2 percent of the vote. In his next primary Aiken rallied the party behind him and won 89.3 percent of the vote.

over several of the Gibson reform measures and further alienated liberals who remembered his 1948 campaign against Gibson. The charge was heard that Emerson was "trying to undo all
Gibson had done."[31]

Added to all the anti-Emerson feelings was the fact that
Emerson was the first Governor to represent the northern half
of the state since the institution of the primary. Thus anti-
Emerson feelings within the party were compounded by sectionalism. In the previous two Emerson primaries, the vote was
defined along sectional lines. What Lockard and others have
confused as a bifactional split between Gibson and Proctor candidates during this period was in reality the coalescence of a
north-south regional dichotomy. (It should be remembered that
Mortimer Proctor by this time was in a very real sense in the
liberal ranks of the Republican Party.) Any bifactionalism in
Vermont in 1952 was sectional and ideological in nature. It was
in no sense an extension of an enduring and personalistic bifactional system of the southern variety.

Whatever the varieties of anti-Emerson feeling actually were,
the fact remains that there was a strong correlation between the
Democratic gain in the vote between 1950 and 1952 and that of
Vail (the anti-Emerson Republican) in the 1952 primary. Hodgkin reports a positive rank-order correlation of .73.[32] The
depth of the anti-Emerson feeling is revealed by the heavy
write-in vote Vail received in the general election. This write-in
vote together with the Democratic gain, defined as an establishment protest vote, correlates with the Democratic gain with a
coefficient of .87.[33] Hodgkin concludes from this correlation
that "it is . . . evident that Vail's primary supporters abandoned
the regular Republican nominee in 1952 to vote either for the
Democratic candidate or for Vail in the general election."[34]
Perhaps Republican disunity had finally caught up with the
party.

Frederick Maher, however, sees Democratic gains in the 1952
election as a result of increased turnout. The argument is essen-

31. Hodgkin, pp. 79-80.
32. Ibid., p. 81.
33. Ibid., p. 82.
34. Ibid., p. 83.

tially that the candidacy of Eisenhower in 1952 stimulated a marked increase in voting and that the Democrats, not the Republicans, were the beneficiaries. Maher's figures show a correlation of .51 between the Democrats' share of the increases in the Presidential vote between 1948 and 1952 and a correlation of .97 between 1948 and 1956. He concludes:

> A principal ingredient of the upsurge was the increased turnout which was itself presumably due to the Eisenhower appeal since he received the benefit of virtually all the turnout at the Presidential level, while the state Republicans were unable to gain from the new plateau of normal voting turnout established in their period.[35]

Which of these accounts is more in tune with reality is difficult to gauge, since both scholars use Vermont's counties (there are only fourteen) as observations for their correlational techniques, and that makes for statistical difficulties. Also the use of aggregate voting data is apt to obscure essential relationships. For example, was it Eisenhower Republicans voting for Democrat Larrow in 1952 or Larrow Democrats voting for Ike? Nevertheless, there seems to be much truth in both analyses. First, a retest of Hodgkin's relationship between Vail support in the primary of 1952 and Larrow strength in the general election using towns rather than counties as observation (N increases from 14 to 245) shows that Vail supporters could very well have voted for the Democratic candidate in the 1952 general election for governor ($r = .29$). On the other hand Maher is correct when he claims that Vail-inspired Republican defection lacked depth and staying power and probably could not have produced the enduring plateau of Democratic strength that appeared in 1952. Given two intervening elections, the effect of the Vail defection had disappeared. The correlation between Vail support in the towns and the Democratic totals disappeared completely.

On the other hand, Maher's conclusion that the breakthrough could not have occurred without a substantial increase in voters at the polls is accurate. It is important to realize, however, that both total turnout and the Democrats' proportion of turnout

35. Maher, p. 187.

had dropped to extremely low levels during the war and especially in 1948, Maher's anchor year for making correlations. This drop, coupled with the observation that turnout at the 1952 level was new only if you compare it to the war years, seems to suggest that what happened in 1952 was the actualization of a latent Democratic vote that had surfaced during the Depression but had then submerged during the 1940's.

Even more fascinating is the complete reversal of the high turnout–high Democratic percentage pattern that had been dominant ever since 1938. In each of the presidential years 1940, 1944, and 1948, turnout jumped dramatically, and the Democrats had benefited from the increase. After 1952, however, a decrease in turnout meant an increase in the Democratic percentage. The crucial factor in the 1952 election is not just that the Democrats increased their fortunes but that they did so in such a large way, and that this plateau held. At the state level the Vermont Democratic Party had become self-conscious. No longer was Democratic attendance at the polls magnetized primarily by the presence of a candidate for president on the ticket. Now the governorship was a prize to be seriously considered. If we may credit, as Maher does, the reinstatement of higher turnout to the Eisenhower ticket, it seems reasonable that the deep commitment of Democrat Robert Larrow to the campaign for governor in 1952 was the stimulant that prompted Democratic forces to muster on the off years as they had never done before. It was this fact coupled with the Republicans' tardiness at the polls during nonpresidential years that was to stir ill winds for the GOP over the next decade.

There was another, less easily traceable force at work in northern New England during the 1950's, which had its own impact on the changing character of Vermont's political system. It was what Key called "the erosion of sectionalism."[36] All across northern New England the Democratic Party was making inroads, while participation by the states of the area in national elections began more closely to approximate national voting patterns. (See Figure VII.) Vermont, New Hampshire, and

36. V. O. Key, Jr., "An Autonomous State Politics," in John R. Owens and P. J. Staudenraus, eds., *The American Party System* (New York: Macmillan, 1965), pp. 76-92.

Figure VII
Deviation of Republican Percentages of Total Vote in Vermont and Florida from Republican Percentages of Total National Vote, 1896-1968

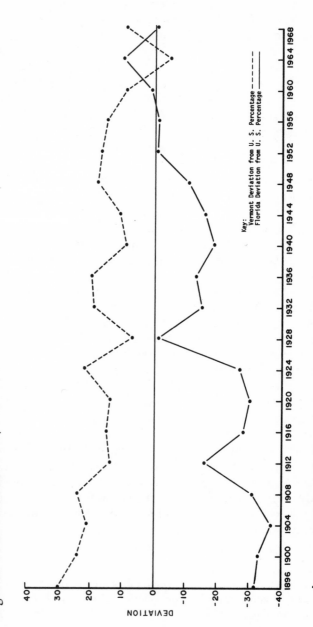

Key:
Vermont Deviation from U. S. Percentage ———
Florida Deviation from U. S. Percentage ———

[a]The format and data through 1952 are from V. O. Key, Jr., "An Autonomous State Politics," found in John R. Owens and P. J. Staudenraus, eds., The American Party System (New York: The MacMillan Company, 1965), p. 81.

Maine began to feel the impulses which have been at work in southern New England since the war and which will, if Kevin Phillips is to be believed, ultimately cast all New England in a Democratic mold.[37] Although there is no accurate way to measure this phenomenon, logic suggests that the new nationalization of the vote for president and the subsequent breaking down of geographic political bastions should have its effect on the balance of power at the intrastate level.

From what sources sprang the new-found strength of the Democrats? Hodgkin's data indicate that it came generally from the more urban counties with high percentages of white-collar employees in the work force. The rural and agricultural counties correlated negatively with Democratic percentage increases. It is interesting to note that the breakthrough did not come in the low-income areas of the state—which simply emphasizes the fact that low-income areas in a rural state like Vermont are usually in the back beyond and not in urban centers. The figures seem to indicate that the Democrats established their base in 1952 within the middle and upper middle classes of the larger towns. The poorer rural and agricultural areas remained essentially Republican. Yet Maher contends that Democratic gains after the breakthrough were not nailed to particular areas of the state—especially to different-sized towns: "These Democratic gains were not selective in the sense of being composed of large gains in some sections of the state while making no progress in other areas. The improvement was an across the board increase and all categories into which the vote had been broken down showing the Democratic percentage as being much higher in recent years . . . "[38]

With the questionable practice of using Vermont's fourteen counties as observations for internal measurements and Hodgkin's relatively weak coefficients, Maher's findings, which were based on an ordinal classification of Vermont's 245 towns, seem more credible. There is too little evidence to suggest that the breakthrough was a product of urbanism or alterations in socio-economic conditions. Moreover, in terms of the long-range

37. Kevin P. Phillips, *The Emerging Republican Majority* (New Rochelle, N.Y.: Arlington House, 1969), p. 186.
38. Maher, p. 77.

gains, at least, Hodgkin's findings coincide with Maher's. In 1962, when the Democrats won the governorship for the first time in a century, the Democratic vote did not correlate so strongly with urbanism as it had in 1950 or 1952. The correlation with white-collar workers dropped in a similar manner. Moreover, the agricultural counties had abandoned their strong negative correlation with the Democratic vote by 1962, indicating that the farmers too had been affected by the Democratic breakthrough.[39] Finally, matching up towns that increased in population between 1950 and 1970 with jumps in the Democratic vote for governor between 1950 and 1960 and/or between 1950 and 1962 produces an insignificant negative correlation. The Democratic gains did not come in the towns that were growing in size.

The Democratic breakthrough in Vermont during the 50's appears to have been an indigenous one. The state experienced no sharp influx of people to form the base of a new party alignment. The breakthrough seems to have been a uniform one as well. By the end of the decade the more rural agricultural areas were capable of shedding their anti-Democratic bias in statewide elections. The breakthrough arrived by way of a reactivated Democratic minority, an atypical factional split within the dominant party, and an energetic campaigner who believed he could win. The crucial point seems to be that change did not come because Democrats are found in urban centers and Vermont became more urban, or because farmers are Republican and Vermont lost many farmers. Clearly Vermont has become less agricultural and has lost farmers steadily, but the farmers that remain are not unwilling to vote Democratic. There is no reason to suggest, moreover, that the Democratic gains are linked to those areas where the family farms have suffered most heavily. In short the evidence is that socioeconomic variables had minimal impact in determining political change in Vermont.

A statistic that reveals the willingness of rural people to accept party change is the percentage of state legislative districts held continuously by the same party. (See Table 14). Though Vermont and Maine are generally believed to lack party competition, especially relative to their sister states in New England,

39. Hodgkin, pp. 157-58.

Table 14
Local One-Partyism: State Legislative
Districts Held Continuously by the Same
Party, 1947–1965

State	House	Senate
Maine	41.8%	25.0%
Vermont	43.5%	28.6%
Connecticut	47.9%	27.8%
Massachusetts	61.9%	65.0%
New Hampshire	63.8%	66.7%
Rhode Island	66.0%	55.6%

Source: Dishman and Goodwin, *State Legislatures in New England Politics*, p. 69.

they have considerably fewer "safe" districts than two-party states like Massachusetts and Connecticut. Party labels mean little in local elections. Districts are not tied to the parties in the same way they are in the more urban states. This willingness to vote for the man and not the party clearly could be a causal factor in ending one-party government in Vermont.

In 1952 the Democratic nominee argued with persuasive results that the Republicans could be defeated given the right circumstances. Six years later, in 1958, a Democrat, running against a weak opponent, proved the point by winning the first statewide Democratic victory in Vermont in a century when he captured Vermont's single seat in the House of Representatives. That same year the Democratic candidate for governor lost by a handful of votes and had the audacity to ask for a recount. But the proof of the political pudding in state politics is winning the governorship. That, too, was to come.

The Hoff Phenomenon

The symbolic arrival of two-partyism in Vermont at the state level came when Philip Hoff won the governor's chair in 1962. It was symbolic because the governorship is the most important barometer of state political competition. But the fall of the

executive seat to the Democrats in 1962 represented no breakthrough, nor did this surprise many careful observers of Vermont politics. Looking at the Democratic and Republican percentages for the governorship in Vermont since 1952, we can
see that the Democrats could, indeed probably would, win in
1962 or at the latest in 1966.[40] Ultimate victory was predictable because in off-year elections voter turnout fell sharply in
Vermont and left the GOP in a vulnerable position.

At first glance it might appear that Hoff was the beneficiary
of a primary battle remarkably similar to the primary of 1950
that aided in the original 1952 breakthrough. As in 1952, the
crucial primary came in the previous campaign and was the
most divisive in the history of the party. In 1960 the Republicans split four ways, and F. Ray Keyser won with only 29.6
percent of the vote. As in 1950, the primary was defined
strictly in sectional terms. Friends-and-neighbors politics was
still the most important single pattern in the Republican primary. Each of the candidates received by far his highest percentage from his home county. Increases in home counties over
statewide returns averaged over 100 percent. Moreover, the
friends-and-neighbors effect spilled into adjacent counties. (See
Figure VIII.) Robert Babcock controlled the northwest from
Burlington; Arthur Simpson covered the Northeast Kingdom
from Lyndonville. Keyser's strength from Chelsea radiated
through the central counties, and A. Luke Crispe controlled the
South and Southwest. In 1962, as in 1952, the seeds of Republican disunity in the previous election seem to have borne bad
fruit for the party. There was, however, an important distinction. In 1952 many disgruntled primary voters wrote in the
name of their losing Republican primary candidate in the general election. In 1962 Crispe, unlike Vail, formed a new party,
"The Independent Party," and selected the Democratic candidate as their own. These votes made the difference; Hoff did
not win the election with Democratic tallies alone.

Yet there is no apparent connection between the votes Hoff
received from the Independent Party and the primary of 1960.

40. Miller interview. Miller claims that Bernard Leddy, the narrowly
defeated Democratic candidate in the previous off-year election, would
have run stronger than Hoff in 1962.

Figure VIII
Friends-and-Neighbors Politics in Two Republican Primaries

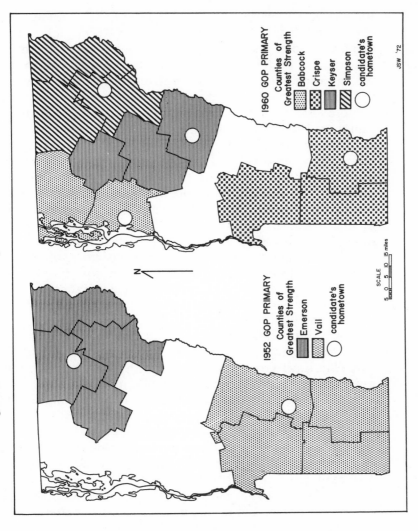

Rank-order correlations reveal no significant relationships between the Crispe vote in the primary of 1960 and Hoff's totals under the Independent column. The counties that voted heavily for Crispe in 1960 correlated at only the .12 level with counties voting strongly for Hoff under the banner of Crispe's new Independent Party two years later.

Moreover, there is no relationship between the Democratic gain from 1960 to 1962 and the Crispe or Crispe-Simpson or total anti-Keyser vote of 1960. The correlation between the Democratic gain between 1958 and 1962 and the Crispe vote was only .13. In other words, the Republican vote for Hoff in 1962 was not an anti-Keyser vote insofar as anti-Keyser feeling was demonstrated in the 1960 primary. The strongest evidence of an anti-Keyser holdover reaction from 1960 occurs in Caledonia County, where Arthur Simpson, defeated for the fourth time in a Republican primary in 1960, supported Hoff. True to their pro-Simpson tradition, the Caledonians gave the Democrats their highest gain, 13.7 percent. The correlation between Simpson towns and the Democratic gain in 1958–62 (.19) was positive and significant at the .05 level. Although the Crispe faction received most of the publicity, Simpson seems to have had a real impact in the Northeast Kingdom (shades of 1946, when Mortimer Proctor suffered mightily at the hands of the same man!). Yet while the Democratic gain of 1952 was tied to an anti-Emerson sectional protest vote, the Hoff gains of 1962 were generally disorganized and could not be laid at the feet of a coherent factional group. Keyser entered the 1962 primary unopposed, while Emerson was forced to re-open party wounds and confront Vail in 1952, barely winning the election. (The Vail candidacy had hardened the north-south factionalism that Emerson had always engendered.) More important, perhaps, are the intense friends-and-neighbors multifactional patterns that split the Republicans in 1960. So divided was the party that it allowed no chance for an enduring anti-Keyser organization to develop. There was much anti-Keyser feeling in 1962, but unlike the situation a decade earlier, it was heterogeneous and unstructured.

The facts indicate that Hoff made his biggest gains in the strong Republican counties. The only relationship that appears in the returns of 1962 is a strong positive correlation between the Keyser vote in the 1960 general elections and the Democratic gain of 1962. There was also a strong positive correlation between the Democratic gain, 1958-62, and the Nixon vote of 1960. It was in the areas of traditional Republican strength that Democratic totals increased the most. This seems to be further evidence that in one-party counties the majority party is seriously hurt in off-year elections when the turnout is low.

The summary of the Hoff victory reads as follows: Hoff was the recipient of a continuing upward trend in the Democratic vote for governor and the benefits of an off-year election. Voter turnout was typically low, and the Democrats made their greatest gains in the heavily Republican counties. Nor was Hoff hurt by the appearance of the Independent Party, which allowed many Republicans to vote for Hoff without voting Democratic. He received a substantial boost from Arthur Simpson which brought in many new Democratic votes from Caledonia County. But in truth the Hoff "phenomenon" was really no phenomenon at all. Following the breakthrough of 1952, two-party politics traveled to the executive seat in Vermont along an ordered and rational path. Erosion of the rock-hard Republican base had continued all across the face of Vermont. Without denying the catalytic effect of local personalities like that of Arthur Simpson, one must conclude that Hoff's victory was a victory of trend rather than of personality or strategy. One fact in particular should not be forgotten: Hoff had 10,000 fewer votes while winning in 1962 than Democrat Russell Niquette gained while losing in 1960. Hoff even trailed fellow Democrat Bernard Leddy, who ran for governor and lost in 1958.

The Hoff win in 1962 may have been no phenomenon, but his six years as Vermont's governor certainly was. The nature of legislative politics was altered dramatically by Hoff, and the state entered a new era of innovative policy changes. At the polls Hoff piled up massive victories. In 1964 his totals skyrocketed as Vermont walked away from Barry Goldwater. This landslide brought the rest of the statewide Democratic ticket to power. Two years later Hoff won big again, and this time the victory was clearly an intrastate coup.

The election of 1966 provides the best yardstick for measuring the character of the Hoff electorate, since it registers his popularity as it hovered above the core Democratic vote of

Table 15

Relationship between Socioeconomic and Political Variables and Indicators of Hoff's Strength: Simple Correlation Coefficients $(N = 246)$[a]

				Indicators of Hoff's strength[b]			
General population characteristics	Hoff vote G.E. 1966	Hoff vote P.E. 1970	Hoff vote G.E. 1970	Hoff loss G.E. 1962–1970	Hoff loss G.E. 1966–1970	Hoff gain G.E. 1962–1966	Average Democratic vote for governor 1968–1970
Population size	.36	–.15	.43	–.01	–.16	–.14	.31
Population increase, 1960–1970	–.09	–.22	.02	.01	–.08	.01	–.08
Population mobility	.01	.03	.07	–.10	–.05	.09	–.06
Native Vermonters	.01	–.25	–.04	.22	.15	–.19	.17
Median family income, 1970	–.08	–.17	–.01	.09	–.10	–.16	–.06
Median family income increase, 1960–1970	–.10	–.20	–.14	.21	.05	–.18	–.11

Population below poverty line, 1970	.09	.14	-.05	.10	.16	.00	.12
College graduates	-.08	.02	.06	-.12	.15	.05	-.19
Population ≥65 years old	-.03	.13	-.02	-.01	.03	.02	.00
Occupations							
Professionals	.00	-.14	.10	-.06	-.12	-.04	-.10
Self employed	-.02	.06	-.09	-.01	.10	.13	-.12
Sales and clerical	.14	-.10	.18	.11	-.19	-.22	.17
Blue collar workers	.12	.22	.01	.04	.15	.04	.14
Farmers	-.16	-.07	-.18	.10	.08	-.02	-.06
Service workers	-.10	-.03	.00	-.19	-.09	.14	-.15
Political variables							
Hoff vote, G.E., 1962	.77	-.20	.52	.51	.04	-.61	.81
Humphrey vote, 1968	.81	-.12	.63	.22	-.08	-.35	.90
Average Democratic vote, governor, 1968-70	.82	-.06	.65	.18	.10	-.31	—
Republican anti-war vote	.08	.24	.09	-.22	.02	.25	.06

[a]Coefficients ≥17 are significant at the .05 level.

[b]G.E. = General election, P.E. = Primary

1962 but below the inflated totals caused by the anti-Goldwater deluge of 1964. As Table 15 shows, the only socioeconomic variable that was a significant indicator of Hoff strength was town size. While we should guard against falling victim to an ecological fallacy in using simple correlation coefficients of this kind, the paucity of social and economic linkages with the vote for Hoff suggests that his support was broad based and heterogeneous. Nor was the Hoff gain a function of social and economic factors, although there is a significant correlation between towns with greater ratios of their population born outside the state and the Hoff gain. There is also a negative correlation between medium family-income increases between 1960 and 1970 and Hoff increases.

This correlation points to a pair of interesting facts about contemporary population patterns in Vermont. First, during the 1960's a negative correlation between medium family income and the native Vermont population was wiped out. This strikes hard at the often heard contention that it was out-of-staters who were reaping the benefits of Vermont's economic prosperity in the 1960's. Secondly, the highest concentration of native Vermonters is in the northwestern region of the state precisely where the highest concentration of ethnic stock (families of French-Canadian origin) is located. These observations bring us to the political dimensions of the Hoff electorate in 1966.

Hoff's gains between 1962 and 1968 correlated negatively with these variables because they correlated negatively with the Democratic vote. And they correlated negatively with the Democratic vote because they came from Republican areas. One of the best predictors of the Hoff gain was the vote in 1962 for Keyser, the man Hoff had originally defeated. The strength of these relationships may be seen by the strong negative correlations between, on the one hand, the Hoff gain (1962 to 1966) and, on the other, three votes: (1) for Hoff in 1962, (2) for Humphrey in 1968, and (3) the averaged Democratic vote for governor in 1968 and 1970. (See Table 15.) What kind of Republicans switched to Hoff? Correlations between the Hoff gain and liberal (or at least anti-establishment) Republicans running in the primaries in 1966, 1968, and 1970 are positive and fairly strong. Note, for instance, that those towns that were to give larger percentages to Tom Hayes, the antiwar candidate in the

Republican primary of 1970, were apt to be those in which a large increase for Hoff is found. The frosting on Hoff's electoral cake therefore consisted of liberal Republican ingredients. But the cake itself was solidly Democratic. We can see this by focusing on the Hoff vote as such in 1966, rather than his gains between 1962 and 1966. The very strong correlations between the Hoff vote of 1966 and his vote in 1962, Humphrey's vote in 1968, and the average Democratic vote for governor for 1968 and 1970 show that his power ultimately lay in traditional Democratic areas and was not in the hands of liberal or discerning Republicans. Hoff's misreading of the Vermont electorate, prompted perhaps by his charismatic qualities and fascination with the frosting to the neglect of the cake, is at the root of the electoral catastrophe that befell him in 1970.

Having served three consecutive two-year terms, Hoff did not seek re-election in 1968. He chose instead to wait until 1970 to try to unseat Winston Prouty, Vermont's junior senator in Washington. On the face of it Prouty was vulnerable. First, he could not match Hoff on the stump and was certain to be outdistanced in the personal campaign. Secondly, 1970 was an off year. There was no Republican presidential candidate to draw out the GOP vote. Most important, Hoff had been one of the most popular political figures in the history of the state. Only four years earlier he had commanded the loyalties of 57 percent of the voters. But as a candidate for the U.S. Senate, he was trounced soundly in 1970. His defeat has the elements of a case study on the politics of defeat.

The postmortem begins with the observation that in 1970 Vermont was still basically a Republican state. To equate the shift of the governorship to the Democrats in 1962 with the arrival of a two-party system in Vermont is like equating a January thaw with the coming of spring. Hoff did little to carry on organizational activities within the party at the grass-roots level. Interviews with knowledgeable persons around the state indicate that Hoff was simply disinterested in political homework of this nature.

Perhaps the best indicator of this lack of organizational activity is the fact that the Democrats made no substantial gains in the number of legislative seats they controlled. Gains were made, but at no time did the minority control as many as 40 percent of the seats. When Hoff entered the statehouse in 1962, his party was accustomed to holding from 20 percent to 25 percent of the seats. When he left six years later, the Democrats held only 37 percent of the seats, despite reapportionment, which substantially increased the number of districts in the large towns where Democrats are strong. Secondly, the Democrats have been unable to mount a serious threat to Vermont's Republican congressional delegation. In no sense have they been able to approximate their success in 1958, when they captured the state's seat in the House of Representatives. In short, the Hoff influence did not radiate to the grass roots of Vermont's political life.

Other interrelated factors that together spell "party split" help explain how Prouty amassed 59 percent of the vote against the Hoff candidacy. First, Hoff was trapped by the dilemma that besets all governors whose party is a distinct minority. To build one's party through patronage pay-offs (both tangible and intangible) will ultimately disturb the majority party in whose hands legislative programs rest. In many respects Hoff's ability to cultivate a bipartisan coalition in the legislature was a high point in his career as governor. Yet by the time his last round with the legislature had been played, it was evident that the Democrats had become badly split.

Division within the party came from sources that are difficult to identify. Two, however, seem clear. One was the failure of some in the Hoff entourage to understand just how important the traditional Democratic vote was to their candidate. If the energy expended to woo George Aiken had been spent on local Democrats, more votes would have been won. To turn one's back on the local organizations was to prove hazardous business. Risking it was perhaps justified if the view that Hoff headed a mass bipartisan popular base is accurate. But it is not.

Another primary source of the split in the Democratic Party is Hoff's flirtation with national power. His early and unequivocal support of Robert Kennedy in 1968, his connection with the Hyannisport syndrome generally, indications that he might be up for a vice presidential bid, his dealings with John Lindsay in New York, and his treatment of the Humphrey forces in the state all served to widen the gap between the Hoff clique (it had become that) and local Democratic power bases. These relationships produced negative spin-offs, chief among which was Hoff's sponsorship of the New York–Vermont Youth Project, which brought black children from New York City to the state during the summer. Some observers were quick to level charges of racism against Vermonters when the program began to encounter opposition. More accurate, we suspect, is the judgment that it was the holier-than-thou almost arrogant "we dare you not to be racists" taunts that seemed to accompany the project which struck discordant notes with Vermonters.

Equally important was Hoff's active involvement with the antiwar movement. Again, it was probably the company he kept rather than the substance of his position that hurt the most. In 1970 there was Hoff in Winooski, the most Democratic city in fact and symbolically in the state (where in 1962 he had led an ecstatic midnight victory parade through the streets), struggling to find a building from which to mount his campaign because the V.F.W. denied him the use of their hall. The conviction that Hoff's loyalties and concerns had drifted out of state, turning sharply left at the border, caused considerable grief among Democrats in Vermont.

Correlation coefficients in Table 15 show the nature of the split in the Democratic Party. In 1970 Hoff was forced into a "nothing to gain, everything to lose" primary with Fiore Bove of Burlington. Although he was able to crush Bove by a 3 to 1 ratio, it took a considerable amount of effort and added substance to the rift in the party. Hoff's performance in the primary was out of tune with both his old electorate and the regular party electorate of the day. His support was no longer associated with the large towns or the regular party vote. It was positively associated only with blue-collar workers and the state's antiwar vote. It was negatively associated with population increases, native Vermonters, higher income, and his own vote of 1962.

In the general election Hoff was able to realign with the party in several ways. Yet there were differences. Although the regular party vote was associated with the native Vermont population, Hoff's was not. His association with the farming towns was negative and significant, while the regular Democratic vote was not associated with farming to any significant degree. Most important, the strength of Hoff's linkage with both his old 1962 vote and the 1968 tallies for Humphrey was much weaker than that of the regular party candidates. Simple correlation coefficients of this nature cannot uncover precise causal relationships, but they do suggest that Hoff was unable to rekindle fires in enough Democratic camps to stand a real chance in the election against Prouty. To win in Vermont, a Democrat must have close to total support of the Party. Table 15 shows that those towns where Hoff lost the most votes from his 1962 totals were positively associated with the vote for other Democratic candidates.

In the final analysis Hoff ran about one percentage point behind Leo O'Brien, the Democratic candidate for governor in 1970, but this statistic hides the losses Hoff suffered within the Party. First, Hoff's vote was inflated by a residue of Republicans that came to him with his gains of 1966. While his gains between 1962 and 1966 were strongly linked to Republican towns, his losses between 1966 and 1970 were not. Moreover, Hoff's losses were negatively associated with the antiwar Republican vote, indicating he picked up support from that area. More evidence that Hoff's total included many more liberal Republicans than O'Brien's lies in the fact that Hoff's vote was positively related to the vote for James Oakes, a leading liberal Republican who ran in the 1968 primary, while O'Brien's vote revealed no such relationship. (Table 15.) Despite the fact, therefore, that Hoff's total included a substantial number of Republicans which O'Brien's total lacked, he still could not match the latter's overall showing.

We argue, therefore, that Hoff was cut down by the very forces that made him. He counted, in the end, on the loyalty of Republicans wooed after his original breakthrough. But all that was left by 1970 was a fringe of antiwar Republicans, and these were too few in number. The senatorial election of 1970 carried with it, however, an importance that transcends the defeat of Philip Hoff and the political and social forces that defined its texture, for this particular contest trumpeted the arrival of a pervasive new force in Vermont's party system—elections of strategy anchored for the most part in the media, especially television. Both strategy and television had been used before, of course, but never in such harmony, never so consciously, never with such profound effects. Hints of the potential impact of a well-planned television campaign occurred when the Johnson tacticians gunned at Barry Goldwater with devastating results in 1964. The Democrats' commercials spilled over into Vermont and brought a coherent pattern of attacks against Goldwater into virgin Republican living rooms throughout the hill country. When it was over, the state (one of only two to vote against F.D.R. in 1936) rejected Goldwater with percentages exceeding the national average.

This was a nationwide campaign, however, packaged outside the state, essentially for non-Vermonters. Intrastate efforts to mesh strategy with the media were still in their adolescence. By the end of the decade, however, both sides were focusing their efforts on the media in more than a haphazard manner. For Philip Hoff this focus allowed promulgation of serious errors of strategy and provided him with a weapon of self-destruction.

The Dawn of Elections of Strategy

In 1970 the Republicans in Vermont won their largest off-year gubernatorial victory in twenty years. Just twenty-four months later they suffered their greatest defeat in the history of the state. The chronology of these events reads as follows: When Hoff decided not to run again for governor in 1968, the Republicans retook the executive seat. Deane Davis, the Republican gubernatorial candidate, running on a ticket with Richard Nixon, won 56 percent of the vote. This total was close to the figure Republicans were receiving in presidential years before the Goldwater election of 1964. Two years later, the year Hoff fell at the hands of Winston Prouty, Davis won again with 58 percent of the vote. In 1972, however, Republican Luther Hackett of South Burlington was soundly defeated by Democrat Thomas Salmon of Bellows Falls. The defeat of Hoff, the second triumph of Deane Davis, and the Salmon victory all point to the increasing importance of antennae strategy in Vermont's electoral system.

Crucial to the development of effective media campaigns is the party's ability to assess and then accurately link up with the state's overarching political agenda. There is, in other words, no way that specific tactics can be successfully developed if the organization's thinking is seriously out of step with the long-range concerns that grip the attention of the polity. An in-depth analysis of the past and future agenda in Vermont will be postponed for Chapter 6, but it is necessary to point out at the early stages of any discussion of comparative strategies that the Democratic Party in Vermont misread the political agenda in the latter half of the 1960's.

Briefly, Vermont's agenda carried no listing that dealt with political inputs. The state is pretty well satisfied with its mechanisms for political participation, its channels of recruitment, its ability to protect minorities, and its clout when it comes to handling harmful penetrations of the system by the "haves" in detriment to the interests of the "have nots." Yet the articulate leadership segment of the Democratic Party in Vermont appeared transfixed by problems of input in the years between 1966 and 1970. Philip Hoff, in particular, carried a torch that seems to have been lit outside the state, where the nation struggled to meet a crisis of alienation that boiled in the cities. While the Democrats circled this flame, the Republicans snatched up the real agenda and made off with it. The real agenda calls for efficiency and precision in dealing with problems of output—in a word, how to manage and finance a state that has decided (1) not to follow in the steps of the great American urban-industrial revolution, and (2) to preserve its abundant social services with a tiny population base spatially distributed in nineteenth century fashion. This goal cannot be reached by a people agonizing over problems of democratic process. It was precisely because the Salmon organization was able to grasp this essential fact in 1972 and then translate it into a coherent plan of action that it was able to pull off the greatest political upset in the history of Vermont. As we discuss the specifics of three recent elections of strategy, it is well to bear in mind that for any party a realistic posture vis-à-vis the agenda is necessary for success.

In the Hoff-Prouty contest the power of television is shown negatively by the suspicion that Hoff would have done better without the medium. That is to say, he probably would not have lost so much of his old following had the avenues for large-scale alienation been absent. Vermonters were not allowed to judge the man by hearkening to memories of his reign as governor. They were asked, instead, to pay attention to more current references promoted in the campaign. For instance, Hoff asked them to accept the judgment that Prouty was less than a good senator by mounting a strong attack on his absentee record in committee.

In a one-party state the wisdom of such a vociferous offensive against the man himself is highly questionable, since there was little to gain (Democrats would vote against him anyway) and much to lose (it would activate the defense mechanisms of the Republicans). But most important is the effect of the media, which allowed the Hoff forces to attack so strongly that they immediately overshot their point of no return. Suddenly, those Vermonters who had had no visceral feeling for Prouty had one—sympathy. Hoff became the young bully and Prouty became the patient old lion, probably misjudged, bravely fending off the jackals.

Of equal importance was Hoff's decision to face up directly to a whispering campaign that seemed to be undermining his credibility. When he went on statewide television to admit that he had a drinking problem and to assure the voters he had solved it, no one doubted his honesty and his courage. But when Vermonters judge their politicians, they demand more than that. The decision to face up to the problem revealed a profound misreading of the Yankee mind, to which honesty is not adequate penance for sin. We suspect that whoever advised Hoff that the people would admire his courage was not a Vermonter. A Vermonter would have added that he would vote against him anyway on the ground of intemperance. The important point is that television allowed him to make this a major error. By appearing, he had nothing to gain (those who knew of the problem would vote against him no matter what) and much to lose (those who didn't know before, now surely would vote against him).

On another part of the ballot Deane Davis was running for re-election to the governorship, and it was television that gave him his second term. Despite the fact that Davis represented a party with which a substantial majority of the voters identified, it was clear that he was in trouble as the election of 1970 came near. It was an off year, and there was no Richard Nixon on the ballot to help draw out the vote. The real difficulty, however, was the fact that Davis had engineered the adoption of Vermont's first sales tax. Governors who bring sales taxes are not re-elected. Early indications were that Davis had a massive negative visibility rating to overcome. In a nutshell, there seemed little chance that the man could win.

The Davis organization's answer to the odds was a masterpiece of advertising that meshed strategy with television. The Governor's pants were rolled up, he was put in a little rowboat half filled with water in the middle of a pond, and he was set to bailing. The audio hammered away at the theme that Davis had bailed the state out of economic disaster. The commercial was short and was broadcast incessantly around the state. With one theme the Republicans had justified the sales tax and had humanized their candidate, a retired insurance executive who suffered from an aura of elitism. There are other reasons for the Davis victory, of course. The Hoff candidacy did not help Leo O'Brien, his opponent, and the Democrats contented themselves with a shotgun media campaign, striking here and there at individual points but failing to follow a coherent plan. Yet it is difficult to find observers in the hierarchy of either party that fail to credit "the bucket" as the prime causal agent behind the re-election of Deane Davis in 1970.

If there were many reasons why Davis should have lost in 1970, there are equally as many why Luther Hackett should not have in 1972. First, there was much good will for the Republican Party around the state. They had won the two previous elections handily. They were well financed and well organized. Their position was matched by an amazing state of disarray among the Democrats. At one point they were having serious difficulties even securing a candidate to run for governor with some statewide prestige, so pessimistically were the chances for victory viewed. Many of Vermont's Democrats looked on the McGovern candidacy with little enthusiasm (to put it mildly), and a very popular Republican was running for President. Hackett had the support of Deane Davis and most of the party regulars. Moreover, as a candidate he was cut from the same cloth as Richard Mallary, Vermont's congressman, who had proved that a quiet, distinctly unglamorous candidate could win by accenting the positive. In both cases, the positive was superior intelligence, sound judgment, and the capability for hard work. Mallary was to reinforce this conclusion when he led the ticket in the 1972 election. Given all this evidence, it is easy to call the Salmon victory over Hackett a profound accomplishment.

There were problems facing the Republicans that should have given the Democrats some hope. At the outset was the fact that the Republicans embroiled themselves in a hard-fought primary campaign. Hackett's opponent, Attorney General James Jeffords, had kept his name in the headlines for several years and went into the campaign with a sizable lead in visibility. In many respects the Hackett victory over Jeffords was an upset much akin to his loss to Salmon in the general election. Jeffords and Hackett were never able to repair the wounds completely. Many in the Jeffords camp felt the nomination had been snatched from them by the machine.

As a matter of fact, however, correlations between the Davis votes in the 1968 and 1970 primaries and the Hackett totals in the 1972 primary were weak and indicated that the machine was pretty much of a myth at the ballot-box level. Nonetheless, there was a strong negative correlation between the Jeffords towns in the primary and Hackett's vote in the general election. In fact, it was the strongest negative correlation of its kind to occur for twenty years. This correlation might be evidence of a large crossover in Vermont's new open primary. There is little doubt that many careful Democrats, feeling Salmon had no chance to defeat Hackett in the general election, voted for the more liberal candidate in the Republican primary. Yet on balance it is simply a matter of disgruntled Republicans jumping the party in the general election.

There were other problems for the Republicans. History showed, for instance, that although increased turnout generally meant help for the GOP, Vermonters were willing to split their tickets. In 1952 ticket-splitting occurred when large numbers of Vermonters voted for Eisenhower and against Emerson, the Republican candidate for governor. Then there was the old problem of visibility. Neither Hackett nor Salmon was well known. Of importance also was the fact that the Democrats, for the first time since their breakthrough, had nominated a Catholic from the southeastern region of the state. This was regional balance of the best kind. They had also nominated an attractive candidate. Salmon's image as a sincere, talented young man with imagination was easily generated from the character of the man himself. Finally, there was the remarkable willingness of the state's Democrats to dissociate themselves from the McGovern candidacy. (They were helped by the McGovern forces, who seemed content to assume a defeatist posture and promote their own death wish.)

But the crucial element in the Salmon victory was the fact that he carried on a superb media campaign and Hackett did not. It was an effort that sewed strategy tightly to television in a manner that showed planning and coherence. To the naked eye, Hackett lacked a media *campaign* altogether. There was advertising, of course, but it was haphazard and spotty. Salmon's messages were brief and repetetive and hammered home one simple point: the state could bring down two birds with one stone. By taxing land-developers (from out-of-state, one assumed), one could help keep Vermont for Vermonters and help solve the property-tax crisis for middle-income people. It was a brilliant mini-articulation of the agenda, since it spoke only to outputs and advocated the protection of the state from outsiders. Much more could be said about the media campaign on both sides, and it should provide a fascinating study for the future, but one thing is clear: without television Thomas Salmon could not have won the election. Moreover, if Hackett had packaged his efforts with the same talent as Salmon, he would have won. The election provides a final and poignant verification of a most dramatic development in Vermont's rural-party system: elections of trend have been replaced by elections of strategy.

Conclusions

Vermont's one-party system was spawned amid the intense heat of abolitionism when a powerful Whig organization lost control of its antislavery faction. Nurtured by a long and vociferous antislavery tradition and driven home by the state's lopsided participation in 'the Civil War, Vermont Republicanism solidified its influence and went on to control Green Mountain politics for over a century.

Though one-partyism in Vermont did not lower levels of participation as it has done elsewhere, and though it did preside

during periods of policy innovations (during the Progressive and
New Deal eras), it nevertheless seemed to deny Vermonters the
benefits of a two-party system. This denial occurred simply
because the Republican Party was not, as many have suggested,
bifactional but rather was characterized by a fraternity of of-
fice-holders that served as an influential magnetic center around
which the opposition flowed but never congealed. The hierarchy was easily penetrated, and the only observable voting
pattern (for the fraternity, as well as the opposition) was
friends-and-neighbors. There was, in other words, no enduring
faction around which to rally the opposition and from which to
demand responsiveness. At the same time Vermonters did not
suffer from an irresponsive system. A lack of party competition
has not caused the kinds of unhealthy outputs that have often
been tied to the one-party situation.

The Republican shell around the statewide elective offices
was cracked in 1952. While important socioeconomic alterations in the character of the state were at large, none seemed to
accompany closely the Democratic breakthrough. Instead, the
phenomenon was largely a political one involving an atmosphere
of Democratic success that settled over the Northeast after the
war, a uniquely energetic campaigner who gave many Vermonters their first glimpse of an honest-to-goodness Democratic
candidate, an increased turnout probably due to the reappear-
ance of a new Democratic core developed during the Depression, and a damaging series of Republican intraparty primary
squabbles. After the take-off, Democrats climbed to the statehouse on off-year election totals, actually winning that office a
decade later in 1962.

Philip Hoff put real teeth in Democratic credibility with two
personal triumphs in 1964 and 1966. Yet Hoff was either unwilling or unable to build a coherent party organization at the
grass roots. His defeat in 1970, the second victory of Davis in
the same year, and the stunning upset engineered by Tom Salmon in 1972, all indicate that rural politics at the ballot-box
level have been cut away from the forces of history and trend.
Though it would be dangerous to classify Vermont as a two-
party state, one thing is clear—a candidate from either party can
win the governorship in any given year. Turnout no longer fluc-
tuates as sharply from election to election. The Democrats' um-

bilical cord to the larger towns has been weakened, and their linkages to the rural towns have been strengthened. Sectionalism within the state has broken down. Most important of all is the fact that political organizations are learning to package campaigns and mesh strategy with the media.

Two final points are worthy of emphasis. The first is that the processes of political change in Vermont have been relatively free of socioeconomic contamination. Neither in the origin of Republican domination nor in the breakthrough of the Democrats were significant alterations in the character of Vermont society at play. In the latter case, especially, the state was changing in certain respects (changes that did not, significantly, include increasing urbanization), but these changes did not seem causally related to the new Democratic successes. This lack of causal relationship strikes a blow at the argument that socioeconomic forces are root causes of political phenomena. Flowing from this observation is the second point, that the rural condition does not preclude innovation in political systems. Breakthrough in Vermont did not arrive piggyback on the shoulders of urbanism. Ruralism and political change were partners.

Four

The Rural Legislature

State legislatures have long been a prime target for public criticism. When the legislature contributes, its contributions are interpreted as reactions, not innovations. Partisanship is viewed as perversity. Independence is obstinacy. But the toughest charge to counter is that of inaction. The tendency of the public (a tendency promoted constantly by the press) is to assess legislative performance strictly in terms of the quantity of legislation passed. To defend a legislature that does not pass bills is to defend a "do nothing" legislature and to appear conservative, a posture that strikes sensitive nerves, especially in academic circles.

The charge is often unfair to the legislature. A case in point: For several years the Vermont legislature grappled with the abortion problem. Hearing followed hearing; roll call after roll call emerged from both houses. The issue produced considerable heat in an atmosphere of usually moderate temperatures. Yet the legislature was uniformly accused of inaction because it failed to change the existing statute. When Vermont's Supreme Court invalidated the existing statute, it did so with a clear call to the legislature to pass new legislation. Vermont's attorney general specifically chided the legislature for not meeting its responsibilities and failing to deal with the issue. Nowhere was heard the one straightforward explanation for the inaction: the legislature (which is more finely tuned to the people's will than is the Court) had decided that the statute was acceptable. In short, the equation that ties change to liberalism and the historical coincidence of liberal domination in both the contemporary press and academia has meant that the legislature has lost a very important option—the decision not to act.

Coupled with the tendency to judge not by what the legislature decides but by how many bills it passes has been a general lack of interest in state legislatures among the ranks of political scientists. Many seem to show impatience with the legislative process. It has been a mood, we suspect, engendered by the belief that the need for checks and balances faded with the dawn of the twentieth century.

In recent years, however, this negative attitude seems to be waning. Exacerbation of problems in the states, increasing interest in a new federalism, and the fact that political scientists are turning to the states in an attempt to establish basic generalizations about the nature of legislative politics have combined to promote a new interest in state legislatures. The result is a growing store of data that should in years to come lend itself to important work in comparative systems analysis.

The raw material used for this book is roll-call votes, and the principal analytical tool is the cluster-bloc technique, a method neglected at the state level[1] but particularly suited for the study of voting patterns in systems marked by an absence of easily definable group pressure. We will also consider such matters as party and district voting behavior, the minority as balancer of power, and policy outputs.

Overview

The Old Legislature

From the 9978 square miles of Vermont's bumpy woods and pasture land, 276 representatives (30 for the Senate, 246 for the House) came in the dead of winter over winding roads to Montpelier, population 8782. Several members knew every one of their constituents by name. The average district for the House of Representatives contained fewer than 800 people; the largest district had 38,000; the smallest had 38; but each has just one representative. Election totals for half the membership did not

---

1. An exception is John G. Grumm, "The Systematic Analysis of Blocs in the Study of Legislative Behavior," *Western Political Quarterly*, 18 (1965), 350-62. For an application of Grumm's technique, see Samuel C. Patterson, ed., *Midwest Legislative Politics* (Iowa City: Institute of Public Affairs, University of Iowa, 1967), pp. 37-66.

exceed five hundred votes. An overwhelming majority were of the same political party. Over 40 percent were newcomers, and only 35 percent had graduated from college. A mere handful were politicians by trade, yet most had held important governing posts in their local communities. They received $70 a week and their stationery. This was how the Vermont legislature looked prior to 1965.

When we speak of the Vermont legislature, we are really talking about two different systems, the body that existed before reapportionment and the newly reapportioned model. In the background of the old, pre-reapportionment, legislature there were four elements: localism, amateurism, malapportionment, and one-partyism.

No exercise illuminates the unique character of the Vermont system as much as the comparison of the legislator-to-citizen ratio with that of several other states. (See Table 16.) In Vermont, prior to reapportionment, there was one representative at the state capital for every 1400 citizens. Of the ten most rural and the ten most urban states in the nation, this was the smallest ratio. Vermont was followed by Wyoming, where the ratio was twice as great. These figures point directly to the highly localistic nature of the Vermont legislature, especially the House of Representatives. (Senators have always been elected on a one man–one vote basis by county.) During several town meetings when I have been present, the town representative asked the people's pleasure on important matters before the legislature. This was not an uncommon practice. Although there is no hard evidence to indicate that these rural legislators acted the role of either delegate or trustee while at the state capital, the very character of their constituencies suggests there was at least a strong potential for the role of delegate. Montpelier lawmakers had an opportunity to know their constituents.

The Vermont legislature was essentially amateur. As stated, usually over 40 percent of House membership was new. In the Senate the percentage of freshmen was only slightly lower. As Table 17 indicates, legislators were somewhat more inexperienced than those in other states. There seems to be very little connection, however, between ruralism as such and experience. Percentages of freshmen lawmakers in the lower chambers of the urban and rural states were nearly the same. Upper houses

Table 16
Metro-urbanism and Legislator-to-citizen
Ratios in Twenty States, 1957

Ten Most Rural States	Metro-Urban Score	Legislator To Citizen Ratio	Ten Most Urban States	Metro-Urban Score	Legislator To Citizen Ratio
Vermont	38	1-1,400	Rhode Island	180	1-6,000
Idaho	48	1-6,500	Massachusetts	179	1-18,000
North Dakota	49	1-3,900	New York	176	1-164,300
Mississippi	49	1-11,500	California	178	1-131,000
South Dakota	56	1-6,200	New Jersey	173	1-74,100
Wyoming	60	1-3,800	Pennsylvania	166	1-53,900
Arkansas	66	1-13,300	Illinois	164	1-42,900
North Carolina	72	1-26,800	Connecticut	164	1-20,400
Maine	73	1-5,300	Maryland	162	1-20,400
Montana	78	1-4,500	Michigan	156	1-54,000

Sources: Council of State Governments, *The Book of the States* (1958-59), and Department of Commerce, *Statistical Abstract of the United States 1961.*

Table 17
Freshman Legislators in Twenty States

Ten Most Rural States	Percentage Freshmen		Ten Most Urban States	Percentage Freshman	
	Upper House	Lower House		Upper House	Lower House
Vermont	37	40	Rhode Island	39	30
Idaho	34	37	Massachusetts	30	23
North Dakota	29	34	New York	16	18
Mississippi	4	5	California	28	49
South Dakota	40	22	New Jersey	14	43
Wyoming	26	27	Pennsylvania	22	22
Arkansas	37	29	Illinois	19	21
North Carolina	66	43	Connecticut	28	36
Maine	39	52	Maryland	48	57
Montana	20	45	Michigan	32	22
Average	33	33	Average	28	32

Source: *The Book of the States* (1958-59).

of the urban states were only somewhat more experienced. Therefore, the inexperience of Vermont's legislators compared to those of other states cannot be traced directly to Vermont's rural nature. Mississippi, another rural state, had almost no turnover. Wyoming had less than Rhode Island, California, and Connecticut. It should be noted also that Vermont's legislative elite was much more experienced than Maryland's, a much more urban state. Grumm's scale of "professionalism" ranks Vermont (along with New Hampshire) near the bottom. Using other criteria such as length of sessions and funds expended for staff facilities, Grumm has type Vermont "nonprofessional." New York on Vermont's western flank and Massachusetts on the southern border, however, are classified near the top of the list with very "professional" lawmakers.[2]

The data in Table 16 show a potential for localism accented by a high degree of malapportionment in the House of Representatives. If one man–one vote had been the norm throughout the state government, each legislator would have represented about 1500 people in 1960. But because each town in Vermont received one representative despite its size, the median constituency was fewer than 800 people, not 1500. This discrepancy points to a third characteristic of the old legislature—its degree of malapportionment. Vermont, like many other states, had a balanced apportionment system, one house based on population, one on geography. In Vermont, however, it was the smaller upper body, the Senate, that was based on population, using the state's fourteen counties for districts, while the lower House, a much larger chamber, was based on the state's constitutional rule of one town–one representative. Because of this rule, the total effect of Vermont's system of legislative apportionment did not produce the intense rural bias known in many other states. The Schubert and Press measure of malapportionment ranked Vermont 24th among the states. The David and Eisenberg formula produced a rather low ranking for Vermont—with the largest counties receiving over three fourths of their potential strength in actual strength, while the smallest had about one half again their fair share of legislators.[3] The Dauer and Kelsay

2. Herbert Jacob and Kenneth Vines, eds., *Politics in the American States,* 2nd ed. (Boston: Little, Brown, 1971), p. 184.
3. Gordon E. Baker, *The Reapportionment Revolution* (New York: Random House, 1966), pp. 34-35.

Table 18
Representativeness of New England Legislatures
prior to Reapportionment

	Ratio of Largest to Smallest "Districts" Per Legislator	Value of Vote in Largest County (Statewide Av. = 100)	Minimum Percentage of Population Needed to Elect Majority
Connecticut:			
House	424.5	68	12.0
Senate	8.1	71	33.4
Maine:			
House	5.5	95	39.7
Senate	2.8	64	46.9
Massachusetts:			
House	13.9	94	45.3
Senate	2.3	90	44.6
New Hampshire:			
House	44.5	95	43.9
Senate	2.6	100	45.8
Rhode Island:			
House	39.0	103	46.5
Senate	96.9	72	18.1
Vermont:			
House	935.0	36	11.6
Senate	5.3	70	47.0

Source: Reproduced in part from Dishman and Goodwin, *State Legislatures in New England Politics.*

measure figured the minimum percentage of the population needed to elect a majority in each house of the legislature. In Vermont, 11.6 percent of the population could elect a majority in the House—a truly remarkable statistic. But in the Senate it took 47 percent of the population to elect a majority.[4] Table 18 compares the Vermont system with the other New England

4. For the details of these various measures, see Glendon Schubert and Charles Press, "Measuring Malapportionment," *American Political Science Review*, 58 (1964), 302-27; Paul T. David and Ralph Eisenberg, *Devalua-*

states according to their degree of malapportionment in 1962. It was noted earlier that in some respects the Senate served as a balance wheel to the House in terms of the character of legislative personnel. Here we see that Vermont's Senate balanced in a sense the grossly malapportioned lower chamber by giving greater representation to the more populous areas of the state.

The Vermont legislature, before reapportionment, had been typed localistic, amateur, and partially malapportioned. The fourth quality was one-sided party control. Both houses have been dominated by Republicans for decades. (See Table 19.) This was essentially the nature of the legislature that served Vermont's rural polity until 1965, when the old legislature was radically altered. In that year the lower chamber reapportioned itself in response to the Supreme Court decisions of *Baker v. Carr* and *Reynolds v. Sims*, which indicated clearly that Vermont's system of one town–one representative would be considered unconstitutional by the Court.

The New Legislature

After reapportionment the Senate remained essentially as it was, but two important structural changes took place in the House: the total membership was reduced from 246 to 150, and the town, ceasing to be the basic unit of representation, was replaced by seventy-two districts, each sending representatives on the basis of one man–one vote.

We will say more later about the impact of reapportionment on legislative politics. It is important to note at this point that coincidental changes in the state's political and socioeconomic systems may have blurred whatever independent impact re-

tion of the Urban and Suburban Vote (Charlottesville, Va.: Bureau of Public Administration, University of Virginia, 1961); and Manning J. Dauer and Robert Kelsay, "Unrepresentative States," *National Municipal Review*, 44 (1955), 571-75. For further coverage of this topic, see Alan L. Clem, "Measuring Malapportionment: In Search of a Better Yardstick," *Midwest Journal of Political Science*, 7 (1963), 124-44; and John P. White and Norman C. Thomas, "Urban and Rural Representation and State Legislative Apportionment," *Western Political Quarterly*, 17 (1964), 724-41.

Table 19
Democrats in the Vermont Legislature, 1947–1971 (percentages)

	1947–49	1951–55	1957–59	1961–65	1966–71[a]
Senate	13.5	12.3	23.3	32.2	25.8
House	12.8	8.9	16.1	21.8	32.7

[a]There was a special election in 1966 to fill the newly apportioned legislature.

apportionment may have had. In the first place, the new district system swept away the old pattern of localism. Large towns were divided into subdistricts, each electing one or more representatives. This means that the city of Burlington now elects twelve members of the House, whereas before it elected only one. At the same time, small towns were grouped together to form districts that covered large tracts of land. For instance, District 63 incorporates nine towns of Vermont's Northeast Kingdom and elects one representative.[5] The 2728 people of the district are scattered over 290 square miles of hills and swampland. Other districts consist of one large town and several small towns. Some towns still hold their identity as separate districts. Before reapportionment, the one town–one representative rule intensified the localism inherent in a system where there were 246 legislators to serve 390,000 people. Reapportionment reduced the House to 150 members and increased the legislator-to-citizen ratio from 1500 to 2600. It did more. By dividing large towns and lumping small towns together, it struck a serious blow against local town government in the New England tradition. The chances for a small town to send local residents to the legislature were decreased. Of the seventy-two newly created districts, fifty-seven are made up of two or more complete towns. Twenty-five of these districts elect two members each, while thirty-two are single-member districts. They represent 219 (89 percent) of Vermont's 246 cities and towns and control 55 percent of the seats in the House. If the district vote were not biased by town lines and friends-and-neighbors

5. These towns are Bloomfield, Brunswick, Canaan, Granby, Guildhall, Lemington, Lunenberg, Maidstone, and Victory. Victory has the smallest population (46) and Lunenberg has the largest (1237).

appeal, residents of the smaller towns should have an equal shot
at these eighty-two House seats. Such is not the case. In the first
four elections following reapportionment the multitown districts have filled a total of 328 chairs in the House. Fifty-two
percent of them went to a group of lawmakers representing the
largest town in their district. Yet towns of this kind made up
only 33 percent of the total number of towns in the districts.
The group comprised of the smallest town in each district also
made up 33 percent of the total, but it filled only 13 percent of
the seats. Put another way, the largest towns in these districts
elected approximately 3.0 legislators per town, while the smallest towns elected only 1.8 legislators per town over the same
four-year period. These data clearly indicate that the large
towns are beginning to dominate Vermont's multitown districts.
No matter what their size, all Vermont's cities and towns were
represented in Montpelier prior to 1966. Between 1965 and
1972, however, over 100 towns failed to produce any representatives, although they had four elections in which to do so.

A second impact the reapportionment process has had on
Vermont's political system is to alter the balance of power that
has been painstakingly maintained over the decades between the
western and eastern regions of the state. If we classify Lamoille
and Washington counties as central counties and omit them
from our calculations, we find that the six remaining eastern
counties lost over half their seats in the House through reapportionment, while the six western counties lost only 25 percent of
theirs. Before 1966 the counties to the east of the Green Mountains sent 112 legislators to Montpelier, one from each of their
towns. The western counties sent 104. This balance was reversed after reapportionment. Now the western delegates out-
number those from the east by seventy-eight to fifty-three.

A third apparent effect reapportionment has had on the legislature is to reduce amateurism and promote professionalism.
The average number of freshmen in the House of Representatives has dropped from 37 percent in the five sessions immediately preceding reapportionment to 24 percent in the two regular sessions following reapportionment. Moreover, the average
years of experience per member has increased from 1.42 before
reapportionment to 1.84 afterward.[6]

6. See Frank M. Bryan, "Who Is Legislating?" *National Civic Review*,
56 (1967), 627-33.

Fourth, as we have indicated in Chapter 3, there have been changes in the kinds of people serving as legislators. In the House the percentages of college graduates, younger legislators, and Catholics increased, although not sharply. Farmers lost membership. In the Senate, however, farmers increased representation, while the percentage of college graduates decreased rather sharply and age levels remained nearly constant.

A final result of reapportionment has been its impact on the political makeup of the legislature. Because most of Vermont's Democrats live in the more populous towns and because reapportionment substantially bolstered the delegations from these towns, it follows that reapportionment should strengthen the Democratic Party. This has in fact happened, although with qualifications. In the first election under the new system (a special election held in 1966), the Democratic percentage of the seats actually fell to its lowest point in eight years. While the Democrats have gained in the House (the 1966 election notwithstanding), an upward trend in their favor in the Senate died quickly after reapportionment. In the three sessions before 1967, they held an average of 32.2 percent of the seats. In the two elections since that date, they have controlled only 25.8 percent. Again the Senate seems not to be in phase with the House. Nor is there assurance that reapportionment played an independent role in increasing Democratic power in the House. Table 19 indicates that Democrats have been gaining seats since 1950. Reapportionment may have simply speeded up a reaction already in process.

Voting Behavior

Academic concern about the nature of legislative politics usually proceeds along paths defined by two questions: what do legislatures do, and how do they do it? What legislatures do is measured by analysis of the kinds of laws that result from the dynamics of legislative government. The question is essentially that simple. Our first concern, however, is with how the rural legislature behaves. We can ask the legislators themselves how they go about their business, and we can analyze their voting behavior. Although the latter method is limited to study of the single act of casting a vote (it cannot, for instance, shed light on intracommittee behavior), it has been generally accepted that the roll-call vote is the best single method of analyzing legislative behavior. Moreover, roll-call analysis is the only way historical research on legislative behavior can be accomplished. It is impossible to interview Vermont's legislators of the 1951 session, but it is possible to see how they acted (irrespective of how they thought about it) through roll-call analysis. We will be dealing with questions such as: What are the power blocs, if any, that emerge in the legislative system? What happens to a minority party tossing in a sea of opposition? Did the large-town delegation cluster and vote as a bloc to enhance its power? Did the ruralites consistently oppose city-oriented legislation? How did the large-town delegations fare when they voted together? What are the dynamics of the rural legislature as a whole? How does it react to alterations in the socioeconomic environment and to changes in the political system outside the capital? Finally, how do the answers to these questions compare with answers to similar questions posed by scholars in the more urban states?

Political scientists use two methods of examining group-voting patterns within the legislative system. One calls upon the researcher to hypothesize that certain members have good reason for voting the way they do. For instance, it is reasonable to assume that members of the same party have cause for voting in unison. Or in Vermont might not farmers group together to promote agricultural interests? Having categorically defined such groups, their internal cohesion is measured on a related set of issues. The second method demands no such prejudgment. It simply reveals which individuals did, in fact, vote together. Given these data, one is called upon to describe the kinds of people voting together in clusters or "blocs" and speculate as to causes for the clustering. This analysis will utilize both approaches but will rely primarily on cluster-bloc analysis. Since that method has had limited application in legislative systems to date, it may be helpful to explain the specifics of the method.

Cluster-Bloc Analysis (The Method)

Computer technology has made available to social scientists a wide new range of research tools, and among these processes is the use of cluster-bloc analysis to identify patterns of voting behavior in legislative systems. Conceived in 1928 by Stuart Rice, this particular technique was placed in a methodological limbo pending the arrival of machines that could cut through the vast amount of quantification and inspection the method demands.[7] In recent years, cluster-bloc analysis has been used in several major studies. Among the more important are David Truman's work on the United States Senate, Arend Lijphart's study of the United Nations, and John G. Grumm's survey of the Kansas legislature.[8]

The strength of cluster-bloc analysis lies in its a posteriori approach to the identification of voting patterns. By empirically establishing the existence or nonexistence of voting blocs at certain levels of cohesion, it bypasses the hypothetical and usually hazardous process of isolating categorically defined groups—something that must be done before standard cohesion tests can be meaningfully employed. The difference is the classical one between inductive and deductive reasoning.[9]

Simply stated, cluster-bloc analysis counts the number of times in a set of roll calls that each legislator in a particular body agrees with every other legislator in that body. There are, therefore, $\frac{N\,(N-1)}{2}$ pairs of legislators in any legislative group (N = the number of legislators). Indexes are then constructed which list the pairs according to the number of agreements on the set of roll calls being examined. It is then possible to select the pairs that match at a certain "level of agreement" and place them on a matrix. This process reveals "clusters" of inter-

7. Stuart A. Rice, *Quantitative Methods of Politics* (New York: Alfred A. Knopf, 1928), pp. 228-41. Rice's work was further refined in 1931 by Herman C. Beyle; see his *Identification and Analysis of Attribute Cluster-Blocs* (Chicago: University of Chicago Press, 1931).

8. David Truman, *The Congressional Party* (New York: John Wiley and Sons, 1959). Arend Lijphart, "The Analysis of Bloc Voting in the General Assembly: A Critique and a Proposal," *American Political Science Review*, 57 (1963), 902-17. John G. Grumm, "Systematic Analysis," pp. 350-62. Bruce M. Russett, "Discovering Voting Groups in the United Nations," *American Political Science Review*, 60 (1966), 327-39.

9. Aage P. Clausen, "The Measurement of Legislative Group Behavior," *Midwest Journal of Political Science*, 11 (1967), 212-24.

agreeing pairs of individuals who voted together at a preselected intensity. (For those who wish to explore in depth the particular variation of cluster-bloc analysis used here, a methodological appendix is provided.) We will be discussing two kinds of clusters as they are uncovered in the Vermont legislature, those which interagree at the 60-80 level and those which interagree at the 70-90 level. In the first case legislators are voting alike on 80 percent of the roll calls on which they are present and voting, and these roll calls equal at least 60 percent of all the roll calls taken during the session. In the second case the clusters are made up of lawmakers each of whom agrees with every other 90 percent of the time on a set of roll calls that equal at least 70 percent of all roll calls taken. Both kinds of clusters are structured in exactly the same manner, the 70-90 level merely representing more intense interagreement among members of the bloc.

In the first example given in Figure X, there are three clusters. Clusters are made up of "blocs" and "fringes." Blocs are simply groups of legislators all of whom interagree at the minimum level (in this case the 60-80 level). Blocs are placed in a solid inked square and broken down by party and district type. Fringes placed in a broken inked square are simply groups of legislators who agree with at least half but not all the members of the bloc. They too are broken down by party and district type. Cluster A of Figure X, therefore, has a bloc made up of three small-town Republicans and three rural Republicans. Each of these six lawmakers agreed with every other member of the bloc at least 80 percent of the time. This bloc has a fringe of three representatives, all rural Republicans. These three lawmakers agreed with at least half the members of the bloc at the 60-80 level.

In short, what we have is a core bloc of six members exhibiting intense and consistent agreement on most of the issues brought before the legislature and three other fringe members who are partially tied to the bloc. In some cases blocs show interagreement as well. The strength of interbloc agreement is revealed by the IBA (Index of Bloc Agreement), which ranges in value from 0 to 100. Figure X, for instance, reveals that in the 1951 session of the House there were three clusters with two sets of clusters (A and B, and A and C) showing interagreement between blocs. The IBA between Cluster A and Cluster B is 18, showing some minor agreement between these two clusters. There is also agreement between Cluster A and Cluster C (the IBA equals 16). There is no agreement between Clusters B and C. There are also times when blocs and fringes actually share members. That is to say, one legislator may be a member of two blocs, a member of two fringes, or a member of one bloc and the fringe of another bloc. When this sharing happens and when the IBA exceeds 40, we have combined the membership of the clusters and labeled them "coalitions." For instance, Figure X shows that in 1953 Clusters A and B were highly interrelated, with a combined membership of two large-town Republicans, one small-town Republican, seven rural Republicans, and one rural Independent.

This method reveals all possible alignments of lawmakers. It can be thought of as a magnet drawing those who usually vote the same into clusters that can be easily identified. It also shows the coalitional formations that these groups develop. There is no hiding from cluster-bloc analysis. If there are groups voting consistently in a similar fashion in the legislature, cluster-bloc analysis will identify them. It is an extremely potent tool in the kits of political analysts.

Cluster-Bloc Analysis (The Findings)

Over the last twenty years, the Vermont legislature has undergone a metamorphosis. The plan of analysis followed here calls for review of these changes through a close inspection of voting alignments at both levels of agreement in the House during three periods that seem analytically coherent: The Early Years (1951–63), The Hoff Era (1964–68), and Aftermath—The Davis Legislatures (1969–72). We will follow this analysis by comparing roll-call voting of the Senate to that of the House. The method is complex but is also rewarding, for it involves executive-legislative relationships, the representative and his district, the impact of reapportionment, coalitional politics, and the minority as innovator.

The Early Years (1951—1963)

For an early, broad view of the nature of traditional pre-Hoff legislative politics in Vermont and the radical revamping of the House since 1963, Figure IX may be especially useful. On it are plotted percentages of the members of the House who have gravitated into clusters. "Fluid" and "unstructured" are apt terms for the House before 1964. At the 60-80 level of voting agreement (that is to say, members must be voting together at least 80 percent of the time on at least 60 percent of the roll calls), the percentage of clustering legislators hovered consistently near or below 10. At higher intensities of agreement (the 70-90 level), no clusters appeared at all.

The assessment of the Vermont legislature provided some years ago by Duane Lockard for this time period ("from time to time, factional alignments do arise, but the usual situation is more fluid and unstructured") appears to be validated by these data.[10] Even the minor pools of solidarity that arose in the amorphous currents of this rural-based legislature are not easily categorized. Neither party nor constituency seemed to be a factor promoting bloc voting.[11] Figure X outlines the cluster structure of the House for the years 1951 through 1963, underscoring this point.

The emergent voting map is characterized by small blocs of rural Republicans with little relation to one another. The 1951 session produced three small blocs, one containing three of only sixteen large-town representatives in the legislature. In 1953, eleven of the 246 lawmakers clustered in two closely aligned blocs. Six Republicans and a Democrat joined together to form another small bloc. The pattern continued in 1955, with four minor groupings, and in 1957, when only one cluster representing 6 percent of the total House membership appeared.

Bloc voting by party surfaced for the first time in the 1959

10. Lockard, *New England State Politics*, pp. 8-45.

11. A threefold classification of district types was used: *large town* districts in which a majority of the population live in urban places as defined by the census; *rural* districts in which a majority of the population live in towns of fewer than 1000 people; *small town*, all other districts. Before reapportionment, the same definitions were applied to each town individually since each town was, in fact, a separate district.

Figure IX
Percentage of House Membership in Clusters with Blocs of Four or More Members, 1951-1972

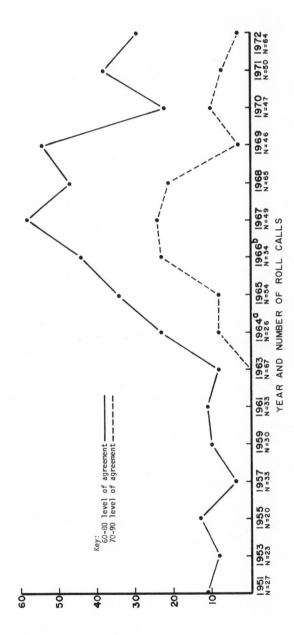

aThe first Legislative program presented by a Democratic governor in Vermont in over a century was brought forth by Phillip Hoff in this special session.

bThe first meeting of the newly reapportioned Legislature.

Figure X
Cluster-Bloc Structure of the Vermont House at the 60-80 Level—the Early Years, 1951-1963

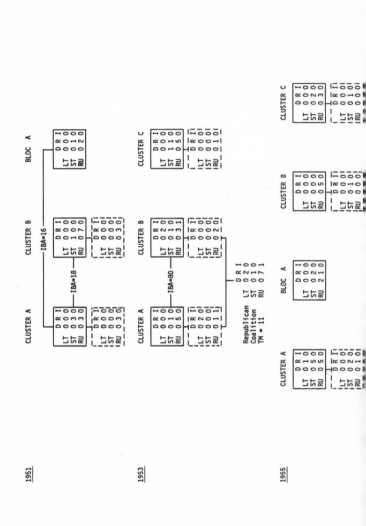

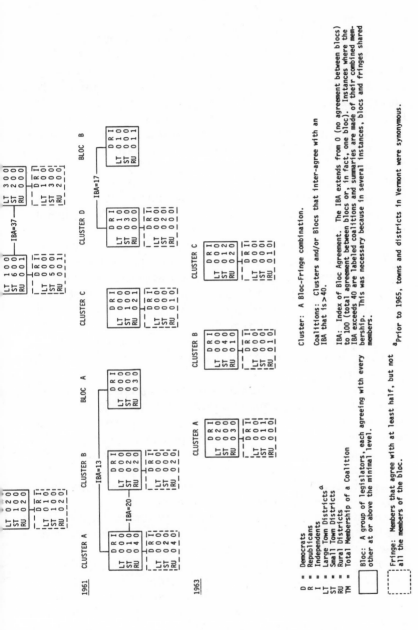

session, when a cluster of thirteen Democrats emerged. This group was in minor agreement with another Democratic cluster of eleven members. Moreover, as we shall see shortly, the cohesion of the Democratic Party as a whole jumped considerably during this session. No meaningful Republican groupings formed in reply to the Democrats, however; by 1961 the Democratic solidarity had melted, and the House settled back into its more natural mold. This momentary Democratic display of party identity may very well have been caused by Democratic success at the polls during the 1958 elections. Jewell has suggested an hypothesis that explains this phenomenon: "Partisanship may be expected to flare up quickly in the legislature when a minority party gains an unusual degree of power."[12] Though it is true that Democrats gained no unusual degree of power in the legislature that year, their performance in statewide elections was astounding in the light of past performances. They captured Vermont's single at-large Congressional seat for the first time in generations and came within a handful of votes of the governorship. It may very well be that the aura of Democratic success that swept over Vermont in that year spilled into the legislature—at least enough to cause some new party identity within the minority.

If neither party nor type of consistency served to identify these minor groupings that congealed in the legislature, were variables such as occupation or education important? Couldn't we reasonably assume, for instance, that members of the farming community would unite to promote values peculiar to an agricultural society? Or might not those few legislators with college degrees see cause for similar behavior manifested in the bills brought before them? Apparently not.

The evidence is sketchy and the search for similarities among cluster members is not particularly rewarding, although from time to time the data produce some suggestive alignments. The chaotic pattern revealed by the roll calls of 1961 contains several. Cluster A (Figure X) has seven Masons among its eleven members, while only 25 percent of the total House membership lists affiliation with that organization. Along with Cluster B this group also shows a regional bias. Most of the legislators come

12. Jewell, *State Legislature*, p. 58.

from adjacent towns in the uplands of Caledonia County or a group of towns in the southern Connecticut River watershed. Yet the most fascinating quality of this tripartite alignment is the nature of the experience levels of its lawmakers. The five-member bloc of Cluster A is highly experienced for this time period, with an average of 3.8 years of seniority per member. The fringe of this bloc, however, is markedly different, with its members having an average of only 1.1 years' experience in the legislature before 1961. Moreover, Cluster B, which is solidly linked to Cluster A, also shows less experience if the eight-years' service of one of the members is discounted. Bloc C as well is tied to the highly experienced bloc of Cluster A (IBA = 13), and it consists totally of freshmen lawmakers. Although there is no way of being sure, it seems as though a core of seasoned legislators stood at the heart of a loosely aligned voting system where attraction weakened as experience levels decreased. Cluster C of 1961 is also of note, since it shows an apparent agricultural and regional bias. Four out of five of its members list their occupation as farming (the other was a carpenter), and all but one live in the Champlain Valley between Rutland and Burlington, the state's two largest cities. Another example of different variables at work occurred in 1953 when the eleven-member Republican coalition (Clusters A and B for 1953 in Figure X) contained only one native Vermonter, and all but one had attended college. This was indeed an atypical group. Clusters of this kind, however, were exceptions to the general pattern.

We find that during fourteen years of legislative politics in the nation's most rural state Vermont's House of Representatives was often charged, among other things, with special hostility toward the state's more urbanized towns and cities. We have seen, however, that no power blocs existed at the higher levels of cohesion (70-90). We have seen that at lower levels of cohesion (60-80) only small and apparently haphazard groups emerged, which bore no consistent markings. We have seen that the only hardening of voting patterns visible was probably inspired politically and was not a function of constituency influence. Statewide electoral success in an habitually minority party may have produced this unique but limited party awareness in the old legislature. In short, what we have seen should help lay to rest the notion that a rural and highly malapportioned legislature will produce congealed rural or farmer voting blocs that continually thwart the designs of urban dwellers and engage in "invidious discrimination."

There is much that cluster-bloc analysis has not told us. It did not and cannot show how particular groups behaved on particular issues. It might be, for instance, that farmers arose to vote with unity on the roll calls that most concerned them and slid into the shadows as a cohesive force when these matters were resolved. Cluster-bloc analysis only paints a broad picture of the entire session at hand and does not point out uniformities on specific issues.

We will address these specifics after dealing with the metamorphosis of the House of Representatives from a large, fluid, unstructured body to one where politics was defined in terms of power, issues were resolved through the workings of power blocs and coalitions, and individual voting gave way to concerted group action. It is safe to say that the immediate and radical turnabout in the nature of legislative politics in the Green Mountain State after 1963 is somewhat rare in the history of American state legislative politics.

The Hoff Era (1964–1968)

The Vermont system began to change in 1964, when a special session of the legislature was called to act on the program of Governor Philip Hoff. In the 1962 election, Hoff had been elected Vermont's first Democratic governor in 109 years. He deferred introduction of executive proposals until the 1964 special session while a series of study task forces were making their reports. Figure XI outlines the bloc structure of the House of Representatives beginning with the 1964 session and continuing through the Hoff era (which included five sessions of the legislature).

In 1964 for the first time two distinct party blocs appeared: (1) A bloc of thirteen Democrats and two Independents with its accompanying fringe of twelve Democrats, three Republicans, and one Independent, and (2) A bloc-fringe combination of twenty-six Republicans—nineteen in the bloc and seven in the fringe. Although the Republican cluster represented only a small fraction of the total legislative party, the twenty-five

Democrats of Cluster A accounted for a substantial portion of the total Democratic contingent. It is of note also that the bloc contained primarily small- and large-town Democrats, and the fringe contained a majority of rural Democrats. The hard-core Democrats were evidently based in the larger towns and rural Democrats found difficulty in voting with them consistently.

During the 1965 session these embryonic voting centers proved to be magnetic and began to grow. A pair of large coalitions appeared. Both were comprised of two closely aligned blocs and their fringes. The larger group of fifty legislators was 70 percent Democratic and 30 percent Republican, with its membership fairly evenly divided among large-town, small-town, and rural districts. The smaller coalition of thirty-three members was both heavily rural and completely Republican. Certainly the development of both groupings was catalyzed by the debate over reapportionment and the many votes forthcoming from that debate. For the struggle served to dichotomize the Republicans, allowing several who supported reapportionment to gravitate into the Democratic cluster. Reapportionment also caused rigidity among rural Republicans who opposed it.

After reapportionment the Democratic coalition, now operating in a body of only 150 members instead of 246, consolidated, emerging in the special session of 1966 as a single cluster of 44 members. It retained its bipartisan character, with nearly 30 percent of the membership Republican. The rural Republicans re-emerged in the 1966 session as well; only now the majority of its members were from the small-town districts. This is easily explained by the constituency makeup of the newly reapportioned body. Rural lawmakers dropped from a majority position into a small minority, while the percentage of large-town representatives increased by some 38 points and the percentage of members from small-town districts increased by 16 points. Appearing as well in this session was a small cluster of nonrural Republicans in very minor agreement with the large Democratic bloc.

In 1967 the Democratic cluster shed its Republicans, replaced them with Democrats, and consolidated its membership into a large core bloc—only 11 of its 42 members were now located in the fringe. This bloc-fringe cluster contained nearly

Figure XI
Cluster-Bloc Structure of the Vermont House at the 60-80 Level—the Hoff Era, 1964-1968

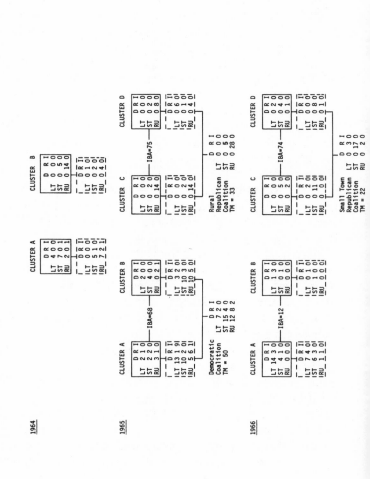

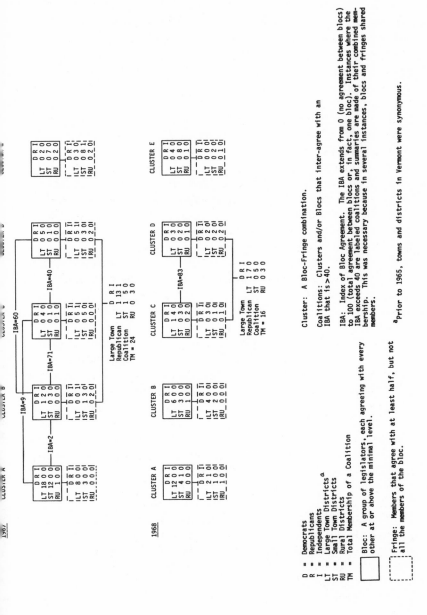

Key:

D = Democrats
R = Republicans
I = Independents
LT = Large Town Districts[a]
ST = Small Town Districts
RU = Rural Districts
TM = Total Membership of a Coalition

Bloc: A group of legislators, each agreeing with every other at or above the minimal level.

Fringe: Members that agree with at least half, but not all the members of the bloc.

Cluster: A Bloc-Fringe combination.

Coalitions: Clusters and/or Blocs that inter-agree with an IBA that is > 40.

IBA: Index Of Bloc Agreement. The IBA extends from 0 (no agreement between blocs) to 100 (total agreement between blocs or, in fact, one bloc). Instances where the IBA exceeds 40 are labeled coalitions and summaries are made of their combined membership. This was necessary because in several instances, blocs and fringes shared members.

[a] Prior to 1965, towns and districts in Vermont were synonymous.

the entire Democratic legislative party. The minority was truly unified and acted as one on most matters before the House—a remarkable turnabout from only a few sessions earlier. Tight party discipline had arrived in rural Vermont. The Republican small-town coalition appeared again in a single bloc-fringe combination of twenty-five members. The 1967 session also saw a third group formed. These were Republicans from the larger towns arranged in three highly interrelated blocs and their fringes with a total membership of twenty-four.

In summary, the four legislative sessions between 1964 and 1967 involved a metamorphosis of voting behavior in which three profoundly new qualities emerged: the growth of a tightly cohesive Democratic minority, the development of a rural bloc within the majority Republican Party, and the parasitic growth of a large-town Republican group that formed within the Democratic cluster and then broke away to form a separate three-bloc coalition. The final session held with Hoff in the governor's chair was, like the session of 1964, a pivotal one for the Vermont House.

Just as Hoff seemed to bring the politics of cohesion with him, he seemed to take much of it away when he announced his departure. During the 1968 session when, having announced prematurely his intention not to run for a fourth term, he sat as a lame-duck governor, the party cohesion that had soared to unprecedented heights only a year earlier came crashing down, and the prevailing bloc formations began to break up. The once highly unified minority party split neatly into two separate clusters, which evidenced no interagreement. The large-town Republican coalition shed many members, appearing as a two-cluster coalition of only sixteen legislators. The rural Republican cluster shrank by over 25 percent. Moreover, the nature of the new Democratic formations began to take on subtleties that cannot be tied strictly to the rural-urban distinctions that had defined the nature of Republican disunity since 1964. In short, the final session of the Hoff era spawned the regional alignments that seemed to govern the character of the Democrats' voting behavior during the Davis administration.

This is not to say that regional variables were independently causal. There is no doubt that the Democratic cleavage in 1968, for instance, was opened in large part by genuine anti-Hoff feeling on the part of party regulars in the legislature as well as in the electorate. It is to say that the regional qualities of the Democratic clusters in subsequent legislatures were too strong to be dismissed as randomly engendered and that the failure of the Democrats, once cut off from executive direction, to maintain party discipline is linked somehow to specific regions of the state and not to rural-urban variations.

This regional bias began during the 1968 session within the vacuum created by neutralization of Philip Hoff's influence. The smaller of the two blocs that held together during that year is called the Franklin County bloc, since a majority of its members lived in that county. (Figure XI.) Equally important is the fact that the bloc is nearly devoid of Burlington Democrats. That city sends by far the largest number of Democrats to the statehouse. (The Burlington delegation made up 20 percent of the entire Democratic membership of the House in 1968.) The larger bloc in 1968 is the important alignment, however, since it is a seedbed for the primary dichotomy that is to stand out within the Democratic legislative party in the four sessions following the end of the Hoff era.

The 1968 Burlington-Rutland axis contained both the "Rutland Triumvirate" of Candon, Esposito, and Debonis and the "Onion River Trio" of Shea, Graham, and O'Brien. The former was to travel unyielding through the maze of interaction that typified the Democratic Party in the House through 1972. It is interesting to note that both Candon and Esposito held important posts in the Party during these years. Candon was the minority leader in the House, and Esposito was the State Democratic Chairman. The Onion River Trio led the Burlington bloc as it struggled to maintain identity amid the kaleidoscopic patterns of the ensuing sessions. Headed by James Shea of Winooski (the nation's most Democratic city ironically situated in the nation's most Republican state), former minority whip in the Hoff legislature, the Burlington bloc was to lose size continually in 1969 and 1970, nearly disappear in 1971, and then regain some limited strength in 1972. Attached to these two threads of unity was a complex patchwork of shifting alignments that also seem linked to territorial imperatives. Nevertheless, the Rutland Triumvirate and Onion River Trio lend some continuity to what was otherwise a chaotic post-Hoff Democratic Party in the legis-

Figure XII
**Cluster-Bloc Structure of the Vermont House at the 60-80 Level—
the Davis Administration, 1969-1972**

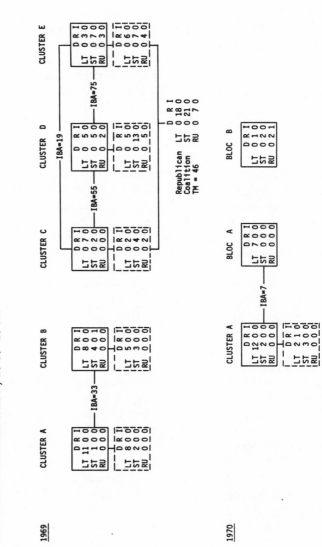

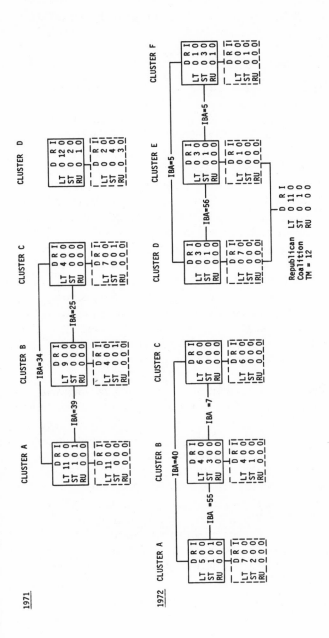

lature. This final observation (of the sessions held after the Republican return to the governorship under Deane Davis) concludes our cluster-bloc analysis of the House at the 60-80 level of roll-call agreement.

Aftermath—The Davis Legislatures (1969–1972)

In the fall election of 1968, the governorship returned to its home ground as Deane Davis snatched it back for the Republicans. The GOP had remained essentially divided during the Hoff years, with the rural and large-town membership parting company on many roll-call votes. What would happen to these clusters with a Republican back in the executive chair? The result seems to be development of a big, new Republican coalition that served to cloud over somewhat the rural versus large-town dichotomy. (Figure XII.) Republican unity was caused in part, no doubt, by the Governor's introduction of sales tax legislation—a move long supported by much of the state's Republican hierarchy. Yet rural-urban divisions still color the Republican intracoalition alignments. The core bloc of Cluster C contains seven large-town and only two small-town legislators, while the core bloc of Cluster E shows the reverse, with seven small-town and three large-town members. There are also three rural representatives in Bloc E and no rural representatives in Bloc C, although the fringe of this bloc does contain two rural members.

Nevertheless, the rural-urban tensions within the majority party were minimized in 1969 as the IBA of 19 between Clusters E and C indicates. Moreover, it was the first time that the GOP had produced a coalition large enough to include nearly half (48 percent) its entire legislative contingent. It would also be the last. If executive leadership was important in 1969, it was clearly ineffectual after that time. Nor did constituency pressures provoke any meaningful clustering. Figure XII tells the story. After 1969, clusters involving large numbers of Republicans simply did not surface in the legislature. One small cluster appeared in 1971 dominated by large-town Republicans. Even this group split in 1972, although the two wings were strongly related (IBA = 56).

Meanwhile, the Democrats failed to amalgamate the core

elements that probably stood in the way of a more unified legislative party, i.e., the seemingly opposed interests of the state's
two largest urban places manifested by the Rutland Triumvirate
and the Burlington-Winooski Onion River Trio. (Figure XIII.)
At the same time these centers failed to create the attraction
needed to build minor solar systems into major constellations of
lawmakers. For three sessions (1969–1971) the Rutland Triumvirate appeared in two blocs with ten other legislators. Although
the membership of this bloc neither increased nor decreased, it
remained in a state of continuous internal flux. Other than its
size, the only permanent thing about these blocs was the absolute lack of Burlington Democrats in its ranks.

In 1969, the alliance was based almost totally in the south
and contained no members from north of the Winooski River.
The next year the membership was scattered fairly evenly
around the state. In 1971 it changed color again, dropping representatives from east of the Green Mountains and showing a
regional bias for the west. Now the Triumvirate was joined by
four members from north of the Winooski but none from the
Connecticut River Valley. In 1969, the bloc had contained four
members from the Connecticut River Valley but none from
north of the Winooski. In the final session of 1972, the Rutland
Triumvirate hung together but was unable to maintain its place
as the largest bloc in the Party, losing nearly half its membership. Interestingly, three of the Triumvirate's colleagues from
Rutland County deserted to form another Rutland dominated
bloc—the Rutland-North Bloc. What we have in 1972, then, is a
splitting of the Rutland County group into two blocs which,
although the two halves were strongly related (IBA = 55), re-
sulted in further atomization of the legislature. In the mean-
time, the Burlington alliance made a comeback as Shea of
Winooski once more surrounded himself with home turf representatives. In sum, the four sessions of the legislature during the
Davis administration were earthquake ones for the cohesive
structures built during the Hoff era.

The House at the 70-90 Level (1951–1972)

This outline of voting patterns has dealt so far with agreement
levels of 60-80. In other words, blocs and fringes were con-

Figure XIII
Democratic Bloc Structure in Detail, 1968-1972

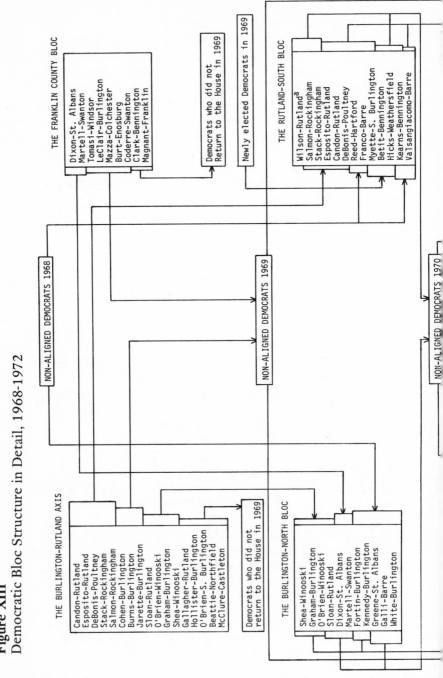

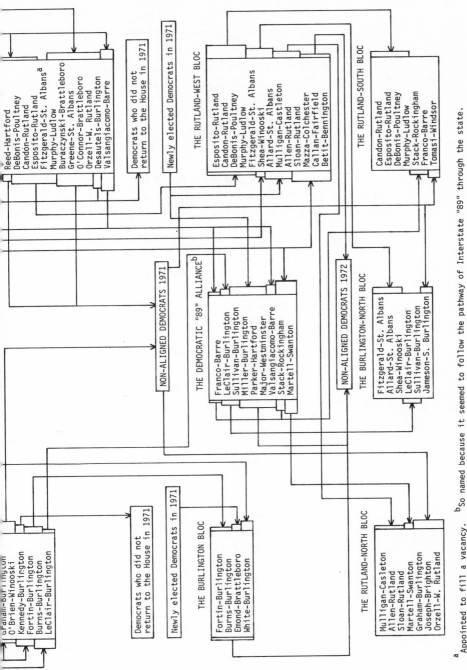

structed using paired legislators that vote the same way 80 percent of the time when they vote together. They must also vote
together and agree on at least 60 percent of the bills before the
House. What happens to these groupings when the level of
agreement is raised from 60-80 to 70-90?

Before 1964 they disappear. In 1964 both the Republican and
the Democratic clusters in evidence at the 60-80 level shrank
considerably when the agreement intensity was raised. After
1964 the Republicans were almost wiped out by the higher
agreement criteria. The rural small-town Republican cluster in
evidence in the 1965—68 sessions disappears completely. The
rural corps could not maintain cohesion at the 70-90 level. The
same can be said for the three-cluster coalition of large-town
Republicans which emerged during the 1967 session. Analysis
of the 1968 session at the 70-90 level produces only a single
group of five large-town Republicans. The higher agreement
level proved completely destructive to Republican bloc structure during the 1969 session.

Only the Democrats were able to maintain cohesion at the
70-90 level in any consistent manner, and their groupings were
much smaller. The 1965 60-80 coalition of thirty-four Democrats and fourteen Republicans was replaced by a single cluster
of eleven Democrats and two Republicans. The 1966 cluster of
thirty-two Democrats and twelve Republicans jelled into a cluster of nineteen Democrats and four Republicans. Moving on to
1967, we find that the pure Democratic cluster of forty-two
tightened its membership into a group of twenty-seven. When
the Democrats split in 1968 at the 60-80 level, they maintained
the dichotomy at the 70-90 level. This is interesting because it
shows that the Democratic split was deeply rooted and the two
factions were not simply divergent outgrowths of a single hard-
core group; rather, each was a hard core in itself. With the
coming of the Davis legislatures, however, nearly all meaningful
clustering at the higher level of agreement ceases. The largest
single group of lawmakers to jell into a recognizable bloc at the
70-90 level emerged in 1971 and consisted of five Republicans
representing enough diversity of social and economic status
indicators to satisfy even the Democratic National Convention
of 1972.

Using the 70-90 agreement criterion adds new perspective to

our analysis in two ways. In the first place, it indicates not only that the emergent Democratic clusters in the Vermont House were larger than any Republican constellations but also that they were more intensely unified, at least through 1968. Simply stated, while many Republicans saw reason for voting together 80 percent of the time, almost none would extend their agreement percentages to 90 percent. Many Democrats, on the other hand, did agree nine out of ten times. Secondly, analysis at the 70-90 level has shown that high intensity agreement disappeared in both parties when the governorship returned to the majority party in 1969.

The Senate 1951–1972

While the House was moving from fluidity to rigidity, a similar reaction was under way in Vermont's smaller upper chamber. There were, however, several variations in the Senate's path through the twenty years under discussion. In the first place, as Figure XIV indicates, changes in total membership that belonged to clusters fluctuated more sharply in the Senate than in the House. This is, no doubt, partly a function of the Senate's much smaller membership (30)—a condition that causes percentages to vary radically with the behavior of relatively few members. Secondly, although the pattern followed by the Senate is basically similar to that of the House, the Senate's maximum cluster participation level peaked a year earlier and fell off more sharply afterward in the Senate than in the House. Thirdly, at no time did the Senate spawn clusters at the 70-90 level— although the House did have over 20 percent in 70-90 clusters during three sessions.

Closer inspection of the actual bloc structures in the Senate (Figure XV) reveals other points of comparison with the House of Representatives. For instance, Democratic cohesion seems to have evolved in the Senate from 1955 to 1961, rather than simply appearing in 1959 as it did in the House. Also, the cluster structure of the Senate in 1965 was not without precedent. In 1961, for instance, *before* Hoff was elected and without the debate over reapportionment, a similar clustering had occurred. This was not true in the House. Before Hoff there had been no

Figure XIV
Percentage of Senate Membership in Clusters at the 60-80 Level, 1951-1972

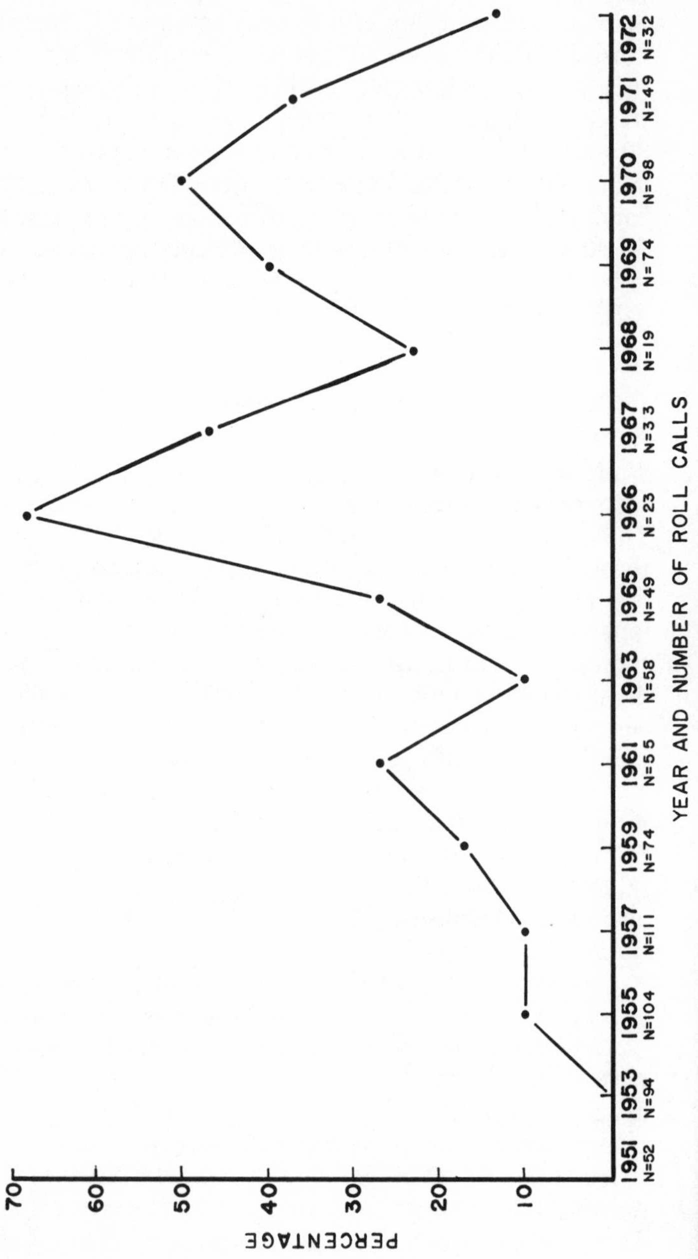

substantial unity in either party. In general, the Senate's development seems to have been less consistent than that of the House of Representatives. The Senate appears to be more capable of substantial change from session to session than the House. (Note the change from meaningful clustering in 1961 to no clustering in 1963 and the tremendous increase in clustering from 1965 to 1966.)

There are similarities, of course. The Senate, like the House, produced a bipartisan coalition during the Hoff years, although it came a year after the House version. Like the House, the Senate's clustering dropped in 1968. Both the House and Senate evidenced new clusters during Governor Davis' first term in office. The general decline of clustering since 1967 has been mirrored by the Senate. Despite this variation, perhaps the most important observation concerning the two Houses is their similarity over the long run. Both seem to have reacted to something during the 60's in rural Vermont, and both reacted in essentially the same manner—a manner involving first a sharp move away from unstructured voting behavior and then a slow movement back toward more fluid patterns, although clustering still remains higher than in the 50's. We will postpone the discussion of just what that something was until we have looked more closely at party and district type as variables affecting voting behavior.

Categoric Group Analysis

The foregoing analysis has been essentially inductive. The cluster-bloc technique has illustrated the changing nature of voting alignments in the Vermont House by empirically identifying groups of legislators who vote together at certain levels of agreement. The following turns the process around and proceeds deductively by measuring the behavior of groups categorically defined.

This new analysis is necessary because cluster-bloc analysis, though providing some understanding of the role of party and constituency as variables of behavior in the context of the legislative body, does not contribute precise commentary on the nature of party and constituency as separate entities. As we

Figure XV
Cluster-Bloc Structure of the Vermont Senate at the 60-80 Level, 1951-1972

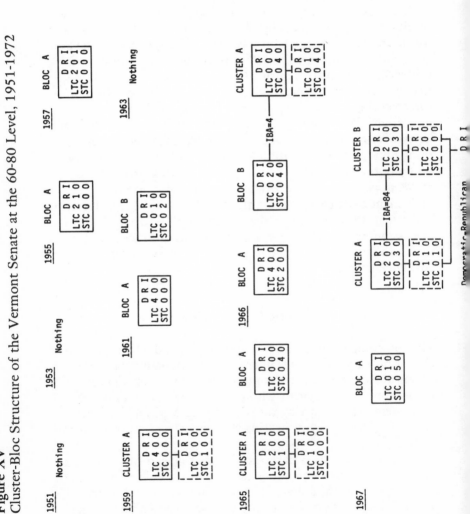

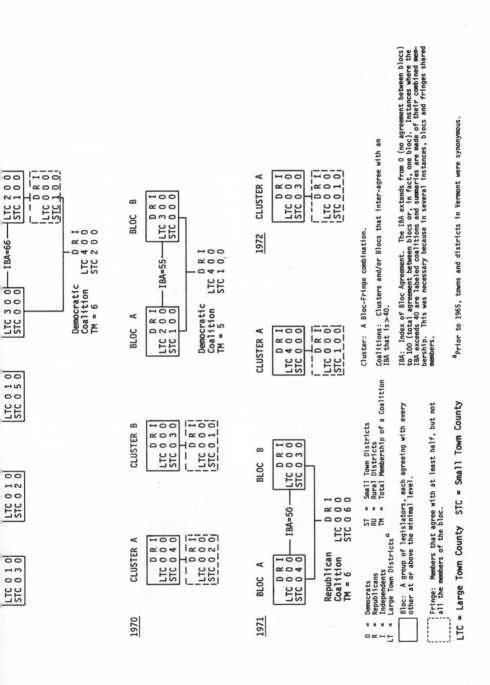

shall see, it is possible for larger numbers of party members to appear in clusters coincidentally with low party cohesion. Moreover, party discipline can vary considerably in both directions at the lower levels of agreement and not show up in a cluster-bloc analysis that builds blocs only at the 80 percent level. Moreover, to abandon the investigation at this point would leave many of the aspects of categoric group activity in Vermont's legislature unsuited to comparison with the findings of those who have studied various other systems. Specifically, we are interested in measurements of party cohesion and conflict and constituency cohesion and conflict.[13]

Party Cohesion and Conflict

Figure XVI shows cohesion scores and the Index of Party Likeness (IPL) in the House from 1951 through 1972. Before 1964 party discipline in rural Vermont's legislature was not a significant force. The Republicans, occupying an impregnable majority position, exhibited no tendency whatsoever toward togetherness. The Democrats seemed to be moving in the direction of party unity in the late fifties, but in 1961 and 1963 cohesion dropped back again to lower levels. Meanwhile, the IPL remained remarkably high, although it did drop somewhat in the 1959 session. This means that party influence was not among the forces that served to promote legislative dichotomies in Vermont. The parties were similar in their behavior on roll calls, and their similarity was coincidental with intraparty divisions. If the Democrats split over an issue (and they often did) so did the Republicans—and in like proportions.

Two dramatic changes occurred within the House of Representatives during 1964. First, party likeness dropped sharply from 88 to 54. Second, cohesion in the minority party leaped 28 points from 38 to 60. Translated, this means that in 1963,

13. The standard Rice index is used for measuring party and district cohesion, expressed as the difference between the percentage of legislators in a group voting yes and the percentage voting no. The Rice index of party likeness is used to measure party conflict. The index of likeness is obtained by figuring the percentage of each party which voted yes or no on an issue, subtracting the smaller percentages from the larger, and subtracting this figure from 100.

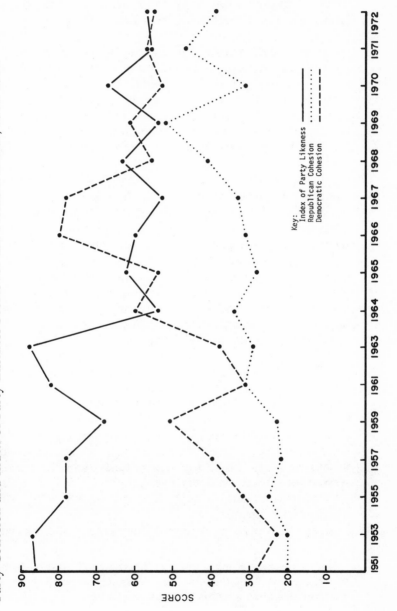

Figure XVI
Party Cohesion and Index of Party Likeness Scores for the Vermont House, 1951-1972

on the average, 69 percent of the Democrats voted on one side of an issue and were opposed by the other 31 percent of the party delegation voting on the opposite side of the issue. A year later, these same Democratic lawmakers averaged only an 80 percent–20 percent split on the average roll-call vote. Eight out of ten were voting alike. This was the special session of the legislature called by Democratic Governor Hoff to introduce the minority's first executive program to the legislature since the Civil War. The Democrats were invoking party discipline (evidenced by the high cohesion score), and in doing so were voting in a manner dissimilar to the Republicans (evidenced by the lower IPL). The latter, however, were not able to maintain a similar unity.

During the 1965 session when the legislature reapportioned itself, this pattern remained essentially intact, although Democratic cohesion dropped slightly and the IPL increased. In 1966, however, when the first newly apportioned legislature met in a special session,[14] Democratic cohesion soared again to a still higher plateau, resting at 80. This score means that on any given vote, 90 percent of the Democrats could be counted on to vote in unison. The Democrats maintained unity at this level (78) in the 1967 regular session. During these two sessions Republican cohesion varied little, hovering somewhere near 30, as it had during the previous four sessions.

It is at this point that the value of cluster-bloc analysis must be underlined. Though raw cohesion scores indicate only a negative state of affairs—that is, no movement within the Republican Party toward unity—cluster-bloc analysis (Figure XI) has shown that there was within the Republican Party a profound dynamism based essentially on district types. Low Republican cohesion was a function of a small-town versus large-town split within the Party. The IPL remained fairly stable during the two sessions of intense Democratic cohesion (1966-67). The score of 53 for 1967, however, was the lowest measured during this eighteen-year period.

In the final sessions analyzed, Democratic cohesion fell from

14. By this time yearly sessions were becoming the rule in Vermont. "Special sessions" and then "adjourned sessions" were called to bypass the constitutional provision prohibiting annual sessions.

its high plateau to levels more similar to the very early Hoff
years. Omit the sessions in 1966 and 1967 and Democratic
cohesion hovers within a ten-point spread between 64 and 72.
During Hoff's final session, Democratic cohesion dropped from
78 to 56, and the IPL increased ten points. For the first time,
however, Republican cohesion rose meaningfully. This unique
phenomenon continued in the next session with the return of
the governor's chair to the Republicans under Deane Davis.
GOP cohesion climbed another 11 points to 52. Now three
quarters (76 percent) of the Republicans could be counted on
to gather on the same side of any given roll call. The Democrats
recovered somewhat (by 5 points) and the IPL reacted by dropping 9 points.

Again, reflection on our earlier cluster-bloc analysis helps to
explain this new state of affairs. The Democrats' cohesion fell in
1968 because they split into two separate clusters of voters. In
1969 their cohesion rose as these two clusters became more
united (the IBA was 33). Republican togetherness mushroomed
as the separate rural Republican cluster—in evidence ever since
the 1965 reapportionment debate—shrank in 1968 and disappeared altogether in 1969. The pattern revealed in Figure
XVI is clear. After the initial eruption of Democratic discipline
in the mid 1960's, followed by the slower development of
Republican cohesion, the parties seem to have reached a common plateau, with the GOP resting some 10 to 15 points below
the Democrats.

To provide a more accurate picture of the nature of party
conflict in Vermont's lower legislative chamber, Table 20 presents figures based on four methods of measuring party conflict
that have been used extensively by students of legislative politics. A close look at these figures reveals again the pattern suggested by the use of cluster-bloc methods. Party competition
began to unfold in 1964 during the Hoff-called special session
of the old 246 member House. The MIO (Majority in Opposition) score for that year more than doubled, and the IPL < 50
score leaped from 3 percent to 38 percent. Yet the immaturity
of this competition is documented by the absence of any roll
calls that met the stiffer criteria of the 80 percent and 80-Index
rules. The 1964 figures may also suffer from percentage infla-
tion linked to the smaller number of roll calls recorded in a

Table 20

Four Measures of Party Voting Behavior in the Vermont
House of Representatives, 1951–1972

Measures	Years						
	1951	*1953*	*1955*	*1957*	*1959*	*1961*	*1963*
Majorities in	%	%	%	%	%	%	%
opposition[a]	33	35	50	36	57	42	30
80% rule[b]	0	0	0	0	0	0	0
80 index[c]	0	0	0	0	0	0	0
IPL <50[d]	0	0	0	0	6	0	3

[a]The percentage of roll calls on which a majority of one party opposes a majority of the opposite party.

[b]The percentage of roll calls on which 80% of the membership of one party opposes 80% of the membership of the opposite party.

special session called specifically to deal with an executive program presumably stripped of inconsequential items that would serve to reduce conflict percentages in regular sessions. In 1965 and 1966, both the MIO and the IPL < 50 dropped—even though Democratic cohesion was very high during 1966. In the regular session of 1967, the MIO was still lower than it had been in the 1964 session; but the IPL < 50 score increased to the 1964 level, and several roll calls met the intense competition-criteria of the 80 percent and 80-Index rules.

Where competition was felt, it was felt more strongly. But the record of these sessions also underlines the dangers of counting cohesion alone as a measure of conflict. In the 1968 adjourned session—the year of the Democratic split—competition again fell but not to the levels of 1965 and 1966. Analysis of the 1969 session revealed the most intense party competition recorded. The MIO jumped to 71, the IPL < 50 registered its highest score (43 percent), and there were substantial roll calls that fit the intense competition measures—24 percent for the 80 percent rule and 15 percent for the 80-Index rules, both of which were new highs and have not yet been surpassed.

In the Senate minority-party cohesion developed as soon as

Table 20 (cont.)

				Years				
1964	*1965*	*1966*	*1967*	*1968*	*1969*	*1970*	*1971*	*1972*
%	%	%	%	%	%	%	%	%
76	67	47	65	57	71	64	66	72
0	2	0	10	9	24	0	10	9
0	0	0	10	2	15	0	10	12
38	24	29	37	34	43	13	38	40

[c]The percentage of roll calls on which the majority of one party opposes the majority of the other, each with an index of cohesion of 80 or higher.

[d]The percentage of roll calls on which the IPL is less than 50.

the Democrats became a measurable force in 1955 (Figure XVII). In 1961, a year before the Democrats captured the executive, they achieved a cohesion of 72, a figure not surpassed until the 1966 session. During the first Hoff-led legislature (1963), minority cohesion actually fell to 63, and when the Democratic governor called a special session in 1964 to implement his program, his party could produce a cohesion score of only 49 in the Senate—a low not matched in any other session. A year later the minority recovered somewhat and registered a cohesion score of 56.

To this point voting behavior of the minority party in the upper house was much different from that of the House of Representatives. Cohesion in the Senate began high and dropped to a low in 1959. In the House it began low and climbed to a high in 1959. From a high of 72 in 1961, Democratic cohesion fell in the Senate to a low of 49 in 1964. In the House it rose from a low of 31 in 1961 to a high of 60 in 1964. Following that, cohesion rose in the Senate and fell in the House. After 1965, however, Democratic voting behavior in the two houses became more synchronized. From similar levels in 1965, cohesion rose in both houses to highs of 80 and 82. It then fell during 1967

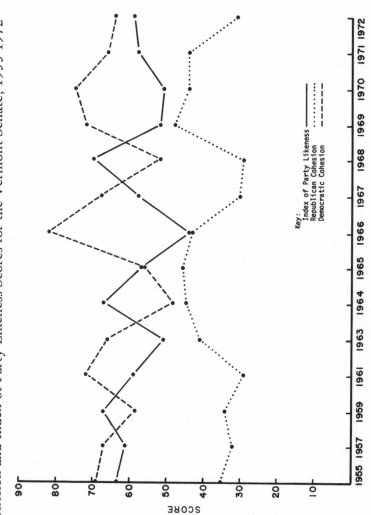

Figure XVII
Party Cohesion and Index of Party Likeness Scores for the Vermont Senate, 1955-1972

and 1968, to rest at lows of 52 and 56. In 1969 minority-party cohesion rose in both chambers—to 71 in the Senate and 61 in the House.

With variations, the Republicans maintained fairly consistent voting behavior between the two houses of the legislature—the only sharp deviation appearing in 1967 and 1968 when Republican unity fell to distinct lows in the Senate while it grew in the House. As in the House, Republican cohesion in the Senate was much lower than Democratic cohesion.

The IPL was generally lower in the Senate than it was in the House. Similarity between the parties was high in the Senate in the 1959, 1964, and 1968 sessions. In the House it was high in the 1963 and 1968 sessions. Before 1964 it was consistently higher in the House than it was in the Senate.

The most interesting point of comparison of party behavior between the two houses is that before reapportionment both seemed to walk separate paths; but, despite variations, party behavior since reapportionment developed in a more parallel fashion until in 1969 it produced a very similar pattern in both houses. In that year Republican cohesion in the Senate was within four points of Republican cohesion in the House, the IPL was only separated by three points, and Democratic cohesion scores were only ten points apart. The dramatic drop in Republican cohesion in the House in 1970 and the sharp increase in the IPL score that accompanied it threw the two houses out of alignment for that year. In the final two sessions of 1971 and 1972, however, the statistics meshed once more. None of the six comparative data sets show variations that exceed 10 points. In the final two sessions measured, the IPL spread between the two houses was only two points, the Democratic cohesion scores differed by only nine, and the Republican alignment was even closer.

Other measures of party competition shown in Table 21 reinforce this conclusion but also provide variations. Generally, the data points for the two scores for which there are consistent data (the MIO and IPL < 50 measures) deviate less after 1964. If we consider the MIO scores to indicate surface competition, while the 80 percent and 80-Index rules show depth—that is, hard-core party struggle—there are differences between the two houses even after reapportionment. In the special session of

Table 21
Four Measures of Party Voting Behavior
for the Vermont Senate, 1955–1972

Measures   *Years*

	1955	1957	1959	1961	1963	1964	1965
Majorities in	%	%	%	%	%	%	%
opposition	53	44	46	45	67	47	65
80% rule	4	3	3	5	9	7	8
80 index rule	0	1	0	2	4	0	4
IPL <50	25	31	22	23	50	26	43

Key: See Table 20.

1966 the Senate experienced deep party divisions on a large number of roll calls while maintaining substantial surface competition as well. In the House, however, interparty strife was minimal. On fewer than half the votes did the parties vote on opposite sides of the issue, and there were no strict party votes whatsoever. But in 1967 the precise opposite occurred, with the parties catching fire in the House while only quietly smoldering in the upper chamber. Then in 1968 and 1969 the two bodies behaved in a similar manner, in conflict in 1969 and more at rest in 1968. The following year they maintained equal levels of surface competition but varied in in-depth hostilities when parties in the lower house refused to carry their differences to the extreme. Finally, in the last two sessions, both bodies were similar in in-depth party competition but the Senate minimized its incidence of simple party roll calls.

Adjusting our focus to a point where these subtleties are blurred, broad outlines seem to emerge: There has been a general minimizing of the differences between Vermont's two legislative chambers as regards party cohesion and competition. The House and the Senate have slowly yielded more similar statistical results since the mid-1960's. The latter has shown a perceptible but slow and erratic movement toward more interparty

Table 21 (cont.)

Years

1966	1967	1968	1969	1970	1971	1972
%	%	%	%	%	%	%
65	45	58	71	64	47	56
22	0	10	22	19	18	14
13	0	0	11	2	8	9
61	33	21	50	46	37	25

competition based on an increase of party cohesion. The House, on the other hand, reacted violently in the mid-60's, showing remarkable changes in the direction of more party competition and cohesion.

The Minority as Balancer of Power

This analysis of party voting behavior will conclude by focusing momentarily on the power status of the minority. We would expect that cohesion within the minority party would swell as the rewards of unity increased. What are the incentives for party voting by a minority that holds no more than one third of the seats in the legislature? Very little, unless the majority was fairly evenly divided on most issues.

Figure XVIII offers data designed to measure the potential of the minority to control votes in the Vermont legislature by tracing the percentage of roll calls on which a fully unified band of Democrats could have swung the roll call one way or another. This simple figure incorporates both dimensions that concern us here: (1) the strength of the minority (Democratic) party in the legislature, and (2) the intensity of majority (Republican) unity.

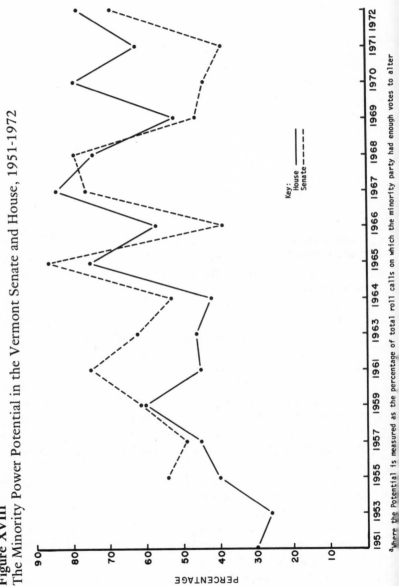

Figure XVIII
The Minority Power Potential in the Vermont Senate and House, 1951-1972

Key:
House ——————
Senate ————————

PERCENTAGE

1951 1953 1955 1957 1959 1961 1963 1964 1965 1966 1967 1968 1969 1970 1971 1972

[a]Where the Potential is measured as the percentage of total roll calls on which the minority party had enough votes to alter

Before reapportionment, Senate Democrats were in a more advantageous position than their colleagues in the House. After reapportionment, however, positions were reversed and the lower chamber began to offer a greater chance for the minority to wield power. As a general rule, House Democrats were in a pivotal position between 40 and 50 percent of the time in the decade between 1954 and 1964. Before this time, they could have controlled less than 30 percent of the votes. After this time, their position strengthened, varying within the 60–90 percent range. Since 1964 their pivotal position has been weakened twice—each time for different reasons. In 1966 the majority was split, but the Democrats had lost seats in the election and were unable to deliver a punch strong enough to take advantage of the situation. In 1969 they were much stronger numerically, but now the Republicans were more unified and refused to hand the Democrats the opportunity to control roll calls.

In the Senate, Democrats were in the balancer position from 60 to 70 percent of the time between 1955 and 1964. Previously their strength in the Senate had been negligible. After 1964 balancer roll calls dropped from 86 percent of the total in 1965 to 39 percent in 1966, when the Democratic Party lost nearly half its membership in the 1966 special election. Mirroring the House, the Senate's pivotal roll calls increased substantially in the 1967 and 1968 sessions, because of Republican disunity and the increased numerical strength of the Democrats. As in the House, they dropped radically in the face of the Republican cohesion of 1969. But unlike the House Democrats, the Senate Democrats remained wounded in the following two sessions (1970 and 1971), because Republican unity held fast. In 1972 Republican cohesion fell in both houses, allowing the Democrats to regain some advantage.

Our hypothesis, to this point, is that a minority will be stimulated to cohesive action if it can control votes by playing the role of balancer in a legislature whose majority is dichotomized. Did this happen in Vermont? How did the Democrats react to increased opportunities to play the pivot in the legislative game?

Generally speaking, the Democrats' willingness to play the pivot increased as the opportunity to do so increased before reapportionment. Figure XIX shows the votes on which the

Figure XIX
The Minority Party as Balancer of Power in the Vermont House and Senate, 1951-1972

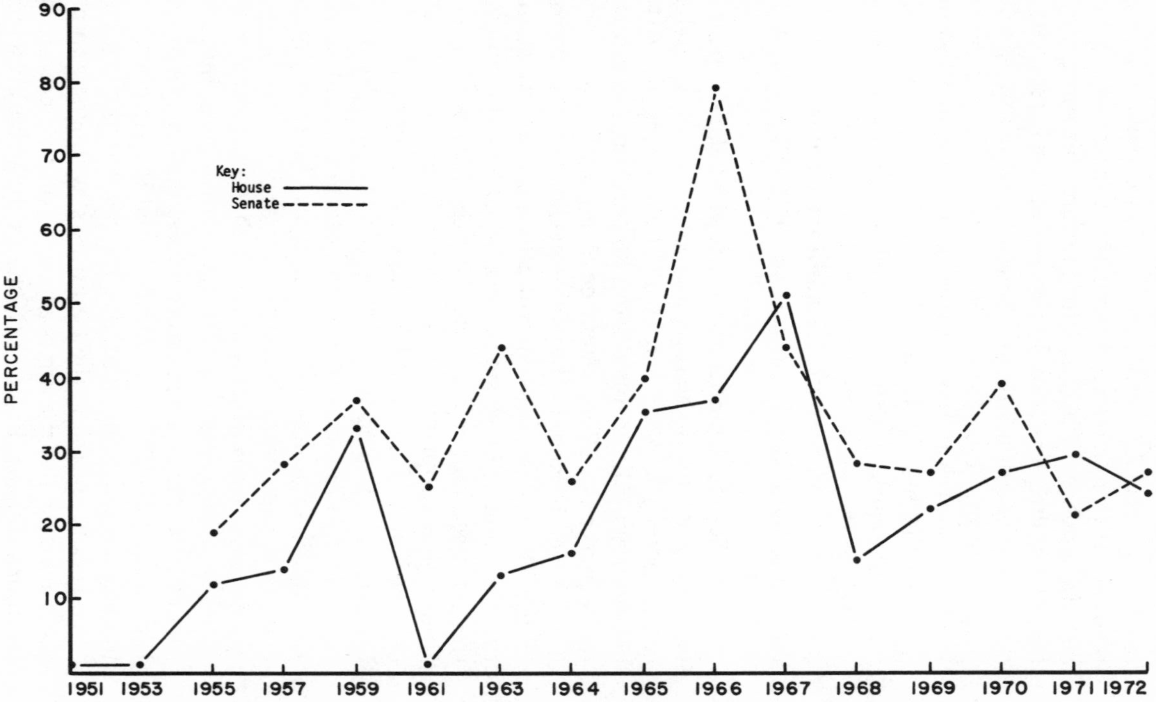

Key:
House ———
Senate — — —

PERCENTAGE

1951 1953 1955 1957 1959 1961 1963 1964 1965 1966 1967 1968 1969 1970 1971 1972

aplotted as the percentage of the votes on which the Democrats could have altered the outcome by voting together and did so minority did change the outcome, as a percentage of the roll calls on which it was possible to do so. In the 1951 and 1953 House sessions, Democrats declined to vote so as to alter the outcome on any roll calls, even when the potential was present. During the next two sessions they began to play the balancer from time to time. Yet on 85 percent of the votes taken, where a unified minority could have changed the vote, the Democrats did not act. In 1959, however, the Democrats took advantage of their position on one third of the balancer roll calls. This increased wielding of power by the Democrats tops off the findings of the cluster-bloc and cohesion analysis above by indicating that increased Democratic activity in that session was not in vain.

When the potential for the Democrats' success fell off in the early 1960's (Figure XVIII), so, too, did their willingness to swing votes even when it was possible—the coming of a Democratic governor notwithstanding. In 1964 a record jump in Democratic cohesiveness (Figure XVI) failed to stimulate the Party to exploit Republican diversity when it could. This record again is evidence that a minimal potential for victory will invoke a "what's the use" attitude that spills over into situations where unified action would be profitable. (In 1964 the Democrats were in their weakest position since 1955.) Conversely, when the minority's position looked generally better in 1965 (balancer roll calls increased from 42 percent to 75 percent in the House), Democrats took heart and overruled Republican majorities 35 percent of the time.

After reapportionment the minority in the House was at first relatively smaller in a smaller chamber (150 members now, not 246). When the percentage of pivotal roll calls fell as a result, however, the Democrats' propensity to give up hope did not arise. They continued to invoke their will when they could at a rate of 37 percent (a high figure; it must be realized that "balancer roll call" is defined as one where only perfect unanimity could change the outcome). In 1967 this figure was increased to 50 percent. More evidence to suggest that our "what's the use" hypothesis no longer held after reapportionment appears in the 1968 session. Democratic willingness to play the pivot did not fall because their chances of winning seemed slim. It fell because, as cluster-bloc and cohesion tests have shown us, the bottom fell out of Democratic unity altogether as the party split into two opposing blocs. In 1969 the minority recovered some of their lost unity and played the balancer roll a bit more often—despite the fact that the new Republican unity sharply lessened their opportunities to do so. In 1970 and 1971, balancer opportunities remained constant, and so did the Democrats' propensity to seize them. In 1972 there is further evidence that the theory linking potential to action is false. In 1972 opportunity after opportunity arose for the Democrats to change the outcome on votes. On nearly 70 percent of the votes the minority, if united, could have invoked its will. But the percentage of the times it did so actually decreased from 29 to 24.

In 1966 Senate Democrats had relatively little opportunity to invoke the power of the balancer. On only 39 percent of the roll calls was it possible for them to swing the vote. Yet on these, they rose to the occasion 78 percent of the time. In 1967, however, when the Republicans were vulnerable on 76 percent of the roll calls, a disunited minority could muster enough cohesion to govern the outcome of only 44 percent of the votes. In 1968 the power potential of the minority increased still more, and Democratic willingness to capitalize on it fell sharply again.

Unlike the House, the Senate at no time seemed to adhere to the "what's the use" hypothesis—evidence, it would seem, that the size of the chamber may be an important variable. Only when the House shed some ninety-six members did the tendency to lose hope when opportunities for action were slim disappear. Although there is no way to postulate a formal causal relationship, the evidence suggests that the metamorphosis of this rural legislature involved some awareness on the part of the minority that concerted action could swing pivotal votes—and this awareness was partly a product of increased opportunities to do so. Once established, the strategy of the minority balancer could withstand periods of inactivity (because of a loss of membership or of majority unity) to appear from time to time as the occasion arose. On the other hand, no amount of opportunity for use could revitalize the strategy if internal cohesion was lacking in the party. Now in the smaller body, Democrats may refuse to act even when the potential to do so increases, as their behavior in the 1972 session indicates.

Review of the issues on which the Democrats opted to invoke their will reveals that they did not waste their efforts on inconsequential items. In the hey-day of their roll as balancer of power—the 1965, 1966, and 1967 sessions—they were a pivotal force on a series of key issues. In 1965 they swung several votes leading to the creation of a legislative council. The establishment of day-care facilities, appropriations, regional development, a state sweepstakes, and blue laws all prompted the Democrats to change the outcome of roll calls with concerted party voting. During the special session of 1966 they joined forces on H.5, a measure to repeal the poll tax as a qualification for voting; on H.7, the fair housing bill; and on H.40, a bill establishing a Scenery Preservation Council. During the next session the Hoff forces played their trumps a record twenty-one times. Nine of these went to back H.72, a major civil rights act. Others were used to regulate cable television, to establish minimum wages, to deal with unemployment compensation, and to provide social welfare measures.

In 1968 when party cohesion fell dramatically and the Party split in half, they still managed to join together and play an important roll in the future of the critical equalization formula for state aid to education. They also swung three roll calls concerning the state's minimum wage. During the Davis administration they have risen as a cohesive force to decide many votes, especially roll calls dealing with education, labor, and welfare. Yet, as Figure XIX indicates, they have failed to regain the power they once knew in the mid-1960's when they held the governorship.

District Cohesion and Conflict

Implicit in the demands to revamp state legislatures in line with the one man—one vote criterion was the suggestion that the historical packing of state legislatures with rural lawmakers had served to inhibit the passage of legislation that was favorable to metropolitan interests. Since *Baker v. Carr*, this hypothesis has been severely questioned by several studies that have compared degrees of malapportionment in state legislatures. The conclusion is generally reached that there was no positive relationship between anti-city legislation and malapportionment.[15]

15. Thomas R. Dye, "Malapportionment and Public Policy in the States," *Journal of Politics*, 27 (1965), 586-601. Richard Hofferbert, "The Relation between Public Policy and Some Structural and Environmental

Table 22
Cohesion of Constituency Types for the Vermont
House of Representatives, 1951–1972

Constituency type[a]	Years						
	1951	1953	1955	1957	1959	1961	1963
Large town	39	37	34	42	38	33	46
Small town	23	24	24	22	21	25	34
Rural	22	24	26	23	20	29	28

[a]District types are drawn using the criteria utilized for cluster-bloc analysis.

That this was the case had been suggested much earlier, however, by David R. Derge, who looked not at what malapportioned legislatures do but rather at how they do it, and concluded for Illinois and Missouri that, measured in terms of rollcall votes, urban-rural conflict was a myth. Moreover, metropolitan legislators seldom vote cohesively, but when they do find cause for unity, their position usually prevails.[16] Derge's work must be interpreted as an important attack on the "invidious discrimination" thesis that stood behind much of the agitation for reform. It is, moreover, precisely because of findings such as these that constituency behavior becomes so important in any study of the legislative system. What has been the pattern of voting cohesion among delegations from like districts in Ver-

Variables in the American States," *American Political Science Review*, 60 (1966), 73-83. Herbert Jacob, "The Consequences of Malapportionment: A Note of Caution," *Social Forces*, 43 (1964), 256-61. A more recent interpretation is Allen G. Pulsipher and James L. Weatherby, Jr., "Malapportionment, Party Competition, and the Functional Distribution of Government Expenditures," *American Political Science Review*, 62 (1968), 1207-19.

16. David R. Derge, "Metropolitan and Outstate Alignments in Illinois and Missouri Legislative Delegations," *American Political Science Review*, 52 (1958), 1051-65.

Table 22 (cont.)

| | | | | $Years^b$ | | | | |
1964	1965	1966	1967	1968	1969	1970	1971	1972
44	47	45	40	36	26	24	27	22
20	24	31	18	36	26	29	32	32
32	24	35	32	44	53	49	57	45

[b] Figures presented are average cohesion scores by year.

mont over the last decade? Has reapportionment affected this pattern?

Cohesion scores for constituency types in Vermont (Table 22) indicate that district alignments, as defined here, have not served as an enduring basis for unified voting behavior.[17] Moreover, reapportionment caused no profound alterations in the voting behavior of legislators based on the kind of district they represented. In the House the large-town group exhibited the highest cohesion prior to reapportionment and continued to do so until the 1968 and 1969 sessions. Higher cohesion on the part of large-towners after reapportionment was evidently a result of the large-town Democratic–Republican coalition that appeared in the cluster-bloc analysis outlined above. When this coalition fell apart in 1968, when the Republicans began to vote more in unison in 1969, and when the Democrats split ranks, large-town cohesion broke down as well.

Growing Republican unity also functioned to increase cohesion scores for the lawmakers from the rural districts—the rural

17. For supportive findings see: Murray C. Havens, *City vs. Farm* (Tuscaloosa: Bureau of Public Administration, University of Alabama, 1957). Probably the most extensive study of rural-urban voting behavior in a one-party state legislature was this analysis of Alabama's House of Representatives. Haven finds no rural-urban alignments that are durable.

bloc being almost entirely Republican. Though it is certainly true that since reapportionment there has been a general decrease in large-town cohesion and an increase in rural cohesion, this state of affairs is more likely a result of party behavior than a conscious awareness of legislators from similar districts that they should vote together. Cluster-bloc analysis has shown us, however, that the intra-Republican dichotomy of 1964-67 was based on a rural versus large-town cleavage.

In summary it appears certain that major voting distinctions based on district types in the rural legislature surfaced only momentarily as an upshot of the reapportionment struggle. Manifested in two Republican voting clusters, one populated by members from the more rural districts and one having more lawmakers from the large towns, they remained visible through several sessions. As a delegation, however, rural members became unified only when their party did so. It has been pointed out by many scholars of the legislative process that constituency homogeneity serves to reinforce party discipline. Some have even gone so far as to suggest that party cohesion is impossible without it. A noted scholar in the field of comparative state politics has suggested, for instance, that:

> It is unlikely that party organization and discipline alone is the cause of party voting, for organization and discipline can only be effective under certain conditions. The evidence seems to indicate that party influence is only effective where the parties represent separate and distinct socio-economic conditions. Where the constituencies of a state are divided along socio-economic lines and where party divisions coincide with these constituency divisions, only then will party program and discipline be effective in shaping policy in legislative chambers.[18]

In Vermont, as we have said, the Democrats have traditionally represented a somewhat distinct sociocultural segment of the state's population. They have come for the most part from large towns where there are more Catholics and other minority groups. The Republicans, on the other hand, are divided by

18. Dye, *Politics in States and Communities*, p. 138.

constituency types—their membership is fairly evenly spread among the three kinds of districts. For a time this state of affairs seemed to exist coincidentally with the predicted results— the Democrats produced high cohesion scores while the Republicans were split. Yet the time when the Democrats were most unified (the mid 1960's) was precisely the time when their traditional constituency homogeneity was breaking down and their appeal was becoming more cosmopolitan. It is also important to note that such constituency similarity as there was evidently could not keep the party glued together after 1967. Conversely, the more heterogeneous constituency of the Republicans did not stand in the way of increased majority unity, given a Republican governor and a potent issue—the sales-tax debate in the 1969 session. This evidence would suggest that party discipline, not district homogeneity (as Dye suggests), was the cause of variations in party cohesion—at least in rural Vermont.

In his analysis of Missouri and Illinois, Derge presents figures that lead him to conclude that "metropolitan legislators are usually on the prevailing side when they do vote together with high cohesion."[19] In short, Derge isolated the roll calls on which the metropolitan delegation voted together and tested to see if they voted on the winning side. This seems to be a valuable exercise, as it shows how successful metropolitan delegations were when they felt the need to be successful. Using Derge's measure of cohesion to provide consistency in our comparison, we see that the figures for the Vermont House of Representatives (Table 23) before reapportionment are remarkably similar to Derge's figures for metropolitan delegations in Missouri and Illinois. In other words, legislators from the more populous areas in all three states won most of the time when they voted in a unified fashion.

Because Derge's 67 percent cohesion score is somewhat low, it was necessary to test further this conclusion at higher levels of unity. To do so, the criterion for delegate cohesion was made relative to the average cohesion of the large-town delegation in each particular session. This was done by defining a high cohesion roll call as one on which the cohesion of the delegation was at least ten points above the average for that year. It was felt

19. Derge, p. 1052.

Table 23
Frequency of Large-town Delegations Voting with Prevailing
and Losing Side of Contested Roll Calls: Vermont House

| | *When delegation cohesion is ⩾67%*[a] | | | | *When delegation cohesion is 10 points above yearly average*[b] | | | |
| | *Before re-apportion-ment* | | *After re-apportion-ment* | | *Before re-apportion-ment* | | *After re-apportion-ment* | |
	N	%	N	%	N	%	N	%
Prevailing Side	132	80.4	131	98.5	93	83.8	100	100
Losing Side	32	19.5	2	1.5	18	16.2	0	0
Totals	164	99.9	133	100.0	111	100.0	100	100

[a]This table is presented in a fashion similar to Derge's. Derge's 67% figure, used here, is a true percentage, not to be confused with the Rice index of cohesion. Derge *American Political Science Review*, p. 1085.

[b]Cohesion measured by using the Rice index.

that this process would reveal what happens when large-town members voted with a solidarity that was above the norm for that particular session. Table 23 also presents these data and supports Derge's conclusion that delegation success varies positively with delegation solidarity.

Issues and Voting

To this point we have shown that the Vermont legislature was traditionally not a dueling ground for concentrated and permanent power blocs. In more recent years, however, party activity has increased (especially within the minority), and behavior appearing to reflect district similarities surfaced for a while, primarily as a result of the reapportionment debate. In short, the legislature has been transposed from a place where consistent power groupings were nonexistent to a place where they are entirely possible and even expected.

It is not possible, however, to infer from these conclusions that conflict was never present in the old legislature. Nor is it possible to conclude that at times parties never voted in a unified manner. We now should investigate what kinds of issues *did* prompt rural lawmakers to vote along party or district lines, and what kinds of issues are associated with the most heated conflict in general—that is to say, what kinds of issues caused close votes within the total membership. Were these the same as those causing party conflict and constituency cohesion? Has conflict over issues changed as the legislature has matured? In short, we will need to define the list of issues linked to the various kinds of voting behavior in the legislature.

In the House, before the special session of 1964, the year that marked the introduction of the minority's first executive program, issues that caused close votes in the House were (1) "morality" (bills involving such things as drinking on the Sabbath, horse racing, gambling, and public entertainment), and (2) conservation, fish and game, and forestry. Taxes and highways also appeared among the bills that caused at least a 40-60 split in the lower chamber. It is interesting to note that agricultural issues produced no general conflict in the House and that morality questions accounted for twice as many divisive roll calls as any other issue. (See Table 24.)

When parties voted in a dissimilar fashion during these years, it was often on different kinds of issues. Bills dealing with education were as important as morality bills, while politics (such items as electoral laws, rules of order, and other matters that deal with party structure and process) and labor categories, which did not cause general conflict, were prime promoters of party difference. On the other hand, taxes and highways, issues that figured strongly in general conflict, produced little party conflict.

Education, highways, appropriations, and taxes produced most of the large-town cohesion. Morality questions did not register at all as variables of large-town cohesion, although topics of this kind produced much of the general conflict and party differentiation in the House. Political scientists have generally observed that morality questions are peculiar to the rural condition. That they provoked no consensus on the part of Vermont's large-town legislators and yet were most responsible for

Table 24
Issues and Voting in the Vermont House 1951–1972

Time periods	Issues associated with general conflict[a]		Issues associated with party conflict[b]		Issues associated with large-town cohesion[c]	
	Category	%	Category	%	Category	%
	Morality	21.6	Morality	14.3	Education	18.2
	Conservation		Education	14.3	Highways	15.9
	Fish and		Politics	12.7	Appropriations	13.2
	Game		Labor	9.5	Taxes	11.8
Early	Forestry	12.5	Conservation		Conservation	
years	Taxes	8.9	Fish and		Fish and	
1951–1963	Highways	8.9	Game	9.5	Game	9.5
	Others	48.1	Forestry		Forestry	31.4
			Others	39.9	Others	
	Total roll calls = 56		Total roll calls = 63		Total roll calls = 74	
	Morality	11.9	Taxes	18.0	Education	17.2
	Education	11.9	Politics	18.0	Appropriations	9.4

Hoff era 1964–1968

Government regulation of private concerns		
Taxes	10.4	
Civil Rights	8.9	
Others	46.5	
Total roll calls = 67		

Labor	11.1
Appropriations	8.3
Government regulation of private concerns	8.3
Others	36.3
Total roll calls = 77	

Government organization	9.4
Morality	7.8
Social Welfare	7.8
Others	48.4
Total roll calls = 64	

Aftermath: Davis years 1969–1972

Morality	22.9
Education	21.4
Taxes	8.6
Politics	8.6
Labor	8.6
Others	29.9
Total roll calls = 70	

Education	20.8
Taxes	19.5
Appropriations	11.7
Politics	10.4
Labor	10.4
Others	27.2
Total roll calls = 77	

Politics	16.4
Education	10.9
Labor	10.9
Morality	10.9
Social Welfare	9.1
Others	41.8
Total roll calls = 55	

[a] Votes where at least 40% of the House membership voted against the prevailing majority.
[b] Votes where the IPL was at least 10 points below the yearly average.
[c] Votes where large-town cohesion was at least 10 points above the yearly average.

close votes in general suggests that while morality bills were very important in Vermont, causing much division, this division was not tied to population distributions within the state.

When Vermont developed the early workings of a two-party system, elected its first Democratic governor in a century, and reapportioned the legislature, one might well have expected different kinds of issues to have emerged as promoters of legislative conflict. This seems in fact to have occurred. Morality issues no longer dominated the general conflict as they once had done, and the slack was taken up by educational issues. However, both these issues disappeared from the list of major-party conflict roll calls where they had been previously dominant. Issues associated with large-town cohesion changed the least, with education and appropriations still among the top three issues. It may be significant to note that morality issues became important sources of large-town cohesion in the sessions surrounding the decision to reapportion and give new power to the larger towns.

Educational issues are of particular import because they seem to have bridged the gap between the parties. Bills on educational matters were not among those which caused great party difference, but they did promote substantial large-town cohesion. Large-towners in both parties very likely voted in a similar fashion to produce high IPL's and low cohesion scores. Finally, in the newer legislature, bills concerning conservation, fish and game, and forestry all but disappeared as promoters of conflict of any kind. In the old system they had been an important cause of conflict.

The passing of Hoff, the return of the governor's chair to the Republicans, and the breakup of the Hoff coalition in the legislature set the stage for further changes in voting behavior on the issues. The legislature's most recent sessions, however, suggest mixed conclusions. On the one hand, issues associated with general conflict in the House did not change to any great degree. On the other hand, the parties began to take sides on education issues, something they had not done during the Hoff years, and political issues became important new identifiers of large-town cohesion. The incidence of labor issues in the various categories also began to increase.

If we add perspectives not immediately evident in the sterile data, several general observations suggest themselves concerning the struggle to weigh the elements of change versus the elements of status quo. To begin with, change seems to win. On conflict of issues in the House, there are more differences than similarities. One difference is the intensity of conflict over single issues that seem to dominate entire sessions of the legislature. In 1969 the sales tax bill accounted for a dozen roll calls that provoked party conflict, while the bill calling for a constitutional convention referendum dominated large-town cohesion. In 1970 and 1972 the abortion question caused the conflict that gave morality issues the lead among issues causing close votes during the Davis administration. In 1971 three bills concerning state aid to education produced a dozen roll calls in the House which caused general warfare, characterized in large part by interparty combat.

Another important change in the House is the lessening in importance of morality bills. Without the abortion question this issue would not have appeared as a meaningful promoter of conflict of any kind in recent years. There is also evidence of new issues becoming important while others begin to fade out. Labor bills are appearing more often and promoting conflict. Education is much more important than it once was; without the abortion bill it would have been the most important producer by far of general conflict in the last four sessions. Taxes now cause party conflict. They did not before the Hoff administration. Finally, there were subtle but important differences between the Hoff and Davis administrations. The focus of the struggle during the Hoff years seemed to be on the relationship of people to people and people to government. For the first time, the legislature fought it out over civil rights bills. The conflict on social welfare seemed to concentrate on the individual's rights and needs and not on the mechanism of efficient programming. The same was true for labor legislation. During the Davis years, the emphasis was more on program and system— how to provide more and better services more and more efficiently. It would be easy to make too much of these differences; the exceptions embodied in individual pieces of legislation are numerous. Nevertheless, the differences in mood were there even though they are hidden somewhat by our analysis of issues in necessarily generalized categories.

What is immediately striking about Vermont's Senate is the
absence of "morality" as an important issue prior to 1964. Also
markedly differentiating the Senate from the House during this
period was consistency of issues that caused various kinds of
conflict. Labor, education, and politics were strongest in all
three areas. In other words, general conflict, party difference,
and large-town cohesion all appear to be a function of these
three types of legislation. (See Table 25.) Part of this consistency is due to the interlinkage of parties and districts. The
Democrats in the Senate for the most part have been exclusively
from the large-town counties. Therefore, when there is cohesion
among them, there is also cohesion within the large-town county delegation. And while it is possible to have intraparty cohesion without interparty conflict, it is not possible to have high
levels of interparty conflict without cohesion within the parties.

During the Hoff era, however, morality issues became very
important in measuring general conflict and the cohesion of
counties with large towns. Education bills disappeared completely. Once again similarity of issues causing conflict and
cohesion is apparent, although there are exceptions. Labor bills
were very important in defining party differences but much less
important in defining general conflict and large-town county
cohesion. Although morality issues made up a plurality of the
roll calls associated with general conflict and district cohesion,
they were unimportant as an identifier of party conflict.

When the governorship returned to the Republicans, the substance of voting in the Senate shifted radically. Taxes and government reorganization replaced morality and labor as the
major issue categories. As in the previous two periods, three
categories provided the roll calls that accounted for the first and
second rankings in all three voting areas. Government reorganization appeared as a product of a massive new plan by Governor
Davis to revamp Vermont's bureaucracy. Taxes were important
because of the barrage of roll calls forthcoming on the sales tax
debate of 1969. In that single session, the Senate recorded
seventeen roll calls on tax issues that caused a drop in the IPL.
Politics became important because of the Senate's roll as instiga-
tor of constitutional amendments every ten years when the time
lock is opened.

The remarkable fact that separates the House and the Senate

is that issues tied to educational problems did not emerge in any area in the Senate after 1964, although they became very important in the House. The Senate after Hoff seems to portray even more than the House the image of a body deeply concerned with political outputs. It seems to have reached consensus on questions involving the nature of public policy (neither labor nor education caused divisions) and is struggling to decide how best to raise the money to pay services and how best to structure the bureaucracy to implement them. In short, the character of legislative conflict in Vermont on issues suggests that Vermont's public sector has begun to do battle with the dual perplexities that plague the administrative state: finance and process.

Some Comparisons and a Summary

A lack of data on legislative behavior makes comparisons between Vermont and other states hazardous. Types of cohesion scores and measures of party difference are as varied as the scholars who have used them. Probably the best summary of party conflict within state legislatures is provided by Jewell and Patterson, who compare several states by the percentage of roll calls on which a majority of both parties are opposed.[20] Their conclusions are as follows: (1) party voting is not found in legislatures where "a single party consistently has a monopoly or an overwhelming majority of the seats"; (2) there is no correlation between "the intensity of competition for legislative seats and the degree of party cohesion"; (3) "there is a rough approximation between party voting in the legislature and the urban and industrial characteristics of states"; (4) homogeneity of party composition increases cohesion; (5) "issue oriented" party systems may cause cohesion; and (6) strong party organization may produce cohesion.

Keefe and Ogul,[21] scholars of the legislative system, emphasize the rural-urban dichotomy as a symptom of party voting and suggest further that where the "rural-urban cleavage tends

20. Jewell and Patterson, *Legislative Process*, pp. 422-25.
21. Keefe and Ogul, *The American Legislative Process*, p. 316.

Table 25
Issues and Voting in the Vermont Senate, 1951–1972

Time periods	Issues associated with general conflict[a]		Issues associated with party conflict[b]		Issues associated with large-town cohesion[c]	
	Category	%	Category	%	Category	%
Early years	Labor	17.4	Politics	15.6	Education	18.8
	Education	13.0	Education	14.6	Politics	15.3
	Politics	11.9	Labor	12.5	Labor	12.9
	Social welfare	8.7	Appropriations	9.4	Social welfare	10.6
	Others	49.0	Others	47.9	Others	42.9
1951–1963	Total roll calls = 92		Total roll calls = 96		Total roll calls = 85	
Hoff era	Morality	22.6	Labor	34.7	Morality	23.1
	Labor	17.0	Politics	26.4	Politics	11.5
	Politics	17.0	Taxes	10.1	Taxes	9.6
	Taxes	15.1	Others	28.8	Labor	9.6
	Others	28.3			Others	46.2
1964–1968	Total roll calls = 53		Total roll calls = 49		Total roll calls = 52	

Politics	17.4		Taxes	29.9		Taxes	25.0
Taxes	15.1		Government reorganization	26.8		Government reorganization	19.6
Government reorganization	11.6		Politics	13.4		Morality	15.2
Government regulation of private concerns	10.5		Others	29.9		Politics	13.4
Others	45.4					Others	26.8
			Total roll calls = 97				
Total roll calls = 88						Total roll calls = 112	

Aftermath: Davis years 1969–1972

aVotes where at least 40% of the Senate membership voted against the prevailing majority.
bVotes where the IPL was at least 10 points below the yearly average.
cVotes where the large-town county cohesion is at least 10 points above the yearly average.

Table 26
Party Difference in Twenty-Six State Senates: Intrastate
Competition and Metro-Urbanism

States ranked by party difference in the state senate[a]	Mean index of likeness	Rank by intrastate party competition[b]	Rank by metro-urbanism[c]
Rhode Island	3	8	2
Pennsylvania	25	7	7.5
New York	35	12	2
Massachusetts	37	3	4
Delaware	37	1	13
Ohio	39	15.5	11
Connecticut	42	9.5	6
Michigan	46	15.5	10
West Virginia	48	19	23
New Jersey	50	18	5
Washington	55	9.5	14
Indiana	56	13	17
Illinois	56	4	7.5
South Dakota	59	25	24
New Hampshire	60	17	21
Kansas	63	21	18
Iowa	66	24	19
Kentucky	66	22	20

to coincide with major party divisions . . . the conflict between
the parties will be fairly frequent and sometimes intense."
Thomas R. Dye agrees, pointing out that party cohesion appears
to be related to urbanism and economic development. In selecting an independent variable (party organization and discipline
or homogeneity of one-party dominated districts) Dye concludes that without the latter, party cohesion could not exist.[22]
    The conclusions of these scholars are backed by sketchy evi-
dence gathered from random studies of particular states. A
study utilizing more consistent information is Hugh LeBlanc's
analysis of party and constituency influences on voting in state

22. Dye, pp. 137-38.

Table 26 (cont.)

States ranked by party difference in the state senate[a]	Mean index of likeness	Rank by intrastate party competition[b]	Rank by metro-urban-ism[c]
Vermont	66	26	26
Missouri	67	20	15
Oregon	69	23	16
Idaho	70	6	25
Montana	71	2	22
Nevada	73	14	9
Utah	74	5	12
California	79	11	2
		$\rho = .23$	$\rho = .44$
		$p = .133$	$p = .012$

[a]Recorded in either 1959 or 1960.

[b]Measured by the Dawson-Robinson technique, which includes gubernatorial elections and seats held in the legislature.

[c]Measured as the percentage of a state's population residing in SMSA[S] doubled, plus the percentage of the state's population living outside SMSA[S] in urban places.

Source: For the Index of Likeness see LeBlanc, *Midwest Journal of Political Science*, p. 44.

senates. Although limited to upper chambers, LeBlanc's data are important in that they are uniform and are all subjected to identical quantitative measurements. Applying Index of Cohesion and Index of Likeness measures to twenty-six state senates, LeBlanc reaches the following conclusions: (1) "Party cohesion . . . was not a direct function of the narrowness of control of the majority party"; (2) cohesion was unrelated to the "majority or minority status" of the parties; (3) cohesion was not a product of the control of the governor's office; and (4) "The degree of party conflict in state senates appears related to levels of urbanization and industrialization."[23]

23. Hugh LeBlanc, "Voting in State Senates: Party and Constituency Influences," *Midwest Journal of Political Science*, 13 (1969), 33-57.

Using a Spearman Rank-Difference Correlation, LeBlanc established "a relationship between party conflict and indexes of urbanization and industrialization particularly when the index of likeness is used as the test of party conflict." Table 26 ranks the twenty-six states found in this analysis by degree of party difference in the legislature and compares these rankings with rankings for extralegislative, intrastate party competition and metro-urbanism. Rank-Difference Correlations support LeBlanc's conclusions and the conclusions of other scholars in the field. Intralegislative party conflict does appear to be more at home in those states typified by high degrees of metro-urbanism than it is in states with high levels of extralegislative, intrastate party conflict.

Analysis of the Vermont system raises questions concerning the orthodox viewpoint in several respects. Primarily, it suggests that in the formative stages in intralegislative party competition, causal responsibility does not reside in any linkage between district and party, but rather in a minority upstart party which, reinforced by an historically unique breakthrough at the polls, seeks to push its own policies through the legislative system, causing the reverberations that produce party cohesion.

The end of unstructured legislative politics in Vermont was a product of the arrival of an innovative party. Certainly there were other factors involved, but we find it hard to escape the notion that Theodore Lowi's concept of the innovative party is more useful than Dye's hypothesis that party discipline is unlikely without homogeneous single-party districts. In short, party appears to be the independent variable. Here are the reasons why this was true in Vermont:

When party cohesion and conflict first surfaced in Vermont, there was no coincidental shifting of constituency alignments between the parties. The new cohesion sprang from districts that were essentially no different than before. Though reapportionment enlarged many districts, it did not produce homogeneous one-party districts where before there had been none. In the second place, the remarkable jump in minority-party cohesion and the fall in the IPL in the House came in a special session of the legislature called specifically to act on the Governor's program. The districts were still the same. Indeed, the lawmakers were the very ones who earlier had exhibited the *highest*

IPL on record. The only change was the injection of an executive program. Thirdly, although the Democrats have traditionally represented somewhat similar districts, no amount of district similarity could maintain high cohesion when their governor lost control of the party in the 1968 session. Fourthly, when the Democratic cohesion fell apart, it did not tumble into compartments that could be tagged with differing levels of urbanism or industrialization. As a matter of fact, the underlying sources of discontinuity for the Democrats were small blocs of legislators from the state's two largest cities. In this case district similarity may have irritated rather than assuaged the party wound. Fifthly, though it may be true that district heterogeneity stood in the way of higher Republican unity, not allowing them to respond to a new Democratic cohesion for four sessions, a sharp issue, pointed directly at the heart of district conflict (the struggle over reapportionment), was required to produce the rural cluster that hampered Republican unity. Without this kind of catalyst, rural-urban conflict might never have jelled within the party, and cohesion might have mushroomed sooner. Finally, be that as it may, no amount of district dissimilarity could stand in the way of Republican cohesion given a Republican governor and a potent issue, the sales tax.

There is need to emphasize that the point of concern is party discipline in its embryonic stages. And there is evidence here, revealed by cluster-bloc analysis, that constituency types did mark off particular groups of lawmakers, serving to dampen party cohesion levels. For the Democrats there was a bloc-fringe combination in 1964 which was colored by large-town versus small-town differences, and the Franklin County–Chittenden County split in 1968 was toned with urban-rural hues. We need to make a point also about the nature of the regional alignments that have stood behind Democratic disunity in the last three years. Despite the fact that Rutland and Burlington are the state's two largest urban centers, some would argue that Burlington and its subsystem of adjacent towns and cities is more an authentic *metro*-urban place, while Rutland still remains simply a large town immediately surrounded by a rural–small town countryside. Finally, the Republicans were constantly divided by rural-urban tensions in the Hoff years, and the Davis governorship did not wipe them out completely. If this tension continues to crop up to thwart Republican unity, and if the Democrats, who represent somewhat more homogeneous districts, are able to reestablish their voting habits of a few years ago, Vermont will clearly provide further verification for the Dye hypothesis. But at this point, party discipline in Vermont seems to have been conditioned not by the fact that parties and districts do or do not reinforce one another, but rather by issues, executive inspiration, and the spirit of an innovative minority party.

There is substantial evidence to support the innovative-minority theory. Jewell and Patterson point, for instance, to the capture of the Illinois governorship by the Democratic minority in 1949 as a causal factor in increased Democratic cohesion during Adlai Stevenson's term as governor.[24] Earlier, Jewell reported on similar happenings in Kentucky: "the presence of a Republican in the governor's mansion and a larger minority representation than usual gave the party greater incentive for unity. During the two sessions party voting assumed importance in the Kentucky legislature."[25]

Kansas provides another case in point. Grumm relates that during its 1957-59 session, Democrats exhibited a new cohesion when their party held the governorship for "the first time in years" and "the Democratic membership had grown large enough to have some impact on legislation."[26]

One of the most meaningful comparisons with the Vermont example is the case of Iowa. When the Democrats, capturing the governorship for the first time since the Depression, increased party balance in the legislature, their cohesion jumped nearly twenty points in the state's House of Representatives (from 23 to 42).[27] Moreover, when Iowa Democrats recaptured the governorship in 1965 and controlled both branches of the legisla-

24. Jewell and Patterson, p. 429.
25. Jewell, *State Legislature*, p. 32.
26. John G. Grumm, "Party Politics in the Kansas Legislature," paper presented at the Wichita Conference on Politics, April 10, 1959, in Jewell and Patterson, *Legislative Process*, p. 429. See also Grumm, "The Kansas Legislature: Republican Coalition," in Patterson, *Midwest Legislative Politics*, p. 60.
27. Ronald D. Hedlund and Charles W. Wiggins, "Legislative Politics in Iowa," in Patterson, p. 30. Charles W. Wiggins, "Party Politics in the Iowa Legislature," *Midwest Journal of Political Science*, 11 (1967), 86-97.

ture for the first time since the 1930's, Wiggins reports that
party voting was extremely potent, reaching new highs in both
chambers. In the House, party majorities were in opposition
66.1 percent of the time, an increase of 17 points over the previous high (in 1957). In the Senate, the figure was 56.9 percent,
an increase of 3 points over 1957.[28] Wiggins continues:

> Swept into power as the result of a national landslide
> election, the immense popularity of an incumbent gov-
> ernor, and the reapportionment of legislative districts,
> Democrats conformed rigidly in practice to the model
> of an innovative party. Bills were introduced, debated,
> and voted upon which had never or only infrequently
> been considered in previous Republican controlled legis-
> latures.[29]

The result of the Democratic breakthrough in Iowa as reported by Wiggins sounds remarkably similar to what happened
in Vermont. In the Green Mountain State, as in Iowa, an innovative minority produced much new legislation. As I have
written elsewhere:

> the new system has produced a mass of progressive legis-
> lation . . . In a move long demanded by liberal forces,
> payment of the poll tax as a qualification for voting was
> cut down. Child day care facilities, educational televi-
> sion, and penal reform were a few of the other areas to
> receive attention. In the first regular session, the House
> passed a fair housing bill, established a Human Rights
> Commission, conducted reform in the state judicial sys-
> tem, regulated outdoor advertising, attacked water pol-
> lution and passed a measure to assess personal income
> taxes as a percentage of Federal payments.[30]

The conclusion that intraparty discipline (cohesion) and/or interparty conflict is a likely product of minority breakthrough
and the innovative spirit is certainly reinforced by the examples
of Vermont and Iowa.

28. Wiggins, "Party Politics," p. 88.
29. Ibid., p. 89.
30. Frank M. Bryan, "The Metamorphosis of a Rural Legislature,"
Polity, I (1968), 211.

The innovative mood in Vermont did not die with the passing of the Hoff era. The Democratic breakthrough and subsequent party activity may have spurred the Republicans to the new kinds of activity that have typified the Davis legislatures. Although the substance of output was markedly different, it was clearly innovative. Taxation, government reorganization, and environmental concern are areas that have undergone profound changes in Vermont in the aftermath of the Hoff breakthrough. Although no personalities dominate the Republican reaction, as Hoff dominated the Democrats, there was a cadre of young, essentially conservative, and highly skilled Republican legislators at work in Montpelier during this period. Richard Mallary (now a congressman), from rural Orange County, and Luther Hackett, from more urbanized Chittenden County, epitomized the kinds of forces at work in the legislature under the Davis administration. While the Hoff innovations were essentially input-oriented and traditionally liberal and the Davis measures were essentially geared to output and were traditionally conservative, both were unique.

In sum, over the last two decades, the nature of legislative politics has been dramatically altered in rural Vermont's legislative system. The metamorphosis has involved a changing socioeconomic environment, reapportionment, and a minority-party breakthrough. The lower house has been transformed from a large, fluid, unstructured body, where neither party nor constituency served as loci for concerted political activity, into a less diffuse system, where cohesion is apt to be very strong in the minority party, especially when it holds the governorship.

The majority, while badly split in the early days of change, was capable of showing a united front. Vermont's small upper chamber, the Senate, has developed clustered voting patterns in a manner remarkably similar to that of the House, and although there were variations in party cohesion between the two houses before reapportionment, that act seems to have helped to synchronize interhouse party behavior.

It is of particular interest to note that political change in Vermont occurred coincidentally with alterations in the socioeconomic character of the state. Yet environmental changes were not profound, and we certainly find no reason to believe they were independently causal in nature. The changes in Vermont's communications and transportation systems and the decline of her family-farm culture coupled with parallel changes in legislative politics may provide a broad background from which to verify a frequently observed relationship between socioeconomic environments and legislative systems—namely, that structured legislatures are most often found in nonrural states. But it is well to remember that, although Vermont is undergoing certain kinds of socioeconomic changes, a move toward less intense ruralism is not one of them.

Reapportionment seems to have acted as a catalytic agent throughout this process: first, as an issue by solidifying Democrats from the larger towns while helping build an atmosphere for strong party cohesion in the Hoff era; second, as a structural variable by decreasing the membership of the House to a level where the minority could raise its head above the confusion of a 246-member body and see hope in unified action; third, as a political force by turning power to the more populous areas of the state and thus helping the Democrats increase their percentage of House membership; fourth and perhaps most important, as a therapeutic device by signaling the end of the old and the coming of the new and creating a feeling for change that coincided perfectly with the dynamism of Vermont's new governor, Philip Hoff.

Although a changing environment may have provided the environmental atmosphere and reapportionment was the catalyst in Vermont's new legislative system, a highly cohesive and progressive-minded minority party produced the basic reaction. The Democratic Party, led by Governor Hoff, is yet another example of Lowi's concept of the innovative party.[31] Moreover, the return of the governorship to the Republicans and with it an innovative issue, the sales tax, brought new unity to the majority party.

31. Theodore Lowi, "Toward Functionalism in Political Science: The Case of Innovation in Party Systems," *American Political Science Review*, 57 (1963), 570-83.

Five

Rural Politics in Practice

The nation was surprised in the spring of 1936 when the people of Vermont gathered in town meetings around the state and turned up their noses at a federal proposal to build a highway-park complex on the flanks of the Green Mountains from Massachusetts to Canada. There have been speculations as to the forces behind this action, but the controlling factors of the controversy over the Green Mountain Parkway have remained in the shadows. Uncovered, they reveal some striking conclusions about the nature of rural politics.

This book so far has focused on three particular aspects of the rural polity—the ruling elite, the party system, and the legislature. In this chapter we will investigate the formation of public policy by looking at an issue that weaves together at least some of the concerns treated earlier. The case provides an excellent opportunity to contribute to the dialogue on the environmental crisis.

Several factors make the Green Mountain Parkway controversy especially appealing. For instance, the decision was made statewide and therefore has boundaries coincidental with a legitimate and self-conscious polity. Secondly, the issue generated extremely high public attentiveness and served to mobilize a wide range of interest-group activity. This fiery intrastate reaction was fanned by national interest in the project. Most important, the issue cut right to the heart of the prevailing dichotomy that defines so much public decision-making: economic development versus the integrity of nature. Show Vermonters a way out of the Depression but only at the cost of severe alterations in their most prized possession—the Green Mountain chain—and you have the makings of a profound political debate.

The Green Mountain Parkway would have been fashioned after the famous Skyline Drive of Virginia's Blue Ridge Mountains and the Shenandoah National Park.[1] The debate that emerged over whether to build it split the state asunder. The observation by the *New York Times* that the issue was "hotly debated" was an understatement.[2] The *Burlington Free Press* thought that the question could be "generally viewed as the most controversial issue which has been placed before the people in many years."[3] The *Barre Daily Times* commented, "Not for many years, perhaps not since the local option on the sale of liquor 30 years ago, has there been such a controversial issue before the voters."[4] The *Northfield News and Advertiser* reported that the struggle for the parkway was accompanied by "one of the most intensive campaigns which has utilized practically every known medium of reaching the public: newspapers, circulations, pictorial supplements, debates, and radio."[5] Further north in the shadow of the Canadian border Newport's *Palladium and News* said, "There has never been an issue in Vermont which has inspired so much letter writing."[6] Elsewhere it was a "burning," "raging,"[7] "much talked of"[8] issue that "filled Vermont with discussion for several weeks,"[9] provoking "lively interest manifest all over the state,"[10] drawing large crowds[11] and swelling attendance at town meeting where the controversy was finally resolved.[12]

William Storrs Lee writes: "The population divided into two camps that were solidly opposed. Every citizen in the state be-

1. For a description of the Blue Ridge Skyline Parkway see Virginus Dabney, "Skyway in the Blue Ridge," *Review of Reviews*, 93 (1936), 50-55.

2. *New York Times* (March 1, 1936), p. 4.

3. *Burlington Free Press* (February 29, 1936), p. 1.

4. *Barre Daily Times* (March 2, 1936), p. 2.

5. *Northfield News and Advertiser* (February 27, 1936), p. 1.

6. *Newport Palladium and News* (March 3, 1936), p. 1.

7. *Newport Express and Standard* (February 21, 1936), p. 1; (February 28, 1936), p. 1.

8. *Essex County Herald* (March 5, 1936), p. 8.

9. *Northfield News and Advertiser* (February 27, 1936), p. 1.

10. *Middlebury Register* (February 28, 1936), p. 1.

11. *Newport Palladium and News* (February 25, 1936), p. 1; *Waterbury Record* (February 19, 1936), p. 4.

12. *Hardwick Gazette* (March 5, 1936), p. 1; *Waterbury Record* (March 4, 1936), p. 1.

came a parkway or an anti-parkway man."[13] Evidence of this statewide dichotomy is found in the legislature, where "unprecedented crowds pressed into the Senate and House Chambers"[14] to hear debate that was characterized as "the best but bitterest I have ever seen or heard anywhere."[15] Indeed, the controversy penetrated all aspects of Vermont life. Even children and students were involved. The *Brattleboro Reformer* sponsored an essay contest for high school students.[16] Polls were taken on many campuses to determine the feelings of the young people.[17] Interest groups took sides; newspapers squared off and began taking editorial pot shots at one another. "Letters to the Editor" were in abundance as the state's leadership made public their respective positions on the parkway. Interestingly, the only noteworthy manifestation of apathy uncovered in the state's press came from the pen of George Aiken. In an open letter published on the front page of the *Burlington Clipper*, Lieutenant Governor Aiken wrote: "I simply cannot get nerved up for or against the Parkway."

The intense reaction to the parkway proposal within Vermont soon caught the fancy of the nation.[18] "Most of the country began to take sides on the issue confronting the Green Mountains," says Lee. "The decision to be made concerned the nation because a conservative, cautious segment of its people was passing judgment on a policy of Federal benefaction."[19] The issue commanded space in the popular magazines and professional journals of the day[20] and was seized by the out-of-state press.[21]

13. William Storrs Lee, *The Green Mountains of Vermont* (New York: Henry Holt, 1938), p. 157.

14. Ralph Nading Hill, *The Winooski—Heartway of Vermont* (New York: Rinehart, 1949), p. 211.

15. Charles Edward Crane, *Let Me Show You Vermont* (New York: Alfred A. Knopf, 1937), pp. 259-60.

16. *Brattleboro Daily Reformer* (February 12, 1936), p. 1.

17. *Burlington Free Press* (February 7, 20, 25, 1936).

18. Raymond Bearse, ed., *Vermont: A Guide to the Green Mountain State* (20th ed., Boston: Houghton Mifflin, 1968), p. 61.

19. Lee, p. 159.

20. *The Literary Digest* (March 1936) and the *Saturday Evening Post* (October 27, 1934).

21. Most metropolitan out-of-state papers were against the parkway. Crane, pp. 4-5.

Argument in the press traveled a range from absurd polemics to thoughtful critique. The *New York Sun* claimed, for instance, that: "With a 1000 foot swath lined with gas stations and refreshment stands cut through the heart of her most beautiful scenery, Vermont would have been Vermont no longer."[22] The *Burlington Clipper* took time to answer Vrest Orton's claim that the Parkway would turn Vermont into a "Coney Island" with exaggerations of its own.[23] The *Middlebury Register* editorialized that "Vermont does not need to put its head in any government noose."[24] The *Palladium and News* defended its negative advice on the parkway referendum with the following: "In view of all these angles and in keeping with the old adage, when in doubt say no . . . "[25] Most of the talk, however, was more in the spirit of point-by-point debate and reveals some depth in the thinking of the public at large.[26]

When the battle over the parkway ended and the smoke had settled, the postmortems over its defeat began. Everyone had his own reasons for Vermont's thumbs down posture, and the event is used for all manner of speculation as to the character of Vermont's political culture. Historian Earl Newton said that the vote against the parkway was the "first fearful reaction to the unpleasant possibilities of an uncontrolled invasion from the residents of metropolitan or suburban New York and Boston."[27] Richard Judd, the leading scholar of the New Deal in Vermont, claimed that the parkway proposal died because of the Vermonters' "traditional dislike of spending money . . . When in doubt, vote 'no' is the usual Vermont reaction to innovations, particularly when they cost money."[28] Bernard DeVoto claimed that Vermont's special kind of tourism (Vermont has the "lowest hot dog stand density" in the country) could not accommodate the parkway, that it was simply a "difference between ten cents and eleven cents" and Vermonters

22. *Hyde Park News and Citizen* (February 19, 1936), p. 4.
23. *Burlington Clipper* (February 20, 1936), p. 5.
24. *Middlebury Register* (February 28, 1936), p. 4.
25. *Newport Palladium and News* (February 25, 1936), p. 1.
26. Ernest H. Bancroft, "Why People Should Favor Green Mountain Parkway." Arthur W. Peach, "Proposed Parkway a Threat to the State's Well Being," *The Vermonter* (January-February 1936), 5-13.
27. Newton, *The Vermont Story*, p. 27.
28. Judd, "History of the New Deal in Vermont," p. 111.

chose to spend ten and not eleven, and that the defeat was "a recognition of natural beauty put on a sound financial basis."[29] The *Burlington Free Press,* Vermont's largest newspaper, listed three causes for the defeat of the parkway: a refusal to put up the $500,000 that was Vermont's share of the cost of the highway (less than 3 percent of the total expense), fear that the parkway would scar the beauty of the state and thus hurt the summer trade, and a genuine dislike for federal programs and control that threatened the independence of the state.[30] The *New York Sun* pointed to "a strong desire to preserve the beauty of their hills" as the main reason why Vermonters voted no.[31]

Lee, on the other hand, believes with many others that the deciding factor was the state's suspicion of "new deal bargains" and "any political body to whom they would have to suffer anything."[32] Edward Crane sees the defeat of the parkway as a result of Yankee "thrift" and a desire on the part of the voters to "make money their own way."[33] Former Governor Stanley C. Wilson, who had supported the idea, opined that a distaste for "extravagant Federal spending, genuine anti-Federal Government feeling, and some limited fear of spoiling Vermont's natural beauty" were the prime causal factors in the roadway's demise.[34] It is interesting to observe that, except for references to a general anti-federal mood, party politics in the traditional sense was not considered to be a major focus for antagonism in the controversy.

Despite all this speculation, however, and despite the fact that Vermont's action on the parkway is believed to be a symbol of all manner of ideological postures, the variables that shaped the controversy have never undergone rigorous examination. The purpose here is to put some of the very basic notions we have about the nature of the parkway decision to the test. In

29. Bernard De Voto, "How to Live among the Vermonters," *Harper's Magazine,* 73 (1936), 333-36.
30. *Burlington Free Press* (March 4, 1936), p. 1.
31. Lee, p. 159.
32. Ibid., p. 157.
33. Crane, p. 21.
34. "No Green Mountain Hot Dogs," *Literary Digest,* 121 (1936), 19.

doing so we hope to clarify our view of Vermont politics and the factors that promoted Vermont's reaction to this most important individual program.

The task is simplified immensely because the factual record is remarkably clear and complete. There were (1) two roll-call votes taken in the Vermont House of Representatives with which to measure elite response to the proposal, and (2) vote totals for the popular response by town provided by the parkway referendum taken on Town Meeting Day in 1936. Also, soft data abound from the libraries and the press.

Historical Background

One of the programs offered by Franklin Roosevelt's New Deal for Americans focused on the development of public works projects of national character in the various states. Among the appropriations approved by Congress was a sum of $50,000 granted to the National Park Service for a "Study of the Green Mountains of Vermont as a possible location for a great National Parkway." In the final days of April 1934, a team of federal officials from the National Park Service and the Bureau of Public Roads began a ten-month survey to plan the parkway. They had the cooperation of the Vermont Bureau of Public Works. The report of their findings was delivered to Governor Charles M. Smith on January 17, 1935. Smith handed it on to the Vermont legislature two weeks later. The plan for the parkway was outlined as follows:

> It will extend the entire length of the State of Vermont through the Green Mountains and their adjacent ranges and foothills, being located so as to embrace as far as possible typical examples of all forms of outstanding natural scenery characteristic of the Green Mountain region. The minimum right of way for the Parkway will be 1000 feet which will give approximately 500 feet of forest and park land on either side of the Parkway road. At numerous places this width will be expanded into park areas including whole lakes and their shores, stream valleys and their adjacent hillsides and entire mountains

and groups of mountains. The Parkway will thus partake of the character of a great scenic reservation, conserving within its area some of the finest natural scenery in Vermont. The present terminus of the project will be a park area of some 20,000 or more acres of complete wilderness including several peaks of the Jay group and extending to the Canadian boundary.[35]

The political response to this proposal was immediate. In a nutshell, Vermont's 248 members of the lower House turned the proposal down shortly after it emerged from the Judiciary Committee. The vote was close, 126 to 111.[36] The parkway was given a second life in the Senate, where it received quick positive attention, but once again, the House killed the bill. This blow came only a day after the House had recognized praise from the New York *Herald Tribune* for its good "hard sense" in its first killing of the parkway proposal.[37]

The issue was not yet settled, however. In the fall of 1935 Governor Smith called a special session of the legislature, which reconsidered the idea. This time the House (identical in membership to the previous House, since there had been no intervening election) altered its position and endorsed the Green Mountain Parkway project by a vote of 131 to 105.[38] There was a catch, however. The new bill would allow the people at large to settle the issue once and for all in a popular vote to be taken at the annual March town meeting. On March 3, 1936, this referendum yielded a substantial defeat for the parkway by a vote of 42,318 to 30,897.[39] The mountains, as Ralph Nading Hill has said, would not "be hitched together."[40] The task at hand is to discover why. We will seek answers in the two arenas where the decision took place: in the legislature among the elite and in the state at large among the people.

35. *House Journal for the State of Vermont* (Biennial Session, 1935), p. 206.
36. Ibid., pp. 207-08.
37. Editorial, New York *Herald Tribune* (April 2, 1935), p. 4.
38. *House Journal of the State of Vermont* (Special Session, 1935), p. 129.
39. *The Vermont Legislative Directory and State Manual* (1937), p. 315.
40. Hill, p. 111.

The Elite Response—Voting in
the House, 1935

The old pre-*Baker v. Carr* House of Representatives in Vermont was truly a people's parliament, and its members, for the most part, were legitimate and highly respected leaders in their local communities. In the years between 1947 and 1967, 28 percent of the House members had been selectmen in their home towns, and 22 percent had been members of the local school boards. Nearly all had held at least one office in their district, and most had held several. For these reasons an analysis of the 248 lawmakers, drawn from every nook and corner of the state, provides an accurate picture of how Vermont's rural elite viewed the parkway proposal in 1935.

In analyzing their response to the parkway question, two dimensions of behavior were considered. First, would the controversy produce a reaction common to "types" of legislators? For instance, would occupational role be an important factor? Would native Vermonters be more apt to oppose the parkway than immigrants to the state? How about age, education, or party preference? The second dimension was the linkage of the elites to their constituencies. Would legislators whose districts lay in or near the path of the proposed highway react in a similar fashion when asked to vote on its future? Would legislators whose districts were suffering economically tend to see the parkway as relief from the depression and vote accordingly? Would town size make a difference?

To begin with, there was much speculation in the press that the core opposition to the parkway was grafted to a negativism inherent in the character of native, tradition-bound Vermonters. Yet the data in Table 27 show no such thing. Whether a legislator was a Vermonter or not seemed to have little bearing on the vote. Home-grown lawmakers divided evenly for and against the parkway. Although the businessmen in the legislature seemed to support the project (52 percent solidly for it and 29 percent solidly against it, with 19 percent splitting their votes on the two roll calls), occupational background also appears to be inconsequential. Farmers divided evenly on the issue, as did laborers, housewives, clerical types, and professionals. At first glance religion seems to make a difference, since none of the twenty-five Catholics in the House voted solidly against the parkway.

Table 27

Parkway Preference of Legislators by Personal Characteristics[a]

| Legislator preference[b] | Birthplace | | | | | | Age | |
| | Vermont | | New England | | Other | | <40 | |
	No.	%	No.	%	No.	%	No.	%
Solid against	79	42	7	58	9	38	36	40
Mixed	33	16	–	–	2	8	14	16
Solid for	79	42	5	42	13	54	40	44
Totals[c]	191		12		24		90	
Significance test (X^2)	$X^2 = 4.28$ $p = .310$						$X^2 = .626$ $p = .958$	

[a]Source: State of Vermont, Secretary of State, *Vermont Legislative Directory and State Manual* (Montpelier, Vt., 1935 and 1937).

[b]Solid against = legislators voted "no" on both roll calls; Mixed = legislators split

Yet closer inspection of the religion and political-party categories indicates that the Catholic support of the parkway was a function of party support. Catholics were Democrats, and Democrats were strongly for the parkway. Holding "party" constant reveals that religion exerted little influence under the control conditions. This discovery leads to the point suggested by Table 27: the vote on the parkway appears to have been severed from the "kind" of individual the legislator was and linked instead to his party affiliation. Democrats were solidly for it, and Republicans were generally against it, whether they were young or old, farmers or doctors, Vermonters or non-Vermonters.

There is, however, another set of variables often used to solve the complex puzzle of legislative voting behavior: constituency pressures. Were there any observable relationships between the kind of town a legislator represented and the way he voted on the parkway proposal? Table 28 speaks to these questions.

Table 27 (cont.)

Age				Religion				
40-59		>60		Catholic		Protestant		Other	
No.	%	No.	%	No.	%	No.	%	No.	%
54	44	5	36	4	16	68	44	27	55
18	15	2	14	4	16	21	14	5	10
51	41	7	50	17	68	64	42	17	35
123		14		25		153		49	

$$X^2 = 10.84$$
$$p = .028$$

(continued on p. 212)

their votes on the two roll calls; Solid for = legislators voted "yes" on both roll calls.
cTotals do not include legislators who were absent on either vote.

Once again the strength of party politics appears as the most important explanatory variable. District proximity to the parkway had no significant bearing on the way legislators voted. Neither did socioeconomic variables such as town growth or the percentage of the population on the public relief rolls. In the light of speculation as to why the legislature voted as it did, these figures are surprising. During the statewide debate the point was made repeatedly that construction jobs that the parkway would create would end Vermont's unemployment problem and the economic crisis that accompanied it. Governor Wilson, in his final message to the legislature, singled out this very point in his call for support for the parkway. Yet the legislators themselves did not harken to the economic plight of their towns and cities when casting their votes.

In two areas, however, district type did seem to play a role. Legislators from strong farming towns were significantly anti-

Table 27 (cont.)

Legislator preference[b]	Education				Occupation			
	No college		College		Farmer		Laborer Housewife Clerical	
	No.	%	No.	%	No.	%	No.	%
Solid against	78	45	17	32	49	44	26	43
Mixed	25	14	9	17	14	13	10	17
Solid for	71	41	27	51	47	43	24	40
Totals[c]	174		53		110		60	
Significance test (X^2)	$X^2 = 2.73$ $p = .254$				$X^2 = 4.03$ $p = .855$			

parkway, while nonfarming towns were for it. Town size also correlated importantly, with the larger towns more apt to have representatives voting for the parkway than the smaller towns. But closer inspection of these relationships reveals that they were caused by the marked tendency of legislators from the Democratic towns to vote for the issue and their colleagues from Republican towns to vote against it. Since most Democratic towns are large and nonfarming and most Republican towns are small and farming, the powerful draw between party politics and the vote tends to color these other factors. Once again, the process of holding party constant—that is, viewing these other relationships under conditions that control for party influence—wipes out the association of both town size and farmers with the vote.

Table 28 tells the same story as Table 27: party was the determining variable in the way Vermont's legislative corps reacted to the parkway. It is not possible here (nor will it ever be) to determine which of the two political variables was paramount—constituency pressure or actual party affiliation—since

Table 27 (cont.)

Occupation						Political party			
Business		Professional		Other		Democrat		Republican	
No.	%	No.	%	No.	%	No.	%	No.	%
9	29	5	42	6	43	1	2	92	51
6	19	1	8	3	21	4	9	29	16
16	52	6	50	5	36	38	88	59	33
31		12		14		43		180	

$$X^2 = 45.56$$
$$p = .000$$

(as might be expected) strong Democratic towns sent Democrats to the legislature and strong Republican towns sent Republicans. We can speculate that these two variables reinforced one another, but we must leave it at that.

Among a wide range of potential causal variables that took into account both the personal background of the men themselves and the characteristics of the towns they represented, political affiliation was the only variable that emerged as a source for predictive speculation. Though we cannot posit strict causation from exercises of this variety, we can safely conclude that while party was at least potentially causal, the other factors under consideration were not. It is important to make only this statement: party affiliation cut through other variables to influence the vote on the parkway. Yet, given the scholarship that has been developed concerning legislatures of the kind that met during the 1930's in Vermont, the discovery of party cohesion of this nature is doubly intriguing. First, Vermont was a strong one-party state—in fact, the most secure Republican stronghold in the nation. As pointed out earlier, one-party states have ap-

Table 28
Parkway Preference of Legislators by District Characteristics

Legislator Preference	Number of Farms[a]						Distance From the Parkway[b]	
	Low		Medium		High		<10 Miles	
	N	%	N	%	N	%	N	%
Solid Against	18	30	53	40	15	62	39	36
Mixed	11	19	20	15	2	9	17	16
Solid For	30	51	58	44	7	29	51	48
Totals	59	100	131	99	24	100	107	100
Significance Test (X^2)	$X^2 = 7.34$ p = .118						$X^2 = 1.43$ p = .840	

[a]Individual farms per capita. Low = less than or equal to .09 farms per capita; Medium = between .1 and .19 farms per capita; High = more than .19 farms per capita.

[b]Air miles from the Parkway.

peared to be poisonous to party cohesion and discipline.[41] Secondly, Vermont was intensely rural, and some maintain that rural areas lack the magnetic centers that draw and reinforce the interests that promote party discipline. Then there are studies such as this one which have pointed again and again to a lack of party cohesion in Montpelier—at least before the days of the Hoff breakthrough.[42] Finally, and most important, the parkway itself was the kind of issue that could slay party discipline even of the toughest variety. It appealed in different ways to all manner of interests: hiking the Long Trail, business, farming,

41. Dye, *Politics in States and Communities*, p. 137. Jacob and Vines, *Politics in the American States*, p. 187. Jewell, *The State Legislature*, pp. 112-15.

42. Frank M. Bryan, "The Metamorphosis," pp. 191-212. Lockard, *New England State Politics*, pp. 1-42.

Table 28 (cont.)

Distance From the Parkway[b]				Population Growth[c]					
10-25 Miles		>25 Miles		De-creasing		Stagnant		Growing	
N	%	N	%	N	%	N	%	N	%
33	43	14	45	25	53	52	37	9	37
12	16	4	13	6	13	23	16	4	17
31	41	13	42	16	34	67	47	11	46
76	100	31	100	47	100	142	100	24	100

$$X^2 = 4.15$$
$$p = .387$$

(continued on p. 216)

[c]Percent population increase, 1920-1940. Decreasing = less than or equal to −.18% increase; Stagnant = between −.17% and +.09% increase; Growing = more than .09% increase.

tourism. Yet, for the most part, the legislators refused to be influenced by the other pressures and dusted off their party labels when voting on the parkway. Our task now is to turn away from the legislature to see if the people of Vermont acted consistently with their elected leaders.

The Popular Response

While it is a surprise to discover that party was the single best predictive variable on the parkway vote in Vermont's legislature, it is understandable. Legislatures do, after all, provide a focus for party policy concerns, and the representatives themselves are directly accessible to the persuasive techniques of party leadership. If cohesion were to appear anywhere, one would expect to see it first in Montpelier. On the other hand,

Table 28 (cont.)

Legislator preference	Impact of the Depression[d]						Size of Town Population	
	Low		Medium		High		Small	
	N	%	N	%	N	%	N	%
Solid Against	41	49	35	36	10	29	80	43
Mixed	9	11	17	18	7	21	27	15
Solid For	34	40	44	46	17	50	78	42
Totals	84	100	96	100	34	100	185	100
Significance Test (X^2)	$X^2 = 5.57$ $p = .233$						$X^2 = 5.31$ $p = .069$	

[d]Percentage of 1935 population on relief. Low = less than or equal to 2.4%; Medium = between 2.5% and 9.9%; High = more than 9.9%.

[e]Based on an average of the totals for 1930 and 1940.

[f]Average Democratic vote for governor, 1934 and 1936. Low = less than or equal to 19%; Medium = between 20% and 39%; High = more than 39%.

Vermont's 248 towns and villages were scattered over hundreds of square miles of rural terrain, and her people were well insulated from the pressures of party politics. Moreover, the myriad of intervening variables at hand to attach themselves to the parkway vote at the legislative level were far more relevant to the individual Vermonter as he went about his business all around the state.

The primary reason we would not expect to find party an important factor in the vote at the local level, however, is simply that local politics had never been a partisan affair in the Green Mountain State. It is a fact that at the local level Vermont's towns are more apt to change parties in electing their representatives than local districts in other so-called two-party states in New England.[43] While town meetings were often parti-

43. Robert B. Dishman and George Goodwin, Jr., *State Legislatures in New England Politics* (Durham, N.H.: New England Center for Continuing Education, 1967), p. 69.

Table 28 (cont.)

Size of Town Population[e]		Strength of the Democrats[f]					
Large		Low		Medium		High	
N	%	N	%	N	%	N	%
6	21	28	50	50	48	8	15
6	21	10	18	13	12	10	19
17	58	18	32	42	40	35	66
29	100	56	100	105	100	53	100

$$X^2 = 20.29$$
$$p = .001$$

Sources: Vermont State Legislative Directory and State Manual; Vermont State Planning Board, *A First Step in State Planning for Vermont* (Montpelier, 1937); National Park Service, *Green Mountain Park Reconnaissance Survey* (1934); U.S. Department of Commerce, *United States Census of Agriculture* (1935). I am appreciative of Dr. Enoch Tomkin's help in obtaining figures concerning Vermont's farming population during this period.

san enough, the conflict was rarely a part of Democratic-Republican hostility. Even today, when party conflict is more generally prevalent in the state, studies of town meetings show no strong relationship between party competition in the towns and competition at town meeting. Clearly, policy decisions in Vermont towns in the 1930's were not molded by hardened political identities. Cast in such an apolitical context, the referendum vote seemed to promise good hunting for the other variables we felt must have been present in deciding this environmental question. Such, however, was not the case.

Figure XX outlines briefly the overview of the parkway referendum vote and compares it to Democratic and Republican areas of strength across the state. While exceptions are numerous, the general pattern seems clear. In the northwest and extreme southwest, where the Democrats had considerable strength, the parkway "yes" vote was high. In Rutland County the only three localities not to reject the highway at the "20

Figure XX
The Parkway Vote and Democratic Strength

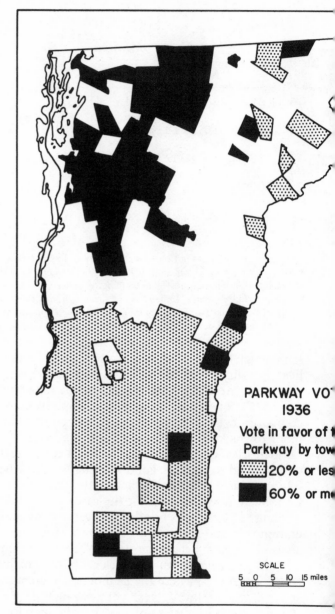

PARKWAY VO
1936

Vote in favor of 1
Parkway by tow

20% or les

60% or m

SCALE

5 0 5 10 15 miles

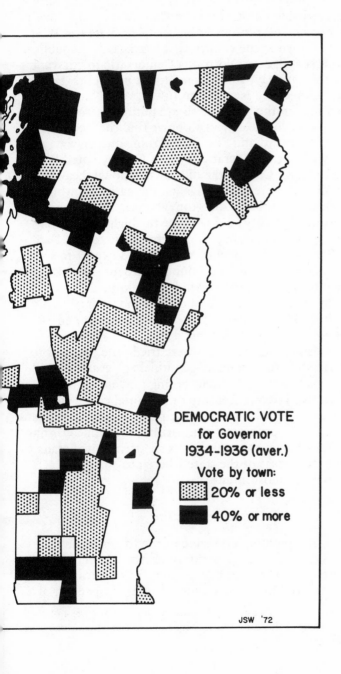

DEMOCRATIC VOTE
for Governor
1934-1936 (aver.)
Vote by town:
20% or less
40% or more

JSW '72

percent-or-less" level were all part of the Rutland (and Route 4 West) Democratic bloc. In Chittenden County the only town to deny the parkway a 60 percent or higher "yes" vote was Westford, the single town in the county that was heavily Republican. In the Northeast Kingdom, Norton, a Democratic town, went strongly for the parkway, while its nextdoor neighbors, Holland and Morgan, both strong Republican towns, voted "no."

The exceptions to the party thesis are both numerous and fascinating. In the Northeast Kingdom we find the Republican strongholds of Stannard and Sheffield turning out a heavy "yes" vote, while the Democratic town of Granby voted "no." In Southwest Orange County the hill towns, though heavily Republican, did not vote heavily against the parkway, while the Barre watershed towns of Washington, Orange, and Groton (the latter in Caledonia County) did not give the highway a strong positive vote, even though they were Democratic towns. Had the party thesis been fully operative, we would expect to see much less opposition in Rutland County. Perhaps the most intriguing town of all is Chester in Windsor County. Completely surrounded by intense parkway opposition and voting heavily Republican in 1934 and 1936, Chester nevertheless voted 383 for the parkway and only 13 against it.

To add precision, two strategies were tried. The first was to view the entire state from long range, utilizing Vermont's 248 cities and towns as observations according to which it was possible to measure the interrelationship of potential causal (or independent) variables and the vote for the parkway (the dependent variable). Next, for purposes of comparison, the scope was narrowed to two of Vermont's counties as an attempt was made to zero in on the two areas of the state where pro and con reaction to the proposal was most intense.

The Statewide Picture

To draw as clear a picture as possible of the forces behind the people's decision to reject the parkway, thirty-four independent variables were constructed and data from 233 of Vermont's 248 towns were gathered to measure them.[44] After inspection of

44. Thirteen towns were not used because accurate data were not available for them. Their exclusion in no way invalidated the conclusions based on the remaining set of 233 towns.

the original correlation matrix, eighteen of these items were
selected for further tests. These variables and the reasons why
they were selected are listed as follows:

I. Political Variables
  A. Raw New Deal Democratic Indicators
    1. Intrastate Democratic strength was measured as the
       percentage the Democrats received in the vote for
       governor averaged for the elections of 1934 and
       1936. This variable was used to show the strength of
       Democratic sentiment when the reference point was
       the State House in Montpelier.
    2. The appeal of the New Deal as such at the intrastate
       level was said to have been revealed by a single elec-
       tion for the United States Senate. The Martin-Austin
       race of 1934 was a remarkably close one in which
       Austin was unabashedly anti-New Deal and Martin
       was vociferously pro-New Deal. Historians agree that
       this election focused on the credibility of the New
       Deal. For this reason we used the percentage of the
       vote cast for Martin in the towns as an indicator of
       the appeal of the New Deal in Vermont at a point
       above the local level (it was a statewide election for a
       national office) and still not tied directly to the popu-
       larity of Roosevelt.[45]
    3. Roosevelt's own personal attraction was also consid-
       ered as a potentially important factor in the parkway
       vote. To measure it we simply used the percentage of
       the vote received by Roosevelt in each town in the
       election of 1936.
  B. Adjusted New Deal Democratic Indicators
    1. To separate the draw of the New Deal from the "nor-
       mal" Democratic strength in that period, we mea-
       sured the percentage increase in the averaged Demo-
       cratic vote for governor (1928-30) and the averaged
       Democratic vote for governor (1934-36). This vari-
       able measures the impact that the New Deal had on
       Democratic tallies in intrastate elections.

45. Judd, "History," p. 95. See also George T. Mazuzan, "Vermont's
Traditional Republicanism vs. the New Deal: Warren R. Austin and the
Election of 1934," *Vermont History*, 39 (1971), 128-41.

2. To determine the draw of the New Deal over and above what the "normal" Democratic vote would be (1934-36), we measured the percentage increase for Martin over the percentage the Democrats received in the vote for governor in 1934 and 1936.

3. The same reasoning applies here. This variable measures the percentage increase in the vote for Roosevelt over the Democratic vote for governor in 1934 and 1936.

C. Political Apathy

1. Here we sought no clear causal understandings. Our purpose was to determine whether the vote was related to a town's general level of political activism. We therefore averaged the percentage of registered voters who voted in 1934 and 1936 and used this average as a statistic indicating levels of political activity in the towns.

2. We used this variable simply to indicate whether the parkway fell because of citizen apathy. Here we measured the turnout on the parkway referendum as a percentage of the registered voters in the towns.

D. Conservatism

In Vermont conservatism has generally meant fiscal conservatism. In order to measure this attitude, the per-capita public indebtedness was figured by town and this figure was taken as an indicator of that town's "conservatism." The argument is simply that, in Vermont towns, "indebtedness" is a highly public and visible statistic—one that is generally debated at length during town meeting. If a town were to allow a substantial town debt to go unpaid, we would consider that town less conservative than a town that balanced the budget. That seemed a fairly reasonable operational definition, which has been used in other studies.[46] This variable may, however, have been more a function of a town's ability to pay its debt than an ideological indicator. It correlated with one of our

46. Thomas R. Dye, "City-Suburban Social Distance and Public Policy," *Social Forces*, 44 (1965), 100-06.

economic variables (per-capita delinquent taxes) with
an *r* of .467. However, the correlation with our welfare relief index was only *r* = .170.

II. Socioeconomic Variables

A. Town Population on Relief

The percentage of a town's population listed on relief
rolls in 1935 was used to reveal any relationships between the economic impact of the Depression in the
towns and their support for the parkway.

B. Per Capita Delinquent Taxes

This figure was taken from the towns in 1935 and
1936 and averaged to obtain the basic statistic. We
felt this figure would more accurately reflect economic conditions in rural areas where the property tax
provides the income source for the towns. Generally
speaking, when people don't pay their taxes in a Vermont community, we can be fairly certain that things
are not well economically.[47]

C. Farming Population

Farmers as a percentage of town population was the
statistic used to identify agricultural communities. We
have no theoretical reason to expect farmers to act in
a unified manner on the parkway issue. However, we
felt that this kind of figure is generally useful for distinguishing autonomic from employee cultures. We
felt that individualistic cultures might promote an
anti-parkway vote.

D. Population Increase

The logic behind the selection of this variable is:
members of declining communities will see the parkway as a means of injecting life into the state and its
localities. As a descriptive device this statistic is often
used as an operational definition for socioeconomic
dynamics.

E. Population Size

As an analytical construct, urbanism seems to be los-

47. Vermont Development Commission, *Financial Statistics of State,
County, and Local Government in Vermont, 1932-1936* (Montpelier,
1938).

ing some of its value. Nevertheless, for the decade of the 1930's in Vermont this statistic, like variable IIC, is a useful device for distinguishing between life styles. Hypothesis: the kinds of people who would be likely to support the parkway proposal were clustered in the more urban places.

III. Other Variables

   A. Town Proximity

Measured as air miles from the proposed route, this statistic was used to identify the people whose lives would be most immediately affected by the new project. It would also account for the people who would be separated from the parkway by miles of rugged terrain and, in some cases, even mountain ranges.

   B. Newspaper Coverage

Research indicated that the state's two major daily newspapers took opposite positions on the parkway and led intensive campaigns to promote their views. Each county where the respective papers were located turned in the state's most lopsided returns in favor of the position taken by the papers. Hypothesis: in Chittenden County (the county that voted most heavily for the parkway) the *Burlington Free Press* had an important influence on the vote. In Rutland County (the county that voted most heavily against the parkway) the *Rutland Herald* had an important influence on the vote. Newspaper impact was measured as the per-capita distribution of the newspaper by town.

   C. Green Mountain Club Impact

Research also indicated that the single most active interest group involved in the struggle was the famous Green Mountain Club, the organization that maintains the Long Trail that rides the top of the state from Massachusetts to Canada. This group violently opposed the parkway, and we hypothesized that their membership would have an impact on the vote. We measured this variable as the percentage of a town's population that was enrolled in the Green Mountain Club.[48]

48. Green Mountain Club, *Revised By-Laws of Green Mountain Club and List of Members* (Rutland, 1930).

Table 29
Product Moment, Spearman, and Kendal Correlations for the
Parkway Vote and Selected Political and Socioeconomic
Variables for 233 Towns, 1936[a]

Independent Variables	Product Moment	Spearman	Kendal
Democratic vote for Governor	.42	.41	.29
Martin vote for Senate	.29	.28	.20
Roosevelt vote	.41	.41	.28
Adjusted Democratic vote for governor	−.06	.01	−.01
Adjusted Martin vote for Senate	−.26	−.37	−.25
Adj. Roosevelt vote	−.11	−.04	−.03
Voter turnout 1934-1936	.25	.26	.17
Turnout for the parkway	.04	.04	.02
Adj. parkway turnout	.13	.04	.09
Fiscal conservatism	−.04	−.06	−.04
Town population on relief	.22	.25	.18
Delinquent taxes in towns	−.01	−.11	−.07
Town population increase	.09	.09	.06
Farmers in town	−.15	−.14	−.10
Per capita farms in town	−.20	−.20	−.14
Town population size	.16	.24	.17
Town population density	.14	.24	.16
Town's proximity to parkway	.17	.15	.10

[a]All measurements were interval except for "Town Population on Relief." Spearman and Kendal measures were used to determine if the ordinal measure employed for "town population on relief" would cause variations in the coefficients. Simple curiosity tempted their inclusion for the remainder of the variables. The consistency of the Pearson and Spearman measures is striking and probably due to the large "N."

[b]Measured as the percentage increase in the Parkway turnout over normal turnout, 1934-1936.

These were only a few of the variables used in the original analysis. Those which were dropped either lacked solid statistical foundations or caused misinterpretations through multicollinearity. Thus the variable "party competition" was dropped because it appeared to be only a function of increased Democratic strength in the towns. The two variables correlated with an r of more than .9. Table 29 shows simple correlation coefficients for the eighteen independent variables outlined above and the dependent variable, the percentage of "yes" votes for the parkway. Once again the political variables are by far the most important. Intrastate New Deal Democratic strength, with an $r = .42$, and Roosevelt's draw, with an $r = .41$, had easily the strongest association with the "yes" vote. Since both were highly intercorrelated ($r = .873$), we can conclude that Roosevelt's popularity in Vermont was not dissociated from the popularity of local Democratic candidates, and that this mutual appeal was strongly associated with the segment of the population which supported the building of the Green Mountain Parkway. Towns with higher levels of voter participation seemed more apt to be for the parkway than those with low turnout ($r = .217$); yet more participation in the referendum would not have saved the proposal, since increased turnout was unrelated to the "yes" vote.

Economic variables did not carry great weight either, although the percentage of town population on relief did show a correlation of $r = .217$ with the "yes" vote. Farmers seemed to be slightly disposed to vote "no" on the issue ($r = -.154$), and large town dwellers slightly inclined to vote "yes" ($r = .157$). These simple correlations thrust political party far above the other variables in terms of associational strength. Since this result was unexpected and represented a highly unusual state of affairs, the analysis was expanded to include partial and multiple correlation coefficients for these same relationships. Yet the party variable seemed to hold its own when stripped of the influence of the other variables, while the latter seemed to pale even more when cast off from the effects of party.

The use of stepwise multiple regression techniques (setting a cutoff point when independent variables failed to contribute an additional one percent explanation in the variance of the dependent variable) indicated that political variables were dominant. Socioeconomic variables failed to appear in the regression formulas. Table 30 shows simple, partial, and multiple correlations for all variables contributing at least one percent of explanatory power in the variation of the parkway vote. Once again the averaged Democratic vote totals for governor for 1934 and 1936 (intrastate Democratic strength) was the only variable that explained a significant percentage of the variance.

Table 30
Simple, Partial, and Multiple Correlations for Selected
Independent Variables and the Parkway Vote (N=233)

Independent variables	Simple correlations		Partial correlations		Multiple correlations	
	r	r^2	ry.n	ry.n^2	R	R^2
Intrastate Democratic strength	.42	.18	*.33*[a]	.11	.42	.18
Voter turnout	.25	.06	*.20*	.04	.46	.21
Proximity	.17	.03	*.18*	.03	.49	.24
Adjusted intrastate New Deal draw	−.27	.07	.01	.00	.50	.25

[a]Significance tests were performed for the partials. Italic coefficients are significant at the .01 level.

Combined with the other three items contributing at least one percent additional explanatory power in the variation of the dependent variable, the Democratic vote was able to account for 25 percent of the total variance. Forcing economic variables into the regression formula with the two strongest political variables underlines the weakness of the former.

As Table 31 indicates, our welfare index did not contribute any explanatory power and was dropped from the final equation. Per-capita delinquent taxes is the only other variable that appears, but its impact is literally nothing. In this case, controlling for only two other variables leaves the partial coefficient for party more powerful than ever.

Focusing on Two Counties

If party politics were the only important predictive variable on a statewide basis, would it hold up under the heat of the parkway struggle in Chittenden and Rutland counties? Here the reaction to the parkway proposal was most intense. Chittenden County produced the strongest vote for the project, and Rut-

Table 31

Simple, Partial, and Multiple Correlations for Selected
Independent Variables and the Parkway Vote: Economic
Variables Forced (N=233)

Independent variables	Simple correlations		Partial correlations		Multiple correlations	
	r	r²	ry.n	ry.n²	R	R²
Intrastate Democratic strength	.42	.18	.38[a]	.14	.42	.18
Voter turnout	.25	.06	.17	.03	.45	.20
Per capita delinquent taxes	−.09	.01	.07	.00	.45	.20

[a]Significance tests were performed for the partials. Italic coefficients are significant at the .01 level.

land County produced the strongest against it. Intracounty
analysis in these two areas is enriched by the fact that there was
every reason to believe that the impact of the *Rutland Herald*
and the *Burlington Free Press* would be significant. The *Herald*'s
dedication to the parkway's defeat, for instance, was remarkable indeed. A review of the *Herald*'s coverage between February 12 and March 4, 1936, indicates that the editors injected
editorial comments in their front-page coverage. Various car-
toons ridiculed the parkway proposal. Scenic pictures of Vermont implied that the parkway would destroy the natural
beauty of the state. Particularly striking were editorial leanings
portrayed in headlines and picture captions.[49] The *Burlington
Free Press* was a bit more restrained in its support than the *Herald* was in its opposition. The *Free Press* restricted its editorial-
izing primarily to its editorial pages. However, the Burlington

49. *Rutland Herald*, February 1936: *13*, pp. 3, 10; *15*, p. 9; *17*, p. 8;
19, p. 1; *20*, pp., 1, 2, 8; *21*, pp. 1, 8; *22*, pp. 1, 8; *24*, pp. 1, 2, 8; *25*, pp.
1, 8, 12; *26*, pp. 1, 8; *27*, pp. 1, 8, 11; *28*, pp. 1, 8; *29*, pp. 1, 8, 9; March
2, pp. 1, 7, 8; March 3, pp. 1, 2, 3, 7.

paper strongly supported the proposal, and we would tend to assume that it had its own positive impact on the vote.[50] Yet our data indicate no relationship between newspaper coverage and the vote on the parkway. If our operational definition of "newspaper influence" (per-capita daily distribution) is adequate, we may conclude that newspaper influence was not an important factor in the vote. In each county the simple correlation coefficient for newspaper coverage and the vote on the parkway were low. Both counties registered a coefficient of .23. Moreover, stepwise multiple regression techniques did not show that newspaper coverage was an important variable. This finding is supported indirectly by much of the literature of political science and public opinion, which reports that the press generally has a minimal effect on electoral results.

Nevertheless, we are unwilling to discard the newspaper hypothesis completely. It may well be that our statistics simply do not measure the phenomenon we are after. Moreover, the "soft" data supporting the hypothesis are compelling indeed. It is probably accurate to conclude, therefore, that newspaper coverage was at least a reinforcing variable and may have had some independent, although limited, impact of its own. We are supported in this view by some members of the Vermont press corps of the day. The editors of the *Bennington Evening Banner* even went so far as to say: "The Parkway difference of opinion is not really and truly a referendum. It is a battle between the *Burlington Free Press* and the *Rutland Herald*. A vote for the Parkway is a vote for the *Free Press*. A vote against the Parkway is a vote for the *Herald . . .* "[51] A similar conclusion was reported in the *Montpelier Evening Argus.*[52]

With newspaper coverage at least statistically out of the picture, what variables do contribute to an explanation of the parkway vote in these two counties? As Tables 32 and 33 re-

50. *Burlington Free Press*, February 1936: *11*, pp. 2, 4, 5; *12*, pp. 5, 6, 7, 10; *13*, p. 5; *14*, pp. 2, 7; *15*, pp. 6, 7; *17*, pp. 6, 8; *18*, pp. 6, 7, 9; *19*, pp. 2, 6, 7; *20*, pp. 1, 2, 6, 7; *21*, pp. 5, 6, 7; *22* (an entire supplement was published supporting the parkway); *24*, pp. 6, 7; *25*, pp. 2, 6, 7; *26*, pp. 6, 7, 8; *28*, pp. 6, 7; *29*, pp. 1, 6, 7; March 1, pp. 1, 2, 6, 7; March 3, p. 1.

51. *Bennington Evening Banner* (February 20, 1936), p. 6.

52. *Montpelier Evening Argus* (February 21, 1936), p. 4.

Table 32
Simple, Partial, and Multiple Correlations for Selected
Independent Variables and the Parkway Vote
Chittenden County ($N=16$)

Independent variables	Simple correlations		Partial correlations		Multiple correlations	
	r	r^2	ry.n	$ry.n^2$	R	R^2
Intrastate Democratic strength	.73	.53	.84[a]	.71	.73	.53
Voter turnout	.26	.07	.58	.34	.77	.59
Town population	.47	.22	.76	.58	.81	.66
Proximity	.26	.07	.76	.58	.88	.77
Population increase	.38	.14	.63	.40	.93	.86

[a]Significance tests were performed for the partials. Italic coefficients are significant at the .01 level.

veal, political party was again the most influential variable in both counties, explaining 71 percent of the variance in Chittenden County when stripped of the influence of other factors, and 48 percent of the variance in Rutland County. In neither county did newspaper coverage appear in the regression. Multiple correlations for these two areas produced combinations that explained 86 percent of the variance in Chittenden County and 67 percent of the variance in Rutland County. As in the state-wide analysis, voter turnout and proximity were important factors. Per-capita delinquent taxes provided five additional percentage points of explanation in Rutland County; town proximity, town population, and population increase were all somewhat important in Chittenden County. Yet the principal conclusion of these narrowed calculations is simply that they reinforce the predominance of intrastate Democratic strength as the prime causal variable.

A final task was to explore the possibility that the Green Mountain Club was able to influence the vote through its vocif-

Table 33
Simple, Partial, and Multiple Correlations for Selected
Independent Variables and the Parkway Vote: Rutland County
(N=26)

Independent variables	Simple correlations		Partial correlations		Multiple correlations	
	r	r²	ry.n	ry.n²	R	R²
Intrastate Democratic strength	.72	.52	.69[a]	.48	.72	.52
Voter turnout	.57	.32	.42	.18	.77	.59
Delinquent taxes	−.23	.05	−.43	.18	.80	.64
Population increase	.27	.07	.32	.10	.82	.67

[a]Significance tests were performed for the partials. The italic coefficient is significant at the .01 level.

erous campaign against the parkway. To do this we established a statistic for Green Mountain Club strength from the percentage of the registered voters that belonged to the Club in each town in the state. However, the results proved to be inconclusive. Further research indicated that much of the cry against the parkway came from out-of-state members of the Club. In fact, the in-state members were about evenly divided on the issue.[53]

Discussion

The Green Mountain Parkway controversy carried with it the kinds of concerns that have long been singled out as the gut elements of political conflict in rural areas generally and Vermont in particular—fiscal conservatism versus governmental

53. From a survey of Green Mountain Club opinion found in the Club archives located at the Norwich Military Academy at Northfield, Vermont. Also see "Aiken Letter," *Burlington Clipper* (February 27, 1936), p. 2.

spending; state autonomy versus federal aid; little things versus big things (in this case little towns versus large ones); negativism versus positivism; conservation versus industrial development; and, more generally, cosmopolitanism versus parochialism. While there is no certainty that the many empirical referents proposed here as operational definitions were entirely accurate, it still seems important to note that none of them was an adequate predictor of Vermont's behavior toward the parkway.

What is clearly important, however, is that the variable with many good reasons *not* to be tied to the parkway vote emerged as the only consistent and reasonably powerful determining factor in our correlational exercises. Partisanship (operationally defined as support for candidates for governor) was the only variable in a long lineup of potential variables that clearly indicated strict linkages with the parkway vote. In an urban-industrial, two-party state this would not have been unusual. However, in Vermont's rural, one-party environment we are surprised to find party politics playing such an important role in elite and mass decision-making. This finding seems further evidence that when the record of Vermont's political history is opened, no assumptions are immune to revision.

A quick summary of the impact of these conclusions might read as follows: Take two Vermont farmers, both working under similar environmental conditions, both beset by the same economic problems, both lifelong Vermonters, with their lives tied to the soil and their perspectives on the world around them colored by the same variables, distances, hard work, solitude, and self-sufficiency; one is a Democrat, the other a Republican. Place before them one of the critical issues in the history of the state, and they are apt to disagree. Take this same Democratic farmer and another Democrat from Winooski, a mill worker who rents his home and whose perspectives on the world at large are governed by remarkably different referents; these two are apt to vote the same on the parkway issue. This overly simplistic example underlines once more two observations that crop up often in this book: (1) in the debate between "political sociologists" and "political political scientists" over the root causes of political behavior (are they generated from variations in the quality of socioeconomic milieu or from political forces independent from environmental contexts), political sociologists have a lot of explaining to do; and (2) the utility of the rural-urban continuum as a construct for political analysis is minimal.

Finally, a word about the current environmental crisis. It is well to bear in mind that the parkway issue was cast, molded, and polished in terms that still define the dimensions of the conflict over environmental decisionmaking, i.e. economic development versus preservation of ecological balances and the integrity of nature. When one consults the debate that filled the newspapers of the day, one is struck by the familiarity of the argument. It is easy to forget that the conflict took place nearly forty years ago.

In Vermont during the mid-thirties both ends of the equation were maximized. On the one side, the state was suffering financial difficulties and, although the pain was not so acute as in other parts of the nation, it was in need of massive economic transfusions of some sort. On the other side, Vermont clearly epitomized the isolated, unspoiled, and uncontaminated natural area, complete with a built-in, supportive, "noble savage" ethic. Inject into this atmosphere a plan to bestow on the state huge economic bonuses at the cost of severe alterations in the character of her most prized possession, the Green Mountain range (whence the name Vermont), and you have the makings of a legitimate and profound environmental debate.

What can we say about it? This analysis indicates that even issues profoundly linked to environmental concerns may not shed the influence of party politics as they are resolved in the political system. We propose two arguments. One is that the case study utilized did in fact pose a societal question in terms that highlight the essential dichotomy defining the contemporary environmental debate—the integrity of nature versus economic development. The second is that the atmosphere that surrounded the case study was, in general, extremely unhealthy for partisanship. If these two propositions are sound, then the empirical results, i.e. the appearance of partisanship as the only consistent and reasonably powerful determining factor in our regression tests, may be important. Clearly this evidence suggests at a minimum that those who seek to alter the nation's relationship to its environment in any substantial fashion should consider dismissing the nonpartisan approach and wrap their programs securely in party platforms, if possible majority party platforms.

Six

Political Life in a Rural Technopolity

Vermont has never been urban, and very probably it will never be. Like other rural areas of the nation, it doesn't need urbanism and will refuse it when offered. We should not assume that this rejection is simply because modern urban America has received a bad press over the last decade and rural people are turning up their noses at what they perceive to be crime-ridden, pollution-stifled environments. Rather, the inhabitants feel no need to group together, regardless of their occupation. Rural areas in the United States, unlike their counterparts elsewhere in the world, have always been machine filled. Now that modern technology has become a part of rural culture, urban-rural distinctions no longer serve as important operational definitions.[1] Despite much thinking to the contrary, the case of Vermont shows that a technocratic society is not limited to the urban condition and that the study of rural society today should be as involved with the culture of scientific progress as is the study of urban society.

Scholars have traditionally molded their definitions of "rural" and "urban" around one of two constructs. One group has been satisfied with a strictly physical definition: mathematical ratios of people to space have provided the criteria to identify urban and rural environments. The spatial approach assumes

1. The utility of the rural-urban continuum has been repeatedly questioned in recent years by political scientists and sociologists. See Howard W. Beers, "Rural-Urban Differences: Some Evidence from Public Opinion Polls," *Rural Sociology*, 18 (1953), 1-11; Otis Dudley Duncan, "Community Size and the Rural-Urban Continuum," in Paul Hatt and Albert J. Reiss, Jr., eds., *Cities and Society* (Glencoe, Ill.: Free Press, 1956), pp. 35-45; and Robert S. Friedman, "The Urban-Rural Conflict Revisited," *Western Political Quarterly*, 14 (1961), 481-95.

that various kinds of socioeconomic groups have interests peculiar to themselves. A second school, unsatisfied with strict quantitative definitions, has sought to discover a set of attitudinal constructs peculiar to the urban situation. Louis Wirth developed what has proved to be a relatively standard typology of urban personality traits (over fifteen) and qualities of social organization (over twenty). Wirth contends that number, density of settlement, and degree of heterogeneity of the population serve as measurable criteria with which to identify the environments where these qualities may be found.[2] More recently Anderson and Ishwaran have listed fourteen characteristics peculiar to "urban man" and foreign to "rural man." For example, urban man is "more favorable to new songs and dances, and does not share the rural proclivity for repeating the old familiar jokes."[3] The weight of evidence over the last twenty years points to the superiority of the first method—the spatial school. Rural areas are sparsely settled and urban areas are densely settled. Urbanism thus defined does produce social characteristics that result from the intensity of population. These factors cannot "spread" to rural areas; they are anchored to the city. The failure to recognize the uniqueness of urbanism has led to the mistaken attempt to attribute what is accurately perceived to be a cultural revolution in the countryside, as a transferral of urban values. What the rural cultural revolution represents is the growth of an indigenous technical ethic in the country that parallels a similar growth in urban situations. What is spreading is technocracy—growing upward, not outward, from a technological life style and acceptance of the scientific ethic.

Richard Dewey has underlined the uniqueness of urban traits in his study of the rural-urban continuum. By assigning certain life qualities to people existing en masse, Dewey is able to define what is urban and only urban. For instance, "anonymity is inevitable for the vast majority of a city's population and impossible at the rural extreme" and "when people interact social-

2. Louis Wirth, "Urbanism as a Way of Life," *American Journal of Sociology*, 44 (1938), 1-24.
3. Nels Anderson and K. Ishwaran, *Urban Sociology* (New York: Asia Publishing House, 1965), pp. 6-7.

ly, they must, except on rare occasions, know the status of their associates, and the pervasive anonymity of the large city demands some measure of identifying the functionaries essential to daily living there." Dewey's qualities of life which he sees as increasing with population density are (1) anonymity, (2) a division of labor, (3) impersonal and formally prescribed relationships, and (4) symbols of status which are independent of personal acquaintance. This cluster of limited attributes appears sound. [4] They have been found in higher proportion as people come together in mass living situations. They have been seen to decrease as man lives and works apart from his fellows.

Technocracy is a life system that accepts, understands, and utilizes science and expertise as controlling variables in day-to-day behavior.[5] It is the immersion of the individual in a sophisticated life pattern anchored in technology. Work and leisure are governed by items whose mechanical workings may be obscure but the outputs of which are well appreciated. The ethic holds that the application of *technique* to life will somehow make life better.

One reason that the technocratic culture is viewed by so many to be "urbanism matured" may well be the failure to place the growth of urbanism in chronological perspective. Urbanism has gone stale; it cannot be given new life merely by suggesting that the technological culture represents a blossoming urban maturity that is spilling into the back beyond. The process of urbanization reached its peak in this country before the *Maine* sank to the bottom of the harbor of Havana. Evidence from American literature shows that the great disillusionment with rural life came nearly fifty years ago with the work of Edgar Lee Masters, Sherwood Anderson, Sinclair Lewis, and others. By 1930 the battle was over in fact and mulled over in print. America was an urban nation.[6]

4. Richard Dewey, "The Rural-Urban Continuum: Real but Relatively Unimportant," *American Journal of Sociology*, 66 (1960), 60-66. I have omitted Dewey's third quality (heterogeneity) as not necessarily linked to urban life.

5. Everett C. Ladd, Jr., "The Changing Face of American Political Ideology," *Massachusetts Review*, 8 (1967), 251-66.

6. William E. Leuchtenburg, *The Pearls of Prosperity, 1914-1932* (Chicago: University of Chicago Press, 1958), pp. 225-26. Robert Friedman

Two other factors underlie our misinterpretations of the nature of contemporary rural society. The first is an overstatement: science and technological innovation have traditionally spawned in the cities. There is no doubt, of course, that the urban complex generates innovative impulses that feed the American technological life style. Yet science and technology are not foreign to rural America. Although arising from a different stimulant (in the city, the need to serve and manipulate man; in the countryside, the need to serve and manipulate nature), the evidence shows that agricultural technology blossomed so quickly and so pervasively in America that it soon put 70 percent of the farmers out of business. The evidence also shows that when it was considered necessary, country people obtained the hardware that science offered them.[7]

One need go no further than Vermont to document the inventiveness of rural society. Before 1860, Vermont inventors produced the first steel square, rotary pump, platform scale, and American globes. A dozen years before Fulton, Samuel Morey of Fairlee, Vermont, sailed a paddlewheel steamboat up the Connecticut River. The most significant contribution came from Thomas Davenport, who invented the electric motor in 1834. Although the evidence is not conclusive, it shows that technological innovation is not rare in rural society.[8]

A second distortion of American ruralism stems from our failure to remember that there never has been an American peasantry. Many of the constructs of our assessment of the rural way of life seem applicable to peasant cultures and inapplicable to American ruralism. Beginning with Tocqueville, the evidence has consistently underlined the peasantless character of American ruralism.[9] Paul H. Landis, while suggesting that there is a

---

has taken note of words written by Arthur M. Schlesinger, Sr. that point to a diminishing of rural-urban conflict in the 1890's. Friedman, p. 484.

7. Paul H. Landis, *Rural Life in Process* (New York: McGraw Hill, 1940), pp. 92-95.

8. Marvin Fisher, *Workshops in the Wilderness: The European Response to American Institutions* (New York: Oxford University Press, 1967).

9. Jack M. Potter, May N. Dias, and George N. Foster, *Peasant Society* (Boston: Little, Brown, 1967). A recent collection of articles on peasant

relative difference between the pace of urban and rural life in America, points out, "This characterization of rural life has never been so true of farm life in America as of peasant cultures elsewhere . . . "[10] Landis also shows that American ruralism has been unique in its absence of "nebulous farm" systems that are so common in Europe.[11]

Moreover, the American tradition of the individual farm has served to promote an innovative technological spirit. Although the nebulous farm type facilitates the introduction of communal services such as electricity,[12] it also produces "stagnant . . . patterns of life" where "community ideas and sentiment become firmly molded and limited in perspective."[13] The individual farm settlement "paved the way for a machine revolution in agriculture such as the Old World has not experienced."[14]

It is hard to read much of the literature dealing with rural-urban differences in this country and not suspect that the writers have cast rural America (at least in part) in the mold of the European peasant-village culture. Viewing rural life this way, it is easy to conclude that technology must "break through" to rural areas, penetrating a self-contained, introspective, and noninnovative society.

In his early and perceptive analysis of the new rural culture, Lane W. Lancaster describes the blurring of what he calls the "rural-urban contrast." The countryside has accepted the folkways of the city, says Lancaster. "In short, we have already a

---

society, this book contains no offering dealing with American rural culture. Yet several articles sound very much like the work of many interpreters of the American rural condition. The excellent bibliography, broken down in part by region and country, lists sources concerned with over thirty nations and many other regions. There are no references given for the United States.

10. Landis, p. 4.

11. Ibid., p. 25.

12. Ibid. This may very well be the major cause of rural America's lag in acquiring electricity. Landis points out that in Utah, where farm organization was nebulous, 20 percent more farms were equipped with electricity than in any of the other states.

13. Ibid., p. 25.

14. Ibid., p. 29.

new society for which we have no accurate descriptive term."[15] Lancaster then quotes Irving A. Spaulding: "We have begun to think in terms of 'continua' of relationships between the two types."[16]

The following paragraphs will attempt to qualify the Lancaster assessment in two ways. First, there is real doubt that ruralism and urbanism have blurred. Rural areas are still places where people live apart from one another. Therefore, to argue that the cultural revolution in rural areas is a transfer of urban folkways seems questionable. Second, to argue that the new pattern is a continuum of life style according to which locales can be judged by the criterion of how urban they are does not square with the observation that there are intensely rural areas packed with the hardware of urbanism.

Consider the following from the work Kingsley Davis has done on the growth of urbanization: "A city of a million inhabitants today is not the sort of place of the same number in 1900 or in 1850. Moreover, with the emergence of giant cities of five to fifteen million, something new has been added. Such cities are creatures of the 20th century. *Their sheer quantitative difference means a qualitative change as well."* [my italics] [17]

Something is missing here. We are first told that contemporary cities of one million people are not like their ancestors. "Giant cities," however, are subject to the effects of quantitative differences; for, given enough quantification (growth), a new qualitative something emerges. It is hard not to interpret a direct causal relationship between increases in numbers and qualitative change. What is the "something new" found in giant cities not present in smaller cities? Davis does not say here, but one would suppose it is what Harvey Cox has called the "technopolis"—the "base on which a new cultural style has developed."

For purposes of comparison we shall make use of a

15. Lane W. Lancaster, *Government in Rural America* (New York: Van Nostrand, 1952), p. 10.

16. Irving A. Spaulding, "Serendipity and the Rural-Urban Continuum," *Rural Sociology*, 16 (1951), 29-36, in Lancaster, p. 10.

17. Kingsley Davis, "The Origins and Growth of Urbanism in the World," *American Journal of Sociology*, 60 (1955), 435.

somewhat contrived word, technopolis . . . Although the term is an artificial one, it reminds us that the contemporary secular metropolis was not possible before modern technology . . . *There comes a point at which quantitative development releases qualitative change* [my italics] and that point was reached in urban development only after the modern Western scientific revolution.[18]

Again, it is hard *not* to perceive a cause and effect relationship between urban growth and the development of the technopolis. Yet Cox has paid heed to those (such as Vidich and Bensman) who have noted the arrival of so-called urban qualities as communications facilities in rural settings.[19] Even so, it is tempting to conclude that Cox has rendered his terms meaningless when he argues that urbanization "is not something that refers only to the city" and that "the urban center is not just Washington, London, New York and Peking, it is everywhere."[20] If urbanism is everywhere, what is it that quantitative development releases? Cox may be overstating his case. He may mean that "technocracy" can be found everywhere, and he is perfectly right. He is also accurate when he paints his distinctions between urban and rural. It is his acceptance of the continuum thesis that forces confusion in language.

A final and particularly acute example of the tendency to identify technocracy as a higher stage of urbanism is found in Anderson and Ishwaran, *Urban Sociology.*[21] The authors find the new urbanism "more informed and sophisticated." They find it to be more "technically oriented" and "global in its perspectives." This in itself is perfectly sound. What follows, however, links this new technocratic sophistication to the urban condition and explicitly denies it to ruralism:

One aspect of modern urbanism is the readiness with which city people, *compared with country people* [my

18. Harvey Cox, *The Secular City* (New York: Macmillan Company, 1966), p. 5.
19. Ibid., p. 4.
20. Ibid.
21. Anderson and Ishwaran, p. 8.

italics] accept change, and are not surprised even to be
told of the most profound discoveries in science or the
most extraordinary achievements in technology . . . The
uncertainties of urban life are those of the market, a
man to man relationship, those of rural life involve a
man to nature relationship. Thus urban man is more
stimulated to be alert and resourceful, to create, which
stimulation does not touch rural man with the same
force.[22]

Here is the continuum theory articulated. The urban condition
emits a sociocultural force-field, derived for the most part from
the matter and spirit of technology. This phenomenon is not to
be found in the country.[23]

Our evidence supports those who have perceived the technocratic ethic to be a development superimposed on *both* rural
and urban environments, thereby serving to cloud the utility of
either urbanism or ruralism as definitions with analytical value.
Vermont has entered the age of technology without urbanization.

The Modern Rural Technopolity

As we have said before, census data show the Green Mountain
State to be more intensely rural than any other state except
Alaska. Vermont's population is minuscule and scattered among
the profusion of hills and valleys. The largest urban complex
boasts only about 40,000 people. Moreover, it is well nigh impossible to walk five miles as the crow flies from any point in
downtown Burlington and not run into barbed wire, whitetail

22. Ibid., pp. 4-5.
23. Ibid., pp. 18-19. Anderson and Ishwaran, like Cox, cover themselves
by suggesting that "another type of urbanism" is possible. Rural people
are sharing more and more such urban qualities of life as "education and
communication facilities." Once more urbanism is viewed as a quality
not grafted to population density. I would argue simply that these indicators of "urbanism" are historically found in rural areas in America, and, at
any rate, when urbanism thus defined is said to be rural-bound, the word
becomes meaningless.

deer, or Lake Champlain. Vermont fits our definition of ruralism. If urbanism is a prerequisite to technocracy, surely Vermont of all states must be nontechnocratic.

Yet this is not the case. A close look at the 6 percent of Vermont's population still engaged in farming shows that the Vermont farmer accepts and understands the technocratic ethic.
The extent to which the farmer's life today is controlled by
technology, too little appreciated in scholarly circles, requires
heavy emphasis if we are to understand fully the culture of rural
technocracy.[24] Certainly to question the propositions of
Anderson and Ishwaran (rural people are overawed with and
react against profound discoveries in science) requires evidence
with backbone.

Consider *Vermont Farm and Home Science,* published by the
Extension Service and Experiment Station of the University of
Vermont and mailed quarterly to Vermont farmers on request.
Typical of the articles in the journal are "A Soil Test to Save
Time, Save Money," "New Maple Lab Honors Pioneer Scien-
tists," "A Look at Vermont's Dairy Future," "How to Prevent
Poultry Diseases," "UVM Research Team Studies Poultry House
Heat Loss," "Test Tube Trees," and "ELFAC Goes All Compu-
ter." Technology and expertise are to be utilized for the better-
ment of life.[25]

In 1965 the Extension Service wrote over 5000 news stories,
conducted 2634 radio programs, and appeared on 269 educational television programs. Extension county representatives
held 485 field demonstrations and studies. The Extension workers conducted over 15,000 educational meetings in the same
year. This organization reaches half of Vermont's households in
some manner every year—and the emphasis is progress through
science.

There can be little doubt that the farmer has been introduced

24. See, for instance, the readings (especially the work of Olaf F. Lar-
son and Everett M. Rogers) in James H. Copp, ed., *Our Changing Rural
Society: Perspective and Trends* (Ames, Iowa: Iowa State University Press,
1964), and Walter L. Slocum, *Agricultural Sociology* (New York: Harper
and Brothers, 1962).

25. See *Vermont Farm and Home Science* (Burlington: The Extension
Service and Experiment Station, University of Vermont, 1962-1968).

to the culture of technology; but has he accepted it? Is the old adage "If it was good enough for my father and me, it's good enough for my kids" really dead? The evidence suggests that it is. If the acceptance of expertise and technology means efficiency and efficiency can be measured in terms of effort expended and output realized, then the Vermont farmer has certainly accepted the technocratic culture. In 1953 Vermont dairy herds numbered 10,788. These herds totaled 267,063 cows for an average of 25 per herd. Twelve years later in 1965, the number of herds had decreased to 6051 with a total of 229,612 milking. The per-herd average increased to 38. Yet although there were fewer cows in fewer herds, the total milk production in this period increased by 25 percent. This means that Vermont farmers increased their milk production per cow by about 40 percent.[26] Other data not recorded here show that utilization of new agricultural technology by Vermont farmers has increased at least 100 percent in the ten-year period between 1951 and 1961.[27]

To appreciate the profound changes in the nature of farm life from the outside is difficult. This writer has personally assisted in a Caesarean section of a dairy cow, applied shots of penicillin and other drugs to cattle, operated hay conditioners that were innovations ten years ago and then seen them become obsolete with new hay mowers that perform both the cutting and conditioning function, and watched the development of ultramodern milking equipment, feeding processes, and living environments for cattle. Does the acceptance and use of a contraption that puts one in debt for years and smashes good hay to pieces on the assurances of some college-educated outsider fit the stereotype of the conservative, noninnovative, parochial, rural farmer? That kind of individual is as rare now as hand milking. The Vermont farmer accepts, utilizes, and understands science and expertise in his day-to-day existence.

What evidence is there to suggest that rural nonfarmers are equally influenced by the technological ethic? Hard data are

26. Dwight K. Eddy, "A Look at Vermont's Dairy Future," *Vermont Farm and Home Science*, 5 (1966), 19-21.

27. James G. Sykes, *Dairy Bench Mark Comparisons, 1951-1961* (Burlington: Vermont Agricultural Experiment Station, 1962), pp. 2-3.

difficult to come by—particularly the kinds that lend themselves meaningfully to comparative analysis. What we will hope to show, therefore, is that Vermont, while being the most rural state in the nation, does not compare unfavorably with the nation at large, or highly urbanized New England, in terms of the incidence of various categories of technological indicators. The weakness of the comparisons is understood. It is suggested, however, that a per-capita comparison of four categories of indicators (transportation, communication, education, and medical services) shows that Vermont does possess a high incidence of technological hardware.

Measured in percentage deviations from New England and nationwide averages, Vermont's educational system compares well. Her small population supports a transportation complex that is relatively much more extensive than the national and New England systems. Vermont's medical facilities are superior on a per-capita basis to those of either New England or the nation at large. Most remarkable of all, however (and perhaps most significant in terms of the political system), is the communications network. Burlington, Vermont's largest community with a population of only about 40,000, supports three commercial radio stations and a television station. Just outside the city there is another television station. Across the lake in New York there is a third. These data are at least suggestive. If urbanism is a prerequisite to a technocratic society, why does not the most rural state in the nation (save Alaska) exhibit strictly nontechnocratic qualities, and how can these items be explained away?

The Vermonter today may not be able to hear his neighbor's rooster crow, but he can hear his chain saw in the winter, the automatic drill that taps his sugar orchard in the spring, his small toylike garden tractor in the summer, and his high-powered deer rifle in the fall. He travels on snowmobiles, he is carried up mountains on ski lifts, he comes down on skis with automatic release bindings, clad in thermal underwear and synthetic slacks. In the summer he rides the lakes behind seventy-five horsepower engines on water skis and surfboards, to the consternation of fishermen who cast their sophisticated lures from rods and reels that are a testimony to the age of plastics. He watches the interstate highways cutting into his back pastures. His home town, probably of fewer than 3000 people, has a weekly newspaper. The county seat has a radio station. He sees his youngest daughter on the local TV children's show. Snowstorms that paralyze the rest of the Eastern seaboard delay him not a moment, for he has studded snowtires, and his state has road crews that use the latest equipment to best advantage. In short, he understands, accepts, and utilizes science to better his daily existence. He is a technocrat.[28]

Rural politics need not be carried on in an environment defined by technological backwardness. Technology is not necessarily urbanism matured. There is no "rural-urban technocracy" dialectic that universally structures societal change. The student of rural politics is confronted by a cult of urban parochialism— generally centered in the younger generation of scholars. At its best this cult dismisses rural political systems as irrelevant to the study of American politics. At its worst it condemns rural society and its political structures as conservative anachronisms, populated by uneducated simpletons mired in the Protestant ethic. In recent years the cult has weakened. It should be hurried toward an early grave.

If rural society in America has never wanted for machines, what then is different about modern rural society? One answer involves the distinction between machines and technology; another concerns communications, cybernetics; and a third focuses on Ellul's concept of la technique.

Machines are individual devices that seek to perform a unidimensional function, while technology is, as Bell notes, "a systematic, disciplined approach to objectives using a calculus of precision and measurement and a concept of system."[29] Writing on automation, Diebold offers an equally appealing definition. It is a way of thinking as well as doing, he says, for it is "no longer necessary to think in terms of individual machines, or even in terms of groups of machines; instead, for the first

28. Noel Perrin, "The Two Faces of Vermont," in T. Seymour Bassett, ed., *Outsiders inside Vermont* (Brattleboro: Stephen Greene Press, 1967), pp. 123-30.

29. Daniel Bell, ed., "Toward the Year 2000: Work in Progress," *Daedalus* (1967), 643, in Victor C. Ferkiss, *Technological Man: The Myth and the Reality* (New York: George Braziller, 1969), p. 30.

time, it is practical to look at an entire production or information-gathering process as an integrated system and not as a series of individual steps."[30] Ferkiss adds another dimension, "depersonalization." Technology is, he says, an "organized means of affecting the . . . environment . . . independently of the subjective dispositions or the personal talents of those involved." [31]

These are the qualities that make up the new machine culture in rural America. The machines are part of an uncentered system. When the hay mower broke down in the field yesterday, it was repaired there or in the farmer's nearby toolshed. Today it lies helpless until rescued by the system. So sensitive is the matrix that a small movement in a meadow along the Connecticut River will set in motion reactions all around the world—a call to St. Louis for parts, an invoice slip made in Georgia, an order to Japan to replace the part leaving St. Louis.

Machines have been depersonalized and man no longer understands their workings. Yesterday the farmer bent to inspect the damage to his hay mower. He knew what was wrong. He had fixed it before. Now he must consult the system. There is little doubt that part of the massive consolidation of the school systems of rural America has been caused by the desperate attempt of rural people to provide technical training for their youth so that they might somehow keep pace with the sophistications of the system. But more and more it is recognized that the system is growing geometrically while education cannot. Rural youth are falling behind and will not catch up. Like youth everywhere, they have become estranged from their machines. At best they can be taught the workings of a particular device. They will survive only on the very fringes of understanding.[32] Of course, the depersonalized system transcends work on the farm. It uses and needs the snowblower, the carburetor, the automatic shotgun, the tape recorder, and the proverbial can opener.

Graft cybernetics to this system and you are one step closer

30. John Diebold, *Automation: Its Impact on Business and Labor*, pamphlet, National Planning Association, Washington, D.C. (May 1959).
31. Ferkiss, p. 31.
32. Morris Philipson, ed., "After the Take Over," in *Automation* (New York: Vintage Books, 1962), p. 123.

to understanding the nature of *la technique*. There is no need to discuss the application of cybernetics to social systems.[33] The important element is the factor of self-regulation or feedback, which is the distinguishing characteristic of cybernetics as process. Rural society is now interwoven into the fabric of a system that patches its own tears, adjusts its own patterns, and establishes its own ends and goals in such a way as to protect the integrity of the system itself. Whereas in the past, machines, because they were free of the totality of the technological system, were constructed to manipulate certain aspects of the environment for the benefit of the individual, now the system dictates that the environment be manipulated by certain individuals for its own benefit. Man no longer controls his surroundings, the system does. Michael puts it this way:

. . . if the building trades were to be automated, it would not mean inventing machines to do the various tasks now done by men; rather, buildings would be redesigned so that they could be built by machines. One might invent an automatic bricklayer, but it is more likely that bricks would not be laid. Automation of the electronics industry was not brought about by the invention of automatic means for wiring circuits but through the invention of essentially wireless, i.e., printed, circuits (though today there are automatic circuit wirers as well).[34]

It is through feedback and self-adjustment that the submatrix of agricultural technology is completely revamping the very topography of rural Vermont. The system, which demands efficiency above all else, has dictated that the hill farm is disfunctional. And so it is under the normative criteria of the system that the face of Vermont is changing. At first the system *suggested* that a four-bottom plow be used instead of a single-

33. See Karl W. Deutsch, *The Nerves of Government* (New York: The Free Press, 1963), and Gregory Batesson, "Cybernetic Explanation," *American Behavioral Scientist,* 10 (1967), 29-32.

34. Donald N. Michael, "Cybernation: The Silent Conquest," A Report to the Center for the Study of Democratic Institutions, 1962, in Philipson, p. 79.

bottom plow. Then it *demanded* the four-bottom plow by making single-bottom plows very hard to come by. Soon all the machines that the hill farmer could "make do" with became obsolete, *not for him* but for the system. One by one the old machines that were made to be used by man to produce milk on Vermont's hillsides began to disappear.

But with amazing ingenuity and grinding hard work, many hill farms continued to function. They bought the system's products and somehow adapted them to their surroundings. The final blow came with the bulk tank. The system asked for uniform milk-gathering techniques, designed not for the farmer but for milk processors. The processors could operate more efficiently if they gathered the milk in trucks from large expensive cooling tanks at the individual farms. But their trucks had no time to travel the back roads to service the hill farmer, and that hastened the demise of the hill farmer. Vermont's high land is closing in with brush. The special character of the state, its pastoral softness, is dying. The farmers do not like it. The tourist industry does not like it. The political system tries to find ways to save what is left. All this because man can no longer build special conditions into the system. Instead of inventing machines to wire circuits, the system did away with wired circuits. Instead of finding ways to keep dairy cows on Vermont hillsides, the system in effect did away with the hillsides. Vermont's dairy industry has been adjusted to the system through feedback from the large, flat dairylands of the Midwest. Vermonters still produce as much milk as before, but they do it on large, flat farms that fit the criteria of the system, along the rivers and on lake shores. Now Vermont has conformed. Symmetry reigns. Single-bottom plows need not be produced, and milk cans are going for $25 each at auctions for use as antique umbrella holders. What is the motor force behind the systemization, depersonalization, and cybernation of the machine in rural America?

The motivation behind the "decision" to restyle the high country of Vermont was captured by Jacques Ellul in his description of la technique. Robert Merton explains what the term implies:

> By *technique* . . . [Ellul] means far more than machine technology. Technique refers to any complex of stan-

dardized means for attaining a predetermined result. Thus, it converts spontaneous and unreflective behavior into behavior that is deliberate and rationalized. The technical man is fascinated by results, by the immediate consequences of setting standardized devices into motion. . . . Above all, he is committed to the never ending search for "the one best way" to achieve any designated objective.[35]

In *The Failure of Technology*, German sociologist Friedrich Juenger, like Ellul, sees this "drive for perfecting" as the prime causal phenomenon of technocratic life. As H. Bleibtreau explains in the introduction to the American edition in 1948:

The urge for perfection, as the author sees it, stems from the technician's rational, factual, utilitarian, and impersonal way of thinking, . . . Perfection is the goal for which the technician applies the methods of an ever more efficient functionalism, not only in the conquest and the exploitation of nature, but also in the increasingly refined structure of modern industrial organization. The ideology of perfection, by its own suggestive powers, has eaten deeply into the realm of human relations in general and of the modern state in particular. The drive for technical perfection is a self-impelled and irreversible process. . . .[36]

The pervading cultural ethic at large in rural America demands an acceptance of an all-out war against imperfection in all aspects of life. It calls upon the application of technologies to end imperfections. These technologies are so meshed as to produce a massive and nebulous matrix in which goals other than the goal of the perfection of the system are lost to view. The system is capable of repairing itself, of isolating and then eliminating the areas of imperfection that arise.[37] Rural man is

35. Robert K. Merton, foreword to Jacques Ellul, *The Technological Society* (New York: Random House, 1964), p. vi.

36. H. Bleibtreau, "Introduction to the American Edition" in Friedrich Juenger, *The Failure of Technology* (Hinsdale, Ill.: Henry Regnery, 1949), p. viii.

37. For a biting critique of the pessimistic literature on the technoculture see Ferkiss' enjoyable volume, *Technological Man*.

now alone with his machines. The internal logic of the system
provides that he direct his attention to the system and not to
his fellows. His neighbors are no longer his principal sources of
aid or community. Each man is more complete and individual.
Technique has isolated him in a way no amount of physical
distance could. When his machines malfunction, he is drawn
back to the system. Whereas earlier he might have gone next
door to borrow his neighbor's bull, now the system provides an
artificial inseminator. Whereas before he swapped access to his
flowing spring in a dry summer for access to his neighbor's convenient wood lot in a cold winter, now the system provides electric heat and artesian wells.

   This understanding of rural society is completely at odds
with the contemporary view of a rural America where interpersonal relations endure, where man can live and grow outside
the chaos and hustle of modern America, where life can be a
communion with nature—simple, understandable, good. The gap
between the myth and reality of Vermont grows ever wider,
pushed by a pastoral ideal that America clings to almost desper-
ately.[38] As the nation's nomadic multitudes grappled with the
cultural shock[39] that has accompanied the growth of technique, they turned their eyes to northern New England and
other rural areas (but especially Vermont) as the national
homeland, supplier of Christmas card scenery, Puritan virtue,
and maple syrup. The Vermont State Development Department
underlined the words of Bernard DeVoto in its advertising
campaigns: "There is no more Yankee than Polynesian in me,
but when I go to Vermont, I feel like I am traveling toward my
own place." The myth reads that Vermont is a land of home
places as recorded in the prints of Currier and Ives. But the
home places are gone. The myth reads that Vermont is filled
with neighbors who fend for themselves, tend their home fires,
and help each other out of snow banks in the winter. But many
of the home fires are dead and the hill people are huddled in
trailer parks, where land speculation has left them. The myth
reads that Vermont is a land of hillside Jerseys, farm boys gnaw-

---

38. Leo Marx, *The Machine in the Garden: Technology and the Pastoral
Ideal in America* (New York: Oxford University Press, 1964).
   39. Alvin Toffler, *Future Shock* (New York: Random House, 1970).

ing timothy, and general stores with big black stoves. But a few beef cows (raised for fun and not especially for profit) have replaced the Jerseys, the farm boys have vanished, and the general stores have turned into supermarkets. The myth promotes the Vermonter as the universal neighbor, outwardly hostile to outsiders and imbued with the spirit of community at home. But the rural dweller is now by himself even more than the city dweller in the traffic jam, the crowded elevator, the waiting line at lunch. Now the rural man is completely alone, entrapped by technology, cut away from interpersonal relations, linked only to the system whence comes the governing criteria of his activities.

What manner of political system will he develop?

Agenda and Conflict

In a recent history of American political parties, Ladd explains his use of "agenda" as an investigatory construct:

Every society generates its different coalitions of political interests, and these in turn make demands on the public sector. The many relationships of contending groups and interests come together in conflict situations, involving the scope and substance of disagreement over public policies and the relative strength of the several sides to these disagreements. The political agenda encompasses those things which the political system is concerned with and the manner, from symbolic representation to formal policy responses, in which it deals with them.[40]

Thus the American agenda in the early years was the "logical working out of equalitarianism." [41] The agenda of the post Civil War period was "the supplanting of rural-agricultural societies by urban-industrial societies."[42] Following this thinking, we may say that the politics of the modern rural technopolity

40. Everett C. Ladd, Jr., *American Political Parties* (New York: W. W. Norton, 1970), p. 2.
41. Ibid., p. 57.
42. Ibid., p. 110.

involves the development of a new syndrome of public interests. The agenda that is passing is the "service" agenda. The coming new one is an "environmental" agenda.

The service agenda involved the creation and maintenance of a superior public service component in a society awakened to the reality that the urban-industrial revolution had somehow passed it by or at least was a long time in coming. Development was promoted, but concern over the fact that it did not arrive was minimal. In a very real sense Vermont had already grappled with the national agenda ("the supplanting of rural agricultural societies by urban-industrial societies", i.e. development) and lost.[43]

With the explosion of railroad building in the mid-nineteenth century, the state had seemed to be answering the economic imperatives at large throughout the country. But the coming of the railroads was not followed by urban industrialism. Population growth stagnated. When the sheep farmers left, they were replaced by dairy farmers. The mills began to disappear from the stream sides. Finally, the railroads themselves began to retract their services. By the time of World War I it was clear that Vermont had been cut off from the urban-industrial revolution. Development-as-agenda died, and the state settled into building its public services in spite of its tiny population base and lack of industrialization. It also began to accent its own distinctiveness, promoting tourism, helping its farmers, and generally relishing the fact that it, indeed, represented the "Last Stand of the Yankees."

Though Vermont escaped the urban-industrial revolution, it has not escaped the technological revolution. It is the pressures of the latter that have caused the shift to the new agenda, which involves the relationship of Vermont's physical-cultural environment to the massive forces from outside the state which seek to alter it. It will develop in two phases. In the first, the political system will be occupied in solving the problem of how to keep Vermont for Vermonters and at the same time preserve the high level of public services to which the people are accustomed. Viewed nationally, the program will seem negative and selfish.

43. Many might now argue that in the final analysis Vermont won that struggle.

Internally, it will be accepted by a large majority of the citizens. During the time of the service agenda, Vermont did not consider urban-industrial development a top priority, but it did promote its recreational industry, its tourist trade, and a cadre of summer people whose places inflated local tax lists.

Vermont was "the beckoning country." Before the maturity of the technological revolution in Vermont, before the techno-culture of megalopolis began to "need" Vermont, the beckoning call of the Green Mountain State had little impact. Busy urban men had no great longing for the rural life, especially when it seemed there was plenty of it to be had. The technocrat, however, with much leisure time, finds rural life appealing, especially since it seems to be a scarce commodity. By the middle of the 1960's it became apparent that communications and transportation within as well as to and from Vermont made the beckoning-country theme potent. The two technocultures, rural and urban-industrial, had finally merged. Vermont became an appendage to megalopolis—its greenery a natural vacuum, its abandoned homesteads natural retreats for the upper middle classes. Given the imperatives of Ellul's technique, what other function would do for this unsettled tract of land resting so handily near the great East Coast population belt?

Vermont's decision to resist became clear with the election in 1972 of Thomas Salmon as governor. His campaign openly promoted the theme of Vermont for Vermonters. On statewide television he called explicitly for an end to the theme of the beckoning country. In his inaugural address he reasserted the position that "Vermont was not for sale," with prolonged applause from the legislature. Spurred by the national concern over the environment and counting heavily on the fact that Vermont is a polity—socialized to accept and promote values as a community with self identity—the state's leadership seems committed to guarding the integrity of the ecological status quo, especially the clean air and water. Indeed, in his last news conference as governor in December 1972, Deane Davis named the reordering of priorities with ecology above development as the major accomplishment in his four years as governor.

This absolute shifting of agenda is a profound occurrence in the history of Vermont. While the old agenda was dominant there was no concerted effort to decry urban-industrial development, simply an awareness that it probably could not be had. At the same time there was a continual attempt to promote the beckoning-country theme as a means of financing the public service component. Now the agenda deal with the problems surrounding a rejection of both urban-industrial and recreational development.

This rejection is totally new for Vermont. Here is a rural area that wants no more city dwellers either as tourists or as summer people and is capable of organized resistance to them at the highest levels. In sum, here is a situation where technology preceded population growth and the reaction of the polity has been consciously to reject development and the "progress" that goes with it. Phase one of the environmental agenda may last for some time. Its staying power is greatly enhanced by the cohesion of Vermont as a society and the fact that much of the land has already been taken up or priced out of the range of most people. There will be no waves of have nots immigrating to Vermont as has been the pattern in much of the settlement of America. Moreover, the stakes of victory are important enough to hone resistance.

Two factors in particular will refocus the changed outlook positively. The second phase of the environmental agenda, which will deal with promoting new connections with the rest of the nation, will come about first, because the state will find it cannot maintain strong services on its own in the age of technology the way it had during the urban-industrial era. Secondly, the dynamics and inherent nature of technology discussed above will invoke the final check on those who opt to hold Vermont for Vermonters. Just as the national technological system destroyed the Vermont hillside through the workings of agricultural economics at the national level, the same system will determine the ultimate role Vermont will play in the future of the country. If that means the nation needs a playground for its East Coast megalopolis and Vermont is the best choice, then Vermont will be a playground. Simply stated, in the end Vermont will be what the nation wants it to be. How long the state continues to protect rather than promote its environment will depend in large part on national interests and the willingness of the people to accept huge tax loads. To the cadre of politicians who are able to detect the shift in the phases of the environmental agenda will go political success. In 1972 Thomas Salmon tied himself perfectly to phase one of the new agenda, and the result was the greatest electoral upset in the history of the state.

Agenda deal with conflict. In the past the service agenda reflected the conflict between those who saw urban-industrial development as crucial to the future of the state (Democrats, for the most part, and some constellations of liberal Republicans), and those who concentrated on promoting Yankee virtues, a healthy agricultural sector, maintenance of existing business concerns, and improved public services (mostly Republicans). The latter were in control of the state and its policies, as the rejection of the Green Mountain Parkway shows. As the service agenda are replaced by the environmental agenda, conflict in rural politics will center on the struggle between holders of the community axiom, which was supportive of the service agenda, and holders of the system axiom, which is supportive of the new agenda.

The community axiom holds that man is happiest when in close contact with others (but not too many others) like himself in places whose boundaries are easily understood and where life styles are in plain view. His political ideology is essentially parochial. That is to say, he sees politics from close up, rejects expertise in social affairs, and places local problems at the top of his priorities.[44] Local problems can best be solved by local people. The community axiom is held by three kinds of people. First, there are the hill people, whose parents lived off the land. Unlike many of their generation they did not leave the state when they graduated from high school. They began to take up residences, many in mobile homes on the fringes of the villages, equipped with a pickup truck, a deer rifle, and a love for and memory of the life of the autonomic hill farmer. Most of these people work in service industries, on the big valley farms, in construction, or on the highways for the state or town governments. They are locals not by temperament but because the issues have forced them to be. They oppose centralism because the state has taken away the deer herd, initiated zoning regulations, and controlled use of the snowmobile. These are not, as many would like to suggest, "easy rider" outcasts hung up on

44. Ladd, "Changing Face," p. 256.

status and fearful of the outer world. They are the nearest thing to populists that rural society has. It would be close to describe them as kin to Litt's Yeoman class in Massachusetts, but they are probably too isolated from the decision-making apparatus,[45] and are more closely related to the Swamp Yankees who allegedly inhabit Massachusetts.[46]

The second group of locals is the old Yankee elite. Litt calls them "Patricians."[47] For these people the community axiom is culture. Most are retired or involved in the ownership or management of some kind of local concern. Unlike the landless, native working class outside the village, their prime concern is nostalgia for the good old days. They still hold most of the leadership posts in local government, attend town meetings with regularity, and will oppose centralization to the bitter end.

The third group of adherents to the community axiom is the intellectual and artisan left. For them the axiom is ideology. These are the forces of Charles A. Reich who believe in "localism now!"[48] Most are newcomers. Young, they have come to rural America in droves in recent years to "do their thing," which involves protecting the integrity of little things—the one-room schoolhouse, the maple sugar place, the town meeting, and anything that does not smack of bureaucracy. They are backed by a growing intellectual cadre of the kind that dreamed of "maximum feasible participation" during Kennedy's days in the White House.[49] Thus help has come to the populist-conservative right from the most unlikely place—the new left. At this particular time, therefore, the community axiom seems to be holding its own. In coming paragraphs we will argue that this cannot last, but for the moment, buttressed by a new intellectualism, the community axiom is holed up in the town meeting hall with lots of water and ammunition.[50]

45. Edgar Litt, *The Political Cultures of Massachusetts* (Cambridge: MIT Press, 1965), pp. 3-27.

46. Lockard, *New England State Politics,* pp. 130-45.

47. Litt, pp. 3-27.

48. Charles A. Reich, *The Greening of America* (New York: Random House, 1970).

49. Daniel P. Moynihan, *Maximum Feasible Misunderstanding* (New York: The Free Press, 1966).

50. Frank M. Bryan, "Town Meeting Support in Vermont," *National Civic Review,* 61 (1972), 348-52.

The system axiom, on the other hand, holds that man is happiest in a rational "arms length" relationship with others—lots of others—preferably of different varieties. Issues should be judged long range from a statewide or national perspective. A Black Studies program may make no sense to the people of Glover or Danby or Woodstock or Barre, but these local understandings must adjust to the broader interest. Having accepted a wider view of the public good, the adherents to the system axiom necessarily continue by calling for program guidelines and criteria that are spawned in national or state consciousness.

Although the system axiom holds that there is a kind of therapeutic value in a developed and enduring sense of community, when measured against objective standards of living such as swift and safe travel on the highways, improved medical facilities, dental treatment in the grade schools, or (and this is the crusher) preservation of the integrity of the state's natural character and pure environment—the very reference point that holders of the community axiom harken to in their subconscious— "sense of community" must take a back seat. Because the system axiom is cosmopolitan, it cannot build programs from an evaluation of any particular societal malfunction. It must universalize. Program sources, therefore, come more and more from intellectual cadres: committees, stables of technicians, foundations, or any programmatic group that is capable of dissociating itself from the particular good to focus on the general. This overarching nature of the programs coupled with a desire to do as much as possible to attain goals (which cost money) means that, notwithstanding built-in feedback mechanisms for evaluation, the only operative guiding principle of the system axiom is efficiency.

The great portion of rural residents is accepting the system axiom. This majority is made up of three groups. First, there are the farmers. Technocrats to the core, they understand that their survival depends on a political system geared to the language of science and progress—in a word, efficiency. It is not the life style of farming they are interested in, it is the economics of agriculture—the technique of producing more pounds of milk per cow and feeding more cows per acre of land. No single group has been forced to accept as many regulations from the system as the farmer. Now he is hardened to it. Now his day-to-day behavior is governed by decisions made by socially remote persons. He may delay his haying a week longer than his neighbor, but, more likely, both will follow the advice of their extension agent, who tells them over the radio during breakfast when the best weather in June will come.

The second group is the tertiary middle class. They operate the technopolity. Strictly speaking, they are the technique incarnate. Their employment makes them acutely aware of the decision matrix that keeps the system breathing. For them the community axiom is a luxury that modern society simply cannot afford.

The technocratic elite is the third class. Well educated, urbane, they govern the superstructure that the tertiary middle class operates. Some are natives who came back after college. Most are escapees from megalopolis. They accept, even promote, the symbols of the community axiom but are fully certain that they cannot have their cake and eat it too. Town meeting should be preserved for community therapy, but decisions that count will have to be made by the system.

There are several good reasons to suppose the system axiom is the way of the future in the rural polity. First, the groups that subscribe to the community axiom do so for distinctly different reasons: the populists for negative reasons, the Yankee elite for nostalgic reasons, the Left for ideological reasons. The axiom in no way serves as a reference point for these groups. There are profound antagonisms among them, and their common linkage to the community axiom is a product of the accidents of history. The Yankee elite turns up its nose at the populists, patronizes the artisan left, and despises the younger new left. The left, in turn, despises the Yankee elite, who live on the high streets in the villages, and relates to—but fears—the populists. The populists give a grudging respect to the Yankee elite but do not get on with them. They intensely dislike the left. Politics does indeed make strange bedfellows.

Secondly, the system axiom has adopted the mythology that has developed around the concept of Vermonter (à la Texan), and this mythology has served to weld them and camouflage their basic antagonism to the community axiom. The technocratic elite, especially, dearly love to promote their distinctiveness as Vermonters. It would be tempting to conclude that this is a parochial detour in their ideational map. It is not. They have built this status referent into the system as neatly as they do their calls for zoning or daycare centers.

Another strength of the system axiom stems directly from this drive for status. Holders of the system axiom see the preservation of the system as the sine qua non of their status. For the technocratic elite it is the status of the country gentleman with his Morgan horse and twenty acres of land. For the tertiary middle class it is the status of job security and an uncluttered ladder upward for their children via education and other benefits that flow throughout the system. For the farmer it is simply the status of survival and probationary membership in a class that only recently was devoid of farmers: the well-heeled, technocratic, upper middle class. All these groups see the system as completely necessary to the preservation of their status, while the holders of the community axiom do not.

Another great strength of the system axiom is that its supporters have a program, a design for the future, and they are capable of articulating this program in a fairly unified manner. Their plan is linked to their status, and calls frankly for a halt to urban-industrial (as opposed to technological) progress. The people of the system axiom are involved with such organizations as Zero Population Growth, the Green Mountain Club, or any group committed generally to protect the environment. They seem to have latched on to the agenda of the rural polity, and it has given them a cohesion of purpose that cannot be matched by supporters of the community axiom. Moreover, most holders of the community axiom also support the agenda in at least some fashion. The Yankee elite knows that property tax relief will come only through planning at the state level and not through decisions made in town meeting. It will take technique. The populists like the agenda because it calls for a slowdown in the influx of out-of-staters. Populists do not particularly like the out-of-staters' exploitation of the land. The left likes the system axiom for essentially the same reason. They know it will take "straight" technocrats to preserve their Walden. It is not so much that they dislike the out-of-staters; it is that they got there first.

The final and most powerful weapon is that the axiom itself is only an atom in the complex molecule that is la technique at large. For the system axiom in the rural polity is the political manifestation of the broader cultural ethic that we have gone to some lengths to explain earlier. The erasure of the community axiom in the last analysis is the consequence of the ascendency of technique.

We suggested earlier that when the metamorphosis of rural society had ended, when the conflict between the community axiom and the system axiom was over, when the new techno-polity had emerged, we might not particularly like what had been created. This statement implies value judgments based on ideals that are inherent in the American political tradition. The point here is simply that the nature of modern rural political systems will run counter to these ideals.

To begin with, as we have said, the agenda of the new rural technopolity calls for closing the doors to outsiders. The ruling majority will define its status in terms of space, atmospheric purity, and solitude, not wealth. There will be no propensity to share the one commodity that will be worth more than gold in America—life in a spacious, noiseless playground equipped with No Trespassing signs. Vermonters are planning an optimum limit on the state's population. Since the state is a self-conscious identity that is known to and articulated by the public sector—and since those in control of the public sector are holders of the system axiom that has prescribed such values as legitimate goals of the polity—there is every reason to suspect that resistance to outsiders will be strong.

Land prices have already skyrocketed beyond the reach of most people. Antipollution laws (they have been called the toughest in the nation) have snatched much of the land from the hands of large developers of both high- and low-income living places. Loopholes are being closed in existing statutes. All across the state the murmur for zoning is growing into a roar. This is not to say there is no conflict over the implementation of the environmental agenda; there is, and much of it is intense. But the balance of power seems to be slipping into the hands of the agenda promoters.

This suggests another not so pleasant characteristic of the modern rural technopolity—a paranoiac attitude. The mythology that has always surrounded the ruralite has shown him to be negative to outsiders. But this was a tongue-in-cheek skepticism, a minding-one's-business aloofness generated more by a natural mistrust of things that are different than hostility to those who are seen to be threatening one's very way of life. When a respected pair of Vermont lawmakers announced recently that they were prepared to man the turnstiles at the state's borders to keep out newcomers, there was some laughter that was too nervous to be genuine, followed by an embarrassed silence. The two had let slip what seems to be on the minds of many rural people: ruralism is a good thing which, by definition, can only be shared up to a point. And that point may soon be reached.

In the twilight of the urban-industrial age the old stigmas have been cut away from rural life and grafted to the forces of status. These forces are as powerful as the ones that have protected white suburbia from the blacks or the rich from the poor. Realization of the enormous strength of status drives, coupled with an understanding of how very pleasant technology has made life in the backwoods, makes it more clear why Vermonters pay the highest per-capita personal tax in the nation coincidental with no visible program to develop the kinds of economic inputs to help lessen the load. Rural people like what they have and are willing to pay heavily to keep it theirs. The rural technopolity will be difficult to enter, and if entered may prove a hostile camping ground. It therefore seems reasonable to argue that modern rural society may come to lose at least one value traditionally ascribed to rural life in America: *receptivity*. Some might call it openness, some liberalism, some even freedom.

Another element of the American political experience that may soon disappear in rural America is what Nisbet calls *sense of community*.[51] Without this quality (now being claimed by ideologues of both left and right), rural society will be typified by a raw individualism, untempered by any collective identity with institutions. Local government and the town meeting may be preserved for therapeutic reasons, but soon they will become a sham, and rural man will be cast off from moorage with his government. It is ironic at this particular point in history to

51. Robert A. Nisbet, *The Quest for Community* (New York: Oxford University Press, 1953).

watch the functional death of the Vermont town and with it the end of a profound history of localism, while in urban America cadres of sociopolitical engineers are working feverishly to install neighborhood decision-making structures.[52] Without la technique pure individualism was impossible in rural America. With technology it appears inescapable.

We will not deemphasize the negative overtones of such a development. The individual linked only to an unseen technological matrix for survival is anathema to the concept of liberal democracy as we know it. The alarm has already been sounded by such unlikely intellectual confederates as Nisbet and Reich and needs no reemphasis here. What does need strong emphasis is that rural man without his *community* (and this situation will be a new one in American history) will maximize dangers already well articulated—dangers centered around the loss of another value of American sociopolitical culture, a *sense* of community.

Finally, two other developments are combining to produce conjectures about the future of the rural technopolity. One is the atomization of the input phase of the political system, and the other is the electorate's increasing interest in outputs. The party system, for instance, which in the one-party era provided visible recruitment channels, is giving way to a network of personality-oriented groups with pronounced kaleidoscopic tendencies. This phenomenon helped in the disintegration of the Republican hegemony in the 1950's, prevented meaningful organizational efforts on the part of the Democrats in the 1960's when they had a chance (but failed) to consolidate their successes, seemed to color the revived Republican Party after Hoff, and clearly was at work when the Salmon forces swept to victory after abandoning George McGovern.

In a recent special primary election for Vermont's lone Congressional seat the Republicans sent six candidates to the voters, the Democrats four. Moreover, the last decade has seen a burst of third-party activity all across the ideological spectrum. Though organized party behavior in the legislature is more pronounced,

52. The literature on this movement is growing swiftly. See, for instance, Milton Kotler, *Neighborhood Government* (New York: Bobbs-Merrill, 1969).

it is falling apart in the electorate. Add to this trend the fact
that the revolution in campaign financing has arrived in rural
America piggyback on technology (neither party can depend
simply on party coffers for campaign funds, and both are turning more and more to monies raised through personal organizations) and the suspicion grows that future politics will be of the
hop-scotch variety: with the party label traveling from one well-
financed clique to the next. Recruiting here and there for people to carry the colors, parties will fail to develop a stable of
potential candidates through internal organizational efforts.
Party discipline in the legislature will be real in name only, and
clustering will develop around personalities. All these changes
will weaken the linkage between citizen and government. This
is no time to rehash the party-discipline debate; yet it is difficult to escape the notion that the rural technopolity will house
the kind of political system and agenda in which the credit and
discredit for policies performed will be linked to relatively spontaneous and somewhat invisible personalistic cadres, rather than
to enduring and visible institutions.

The atomization of inputs is developing parallel to the
growth of an electorate that is increasingly concerned with
outputs. In the phraseology of Almond and Verba the political
culture will become more akin to the "subject" culture and less
like the "civic" culture.[53] Numerically tiny, scattered about,
agreed on the essential character of the outputs (the system
axiom), committed to carrying a tremendous tax load to pay
for services, and infused with the ethic of technocracy, which
calls only for efficiency and perfection—rural populations will
not be capable of sustaining meaningful lumps in the input
stages or the feedback loop of the political system. They will be
concerned more with the "taking form" and less with the "giving to" of the polity. Interpreting Elazar's work on political
culture, Sharkansky underlines this fact. Vermont's political
culture was typed by Elazar as being moralistic (which we have
termed the community-axiom culture). Sharkansky, whose interest is public administrations, concludes that this kind of culture "should coincide with high levels of taxation and govern-

53. Gabriel A. Almond and Sidney Verba, *The Civic Culture* (Princeton: Princeton University Press, 1963).

ment expenditure and with generous levels of public service" and "a Moralist culture should coexist with a large and well paid administration . . . "[54] It is argued here that the participatory mood of the moralistic culture (community-axiom culture) is dying out. Left behind is a residue of output mentality.

In sum, these two phenomena (the atomization of organized input mechanisms and a populace interested primarily with outputs) will spawn hardened bureaucratic political systems in rural America. With it may come the loss of a final quality of American politics, civic participation. Some might call it the loss of popular government, the loss of pluralism, some even the loss of democracy. Outputs will become more bureaucratic, decisions will be delegated by legislators to the administration, and the agencies will pick up the feedback loop and bypass the legislature. Because inputs will not be tied to factions with identities that endure, because electoral politics will be controlled by personalized, and therefore transitory, power centers, because the prevailing ideology will be of technocracy demanding only efficiency and system maintenance through rationalism, and because decision-making will be conducted for the most part by agencies of professional technocrats, the modern rural technopolity will develop into an intensified bureaucratic state.

Although standard thinking tends to link bureaucracy to the urban condition, we might argue that modern ruralism provides the healthiest of environmental atmospheres for the growth of bureaucracy. Now that the "decision audience" (those people whose day-to-day activities are controlled by socially remote people)[55] makes up nearly 100 percent of the population, now that technology has isolated rural man from his neighbors, and now that the community axiom is being erased, government by rationalism will find the living good in rural areas. We might even venture to say that, while community politics are city bound, the politics of efficiency are headed for the back beyond.

54. Ira Sharkansky, *Public Administration: Policy Making in Governmental Agencies* (2nd ed., Chicago: Markham Publishing Company, 1972), p. 198.
55. G. Lowell Field, *Comparative Political Development: The Precedent of the West* (Ithaca, N.Y.: Cornell University Press, 1967), p. 40.

Given populations that are small, scattered, homogeneous, steeped in the technological ethic, and agreed on the agenda of government (to protect personal status defined in terms of space, physical isolation, and environmental purity), rural political systems will become more closed than open, more individualistic than communal, and politically more passive than active. We have suggested, moreover, that they will become too closed, too individualistic, and too passive to be healthy. In making this suggestion we established normative criteria—criteria that have traditionally been labeled *good* in the American political experience. These criteria we then inflated to include such terms as freedom and democracy.

To engage in such intellectual gyrations is defenseless if the intention is to conceptualize from empirical referents found in contemporary rural political systems. Our purpose, however, was simply to accomplish two goals. First, cutting oneself away from value judgments while discussing politics futuristically is, like felling trees in a windstorm, ticklish business. Our hope is only that, through the exaggeration of value-laden propositions, we will strike nerves cleanly and openly. Those who harken to such propositions as "power to the people" or "maximum feasible participation," or to the input processes of the political system will find the sledding tough in the modern rural technopolity. On the other hand, rural areas of the future will beckon to those who are satisfied that the input mechanisms have been adequately treated and that political systems should be about the business of developing more efficient delivery techniques. Government in rural areas will be efficient and bureaucratic. There is no other way to say it, and there are many "good" reasons to be happy about it. (The very fact that we feel obliged to underline this fact points to the difficulties of discussing the administrative state in the face of traditional American political values.)

Surely no one understands the need for and value of perfection and efficiency better than rural man. Those who continually confront and cope with nature are sharply aware of the penalties of dealing with her in a sloppy manner. Nature is harsh and demanding. To appreciate its beauty one must first come to grips with its realities. Soft June evenings may be a torment of black flies. Beautiful black canopies of wintertime stars bring subzero temperatures that freeze fingers and toes. The dark green under the south kitchen window comes only after months of dull greyness that can dim the brightest of spirits. Just as the rural man welcomes the aerosol can of bug repellent in June, thermal underwear and insulated boots in December, and the television in March, so he will also welcome the administrative state.

Secondly, we predict such a bleak future for the modern rural technopolity in terms of traditional American political values because the contrary view enjoys such wide acceptance. If we are guilty of employing doomsday arguments, it is partly because the target is so large. Nearly all contemporary assessments of a journey to rural America picture the experience as a return to the good old days, to traditional American values, to a simple life of interpersonal relations where individuals still control events in society generally and in the government as well. No doubt there is much of yesteryear left in rural America. In Vermont, for instance, you can see an honest-to-goodness cannon-shooting contest in Royalton, an old-time fiddler's show in Cabot or Newbury, and ox-pulling at the Tunbridge Fair. Yet the very fact that these events are produced as exhibitions lends support to our case. A tour of modern rural society is not a return to something that is elsewhere long past. It is a tour of something new—the modern rural technopolity. As a matter of fact, if one is looking for a simple life of interpersonal relations, he might find the hunting better on Bunker Hill Street in Charleston, in the core of Washington, D.C., or in downtown Baltimore.

The first century that followed the signing of the Declaration of Independence saw the nation conquer what Elazar has called the rural land frontier.[56] Preparations are now under way in Philadelphia for the celebration of our Bicentennial. During the last hundred years the people of America drew together through the urban-industrial revolution, until now 70 percent of them live on only one percent of the land. As we embark on still another century of national life, Americans are beginning to inch away from the cities. In the two decades following World War II

56. Daniel Elazar, *American Federalism: A View from the States* (New York: Thomas Y. Crowell, 1966).

the process began in earnest as suburbia expanded and spilled over into megalopolis. Given continued population growth, new societal values focusing on living space, and the technological maturity of rural areas, it seems clear that the next century will involve a reconquering of the "rural land frontier."

This reconquering will be no simple matter of returning home for turkey in November, town meeting in March, and skinny dipping in July. Rural areas have leapfrogged the urban-industrial era into the age of technology and are developing complex and perhaps unique sociopolitical cultures. It will be necessary to understand these cultures as people return to the back beyond.

Appendix

Cluster-Bloc Analysis

Our particular concern regarding the use of cluster-bloc analysis was with the problem of absenteeism in a large legislative body (246 members) when a limited number of roll calls was being analyzed.

In the construction of indexes of agreement, three methods are available. Each provides a different treatment of the "absent" response to a roll call. For instance, the total number of agreements between two members on a given set of roll calls may be recorded as the agreement score. In the following sequence, the agreement score between Legislators A and B would be 6.

Voters		*Roll calls*										
		1	*2*	*3*	*4*	*5*	*6*	*7*	*8*	*9*	*10*	
Voter	A	Y	Y	Y	A	N	Y	N	N	Y	Y	IA = 6
Voter	B	Y	A	Y	N	N	A	N	N	A	Y	

Y = yes
N = no
A = absent
IA = index of agreement

The problem is that treating absences as disagreements may confuse the relationship between A and B. Can it be presumed, in other words, that on roll call 4, if A had voted, he would have disagreed with B? Or can it be presumed that if B had voted on roll calls 2, 6, and 9, he would have disagreed with A? This is called an absolute agreement measure and serves to penalize the habitually absent legislator from high scores with anybody, since absences are considered disagreements with all.

The second method of dealing with absent votes is to consider them missing data. The resulting score may be called a relative index, in that it measures only those roll calls on which both members were voting, by dividing the total number of agreements by the total number of roll calls on which both voted and multiplying by one hundred, as follows:

$$IA = \frac{TA}{T} \times 100$$

Where: IA = index of agreement
         TA = total number of agreements
          T = total number of roll calls
              on which both vote

In the hypothetical case described, the index of agreement is 100. Roll calls 2, 4, 6, and 9 have simply been dropped from the calculations.

A third method of measuring agreement was devised by Arend Lijphart, who argues that abstentions in voting in the United Nations may be considered "partial agreement" with both sides of an issue. He therefore gave abstentions a score of .5 as follows:

$$IA = T + .5PA$$

Where: IA = index of agreement
          T = total number of agreements
         PA = number of partial agreements

The index of agreement score would be IA = 8.[1]

The first problem in deciding which of the three methods described above is best fitted to a particular legislature is to make a judgment on the nature of absences. Are they to be viewed as voting behavior? In Vermont it is reasonable to conclude that absences were not to be considered voting behavior. The environmental characteristics of the legislature lead to the conclusion that absences were haphazard happenings and for the most part not the result of strategic decisions. Once this premise has been accepted, it seems appropriate to use the rela-

1. Lee F. Anderson, Meredith W. Watts, Jr., and Allen R. Wilcox, *Legislative Roll Call Analysis* (Evanston, Ill.: Northwestern University Press, 1966), pp. 60-65.

tive agreement measure (number 2 above) and thus consider roll calls on which either member of a pair was absent as missing data.

Yet there are problems in using a strictly relative measure. If nonvoting is considered to be a chance affair, then the probability of obtaining an accurate view of Legislator A's relationship to Legislator B increases with the number of times they are observed voting together. In other words, the set of roll calls on which any two members voted may be considered a sample taken from the entire set of roll calls reviewed. The larger the random sample, the greater the probability that the sample reflects what would have been the case had both members of the pair voted together on the entire set.

Consider the following two pairs of voters on a given set of ten roll calls:

Roll calls	1	2	3	4	5	6	7	8	9	10	
Voter A	Y	Y	N	N	Y	Y	N	N	Y	Y	IA = 80
Voter B	Y	Y	N	Y	Y	Y	Y	N	Y	Y	

Roll calls	1	2	3	4	5	6	7	8	9	10	
Voter A	Y	Y	N	N	Y	Y	N	N	Y	Y	IA = 80
Voter C	A	A	A	A	A	N	N	N	Y	Y	

Although the relative measure indicates a like relationship between A and B, and A and C, the confidence we place in our estimate of relationship A-B is greater than our confidence in our estimate of relationship A-C. Using a simple binomial distribution test, where agreements are considered "successes," the probability of relationship A-B occurring by chance is $p = .043$, while the probability of relationship A-C occurring by chance is $p = .156$.

Since the number of roll calls used in this study was low in several sets, it seemed likely that members with a high rate of absenteeism might receive high index scores merely by chance. In other words, if the cutoff point were established at 60, then a legislator who voted only five times would appear on the matrix with but three agreements. Not only does a decreasing total impair statistical significance, it jeopardizes the meaning of the entire relationship in terms of the policy referent that the roll calls supposedly reflect. There comes a point when enough missing data undermine the study, statistical validity notwithstanding.

The task at hand seemed to be first to avoid maximizing the dangers of considering absences to be disagreements (the absolute scale) and secondly to avoid maximizing the dangers of statistical insignificance and utilization of meaningless data inherent in the relative measure. To avoid these dangers, both a relative and an absolute measure were employed as cutoff points in constructing the matrix. First, it was required that each pair meet a specific level of agreement on all the votes in the set—the index score. In other words, if 100 roll calls made up the set and the index figure were set at 60, then a pair of legislators would have to agree on at least 60 of the 100 roll calls. Having done this, I recorded a higher percentage figure for each pair. If, for instance, an 80 percent score were used in conjunction with a 60 index score, it would mean that every pair considered agreed 80 percent of the time they voted together, and that these agreements were on at least 60 percent of the total roll calls in the set. This may be expressed as follows:

Where: N = total number of roll calls in the set
X = total number of agreements
Y = total number of times pair voted together

Then: X must be 60% of N
X must be 80% of Y

The following is a table of values which indicates how the relationship operates. (Z) marks values that fail to meet a 60–80 score.

N	X	Y	Index	Percent
100	80	90	80	88
100	60	60	60	100
100	60	70	60	86
100	60	80	60	75 (Z)
100	50	60	50 (Z)	83

In this study two cutoff points are used in order to view bloc structure at different levels of agreement. A very high index 70, percent 90 was used to test for highly cohesive clusters. Next, the level was lowered to index 60, percent 80, to take the survey to lower levels of agreement.

The minimal number of agreements required to place two members on the matrix occurred in the 1955 session of the House, when only 20 roll calls were used. In this instance, the lowest totals acceptable are 13 agreements in 16 "complete" votes—that is, both members of the pair are voting. In other words, members of a pair must agree 13 times (65 percent of the roll calls in the set). But these 13 agreements must represent 80 percent or more of the times they voted together. In this case if they voted together 17 times and agreed 13 times, then the percentage would be 76. That would mean the pair would not meet the criteria and would be excluded from the matrix. The criteria for inclusion was therefore 16 complete votes, which places the percentage figure at approximately 81. The probability of this result occurring by chance, using the binomial test, is $p = .0085$.[2] In this way we have required that our relative measure be based on a sample of agreements that is statistically significant.[3] All this means is that if the entire set had been completed instead of only 16 roll calls, the other four would probably not have changed our view of the relationship between the pair of members. This method seemed to solve both the problem of the chronic absentee and the desire to treat absences as random happenings. It also ensures that the resulting clusters are based on a wide spectrum of legislative roll-call activity.

The use of cluster-bloc analysis is not geared in this study to an investigation of intracluster structure. There is no attempt to identify a bloc nucleus or to build clusters from highest correlative pairs. In other words, no attempt was made to distinguish among agreement scores above the minimal level. Therefore, at the 70-90 level, a score of 86-94 would be considered equal to a score of 70-90. In constructing the blocs, matrixes were scanned and rescanned until the largest possible bloc at the min-

2. J. H. Hodges and E. L. Lehmann, *Basic Concepts of Probability and Statistics* (San Francisco, Holden Day, Inc., 1964), p. 168.

3. Peter Willetts, "Cluster-Bloc Analysis and Statistical Inference," *American Political Science Review*, 66 (1972), 569-82.

imal level was identified. Given this configuration, subblocs
(some sharing membership with the original major bloc) were
constructed using the largest possible bloc criteria. It is felt that
this procedure, which emphasizes the bloc structure of a legislative body as a whole at predetermined levels of cohesion rather
than the peculiarities of intrabloc structure, is adequate. Here
we follow the advice of Professors Anderson, Watts, and Wilcox,
who conclude, "The pairs should be ordered so as to reveal
upon completion of the matrix as complete a picture of the
bloc structure of a group as is possible.[4]"

A word about presentation of the data. Because this study
involves fifteen legislative sessions with two views of each, we
were faced with the prospect of presenting sixty different matrixes. Moreover, in some cases a view of the legislature would
reveal five to six separate blocs. Several of these blocs might
share members. The problem seemed to be that of showing the
nature of interbloc agreement in an uncluttered manner.[5] Given
a matrix situation such as the one in Figure XXI, an Index of
Bloc Agreement was improvised to represent the relationship
between blocs.

The Index of Bloc Agreement (IBA) is simply determined by
dividing the number of actual agreements between the members
of two blocs by the number of possible agreements between the
membership of both blocs and multiplying by 100:

$$IBA = \frac{Aa}{Pa} \times 100$$

Where: IBA = index of bloc agreement
          Aa   = actual agreements
          Pa   = possible agreements

The IBA extends, therefore, from 0 (no agreement between
blocs) to 100 (total agreement between blocs, or, in fact, one
bloc).

4. Anderson, p. 68.
5. I found Lijphart's presentation messy and Truman's overly long. See
Arend Lijphart, "The Analysis of Bloc Voting in the General Assembly: A
Critique and a Proposal," *American Political Science Review*, 57 (1963),
902-17, and David Truman, *The Congressional Party* (New York: John
Wiley and Sons, 1959). For a review of both methods, see Anderson, pp.
69-74.

Figure XXI
A Hypothetical Matrix Situation

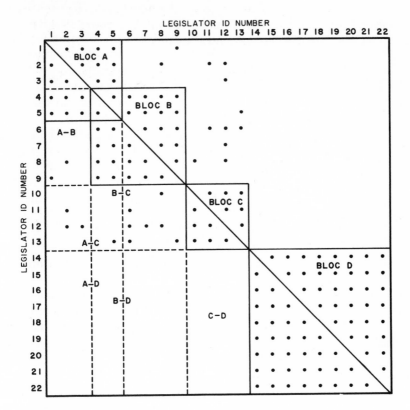

In Figure **XXI** there are four blocs. Three of these are inter-related, and the fourth is independent of all the others. The dotted lines strike off the areas on the matrix where potential agreements between blocs can be found. According to the formula, the IBA for blocs A and B would be:

$$IBA = \frac{20}{30} \times 100 = 67$$

The other relationships on the matrix are as follows:

Blocs	IBA
A-B	67
A-C	20
A-D	0
B-C	33
B-D	0
C-D	0

Bibliographical Essay

This book joins an expanding bloc of studies that is slowly providing both a data base and a wellspring for building hypotheses in the field of comparative state politics. Although the process of scholarship in this area has hardly been sequential, there are certain very simple conceptual handles in the literature that help us to grasp some order from what has been a chaos of publications. I have traced the outlines of this typology in the Introduction to this volume. The purpose here is to display briefly some of the literature that makes up the substance of comparative state politics. I also include some of the other literature that has influenced the development of this volume.

Comparative State Politics

It seems useful to array the literature according to whether or not it is vertical (the "case study" approach, where in-depth analysis of single states is presented in essentially descriptive formats) or horizontal (research concerns are narrowed dramatically to hypotheses geared to comparative techniques using many states as "observations").

The single-state studies are generally of three varieties. First, there are those which use intrastate political subdivisions as observations with which to test hypotheses. The best example of this technique is the literature dealing with the relationship between party competition and size of place. See Heinz Eulau, "The Ecological Basis of Party Systems: The Case of Ohio," *Midwest Journal of Political Science,* 1 (1957), 125-135; Phillips Cutright, "Urbanization and Competitive Party Politics," *Journal of Politics,* 25 (1963), 552-564; and David Gold and John R. Schmidhauser, "Urbanization and Party Competition:

The Case of Iowa," *Midwest Journal of Political Science,* 4 (1960), 62-75. For a review of this literature using cross-state as well as single-state studies, see Philip Coulter and Glen Gordon, "Urbanism and Party Competition: Critique and Redirection of Theoretical Research," *Western Political Quarterly,* 21 (1968), 274-288. West Virginia's counties were used to explain the relationship between certain independent variables and political participation; see Gerald W. Johnson, "Research Note on Political Correlates of Voter Participation: A Deviant Case Analysis," *American Political Science Review,* 65 (1971), 768-776. Secondly, scholars have focused on particular functional components in the political systems of individual states for descriptive purposes and/or hypothesis testing. Most attention has been paid to party systems and the legislature or to relationships between the two.

Studies of state legislatures have clustered around the following topic areas:

(1) *The relationship between independent variables* (such as party discipline and/or apportionment patterns) *and legislative behavior.* See Robert W. Becker, et al., "Correlates of Legislative Voting: Michigan House of Representatives, 1954–1961," *Midwest Journal of Political Science,* 6 (1962), 384-396; Glen T. Broach, "A Comparative Dimensional Analysis of Partisan and Urban-Rural Voting in State Legislatures," *Journal of Politics,* 34 (1972), 905-923 (Broach studies Alabama, Tennessee, Iowa, and Indiana); Frank M. Bryan, "The Metamorphosis of a Rural Legislature," *Polity,* 1 (1968), 191-212; and Alan L. Clem, "Roll Call Voting Behavior in the South Dakota Legislature," *Public Affairs,* 25 (1966), 1-8. Clem's short article is a gold mine of information for this small state and is the kind of effort that is of high value in comparative state politics. See also David R. Derge, "Metropolitan and Outstate Alignments in Illinois and Missouri Legislative Delegations," *American Political Science Review,* 52 (1958), 1051-1065; Thomas R. Dye, "A Comparison of Constituency Influences in the Upper and Lower Chambers of a State Legislature," *Western Political Quarterly,* 14 (1961), 473-480; Thomas A. Flinn, "Party Responsibility in the States: Some Causal Factors," *American Political Science Review,* 58 (1964), 60-71 (Flinn studies Minnesota and Ohio); Sheldon Goldman, *Roll Call Behavior in the Massachusetts*

House of Representatives (Bureau of Government Research, University of Massachusetts, Amherst, 1968); John C. Grumm, "A Factor Analysis of Legislative Behavior," *Midwest Journal of Political Science*, 7 (1963), 336-356; William C. Havard and Loren P. Beth, *The Politics of Mis-Representation: Rural-Urban Conflict in the Florida Legislature* (Baton Rouge, 1962); Murray C. Havens, *City Versus Farm? Urban-Rural Conflict in the Alabama Legislature* (Bureau of Public Administration, University of Alabama, 1957); C. Richard Hofstetter, "Malapportionment and Roll-Call Voting in Indiana, 1923–1963: A Computer Simulation," *Journal of Politics*, 33 (1971), 92-111; Robert J. Huckshorn, "Decision-Making Stimuli in the State Legislative Process," *Western Political Quarterly*, 18 (1965) 164-185; Malcolm E. Jewell, "Party Voting in American State Legislatures," *American Political Science Review*, 49 (1955), 773-791; William J. Keefe, "Comparative Study of the Role of Political Parties in State Legislatures," *Western Political Quarterly*, 9 (1956), 726-742; William J. Keefe, "Parties, Partisanship, and Public Policy in the Pennsylvania Legislature," *American Political Science Review*, 48 (1954), 450-464; Harry F. Kelley, Jr., *Dimensions of Voting in the Tennessee House of Representatives in 1967* (Bureau of Public Administration, University of Tennessee, Knoxville, 1970); Duncan Macrae, Jr., "The Relationship between Roll Call Votes and Constituencies in the Massachusetts House of Representatives," *American Political Science Review*, 46 (1952), 1046-1055; Bruce W. Robeck, "Legislative Partisanship, Constituency and Malapportionment: The Case of California," *American Political Science Review*, 66 (1972), 1246-1255; Robeck, "Urban-Rural and Regional Voting Patterns in the California Senate before and after Reapportionment," *Western Political Quarterly*, 23 (1970), 785-794; William de Rubertis, "How Apportionment with Selected Demographic Variables Relates to Policy Orientation," *Western Political Quarterly*, 22 (1969), 904-920 (de Rubertis' work, like that of Robeck, deals with California). See also Frank J. Sorauf, *Party and Representation: Legislative Politics in Pennsylvania* (New York, 1963).

(2) *Legislative Pressure Group Analysis.* The following studies deal with pressure groups in the legislative arena: William Buchanan, *Legislative Partisanship: The Deviant Case of Califor-*

nia (Berkeley, 1963); Wilder Crane, Jr., "A Test of Effectiveness of Interest-Group Pressures on Legislators," *Southwestern Social Science Quarterly*, 41 (1960), 335-340; Oliver Garceau and Corinne Silverman, "A Pressure Group and the Pressured: A Case Report," *American Political Science Review*, 48 (1954), 672-691; Jay S. Goodman, "A Note on Legislative Research: Labor Representation in Rhode Island," *American Political Science Review*, 61 (1967), 468-473; Bernard D. Kolasa, "Lobbying in the Nonpartisan Environment: The Case of Nebraska," *Western Political Quarterly*, 24 (1971), 65-78. Kolasa's study uses the nonpartisan situation to retest (and verify) the hypothesis that party strength and interest group strength in legislatures are inversely related. See also Samuel C. Patterson, "The Role of the Lobbyist: The Case of Oklahoma," *Journal of Politics*, 25 (1963), 72-92.

(3) *Legislative Elite Analysis.* James D. Barber, *The Lawmakers: Recruitment and Adaptation to Legislative Life* (New Haven, 1965); Harlan Hahn, "Leadership Perceptions and Voting Behavior in a One-Party Legislative Body," *Journal of Politics*, 32 (1970), 140-155; Victor S. Hjelm and Joseph P. Pisciotte, "Profiles and Careers of Colorado State Legislators," *Western Political Quarterly*, 21 (1968), 698-722; Kenneth Janda, Henry Teune, Melvin Kahn, and Wayne Francis, *Legislative Politics in Indiana: A Preliminary Report to the 1961 General Assembly* (Bureau of Government Research, Indiana University, Bloomington, 1961; this brief document provides much useful data); John B. McConaughy, "Certain Personality Factors of State Legislators in South Carolina," *American Political Science Review*, 44 (1950), 897-903; Leonard Ruchelman, *Political Careers: Recruitment through the Legislature* (Rutherford, New Jersey, 1970); Lester G. Seligman, "Political Change: Legislative Elites and Parties in Oregon," *Western Political Quarterly*, 17 (1964), 177-187; John W. Soule, "Future Political Ambitions and the Behavior of Incumbent State Legislators," *Midwest Journal of Political Science*, 13 (1969), 439-454. These studies of elites are concerned with the following states respectively: Connecticut, Indiana, Colorado, Indiana, New York, Oregon, and Michigan.

(4) *Studies on power relationships in state legislatures.* James J. Best, "Influence in the Washington House of Representa-

tives," *Midwest Journal of Political Science,* 15 (1971), 547-562; Wayne L. Francis, "Influence and Interaction in a State Legislative Body," *American Political Science Review,* 56 (1962), 953-960; Malcolm B. Parsons, "Quasi-Partisan Conflict in a One-Party Legislative System: The Florida Senate, 1947-1961," *American Political Science Review,* 56 (1962), 605-614; Samuel C. Patterson, "Dimensions of Voting Behavior in a One-Party State Legislature," *Public Opinion Quarterly,* 26 (1962), 185-200; Patterson, "The Role of the Deviant in the State Legislative System: The Wisconsin Assembly," *Western Political Quarterly,* 14 (1961), 460-472.

Another functional component of the political system that has been studied in individual states is the political party outside the legislature. Representative of these studies are F. Glenn Abney, "Partisan Realignment in a One-Party System: The Case of Mississippi," *Journal of Politics,* 31 (1969), 1102-1106; Numan V. Bartley, *From Thurmond to Wallace: Political Tendencies in Georgia, 1948–1968* (Baltimore, 1970); Robert E. Burton, *Democrats of Oregon: The Pattern of Minority Politics, 1900–1956* (University of Oregon Books, Eugene, 1970; Burton's work is excellent political history and a strong contribution to the literature on breakthrough politics); Thomas A. Flinn, "The Outline of Ohio Politics," *Western Political Quarterly,* 13 (1960), 702-721; Murray B. Levin, "The Atrophy of Party Organization in Massachusetts," in *The Grass Roots,* ed. Erwin C. Buell and William E. Brigman (Glenview, Illinois, 1968); Stephen B. and Vera H. Sarasohn, *Political Party Patterns in Michigan* (Detroit, 1957); Lester R. Seligman, "Political Recruitment and Party Structure: A Case Study," *American Political Science Review,* 55 (1961), 77-86; Allan P. Sindler, "Bifactional Rivalry as an Alternative to Two-Party Competition in Louisiana," *American Political Science Review,* 49 (1955), 641-662; William H. Standing and James A. Robinson, "Inter-party Competition and Primary Contesting: The Case of Indiana," *American Political Science Review,* 52 (1958), 1066-1077; Henry J. Tomasek, "North Dakota's Advent as a Two Party System," *North Dakota Quarterly,* 30 (1966), 57-61; Joseph B. Tucker, "The Administration of a State Patronage System: The Democratic Party in Illinois," *Western Political Quarterly,* 22 (1969), 79-84.

We have divided studies of individual states into those which use intrastate subdivisions as observations for hypothesis testing and those which focus on functional mechanisms in the states (such as the legislature and political parties). There is also a listing of works that present more complete overviews of state systems. The great problem with these studies is that they tend to cluster on the more populous states. California: Winston W. Crouch, John C. Bellens, and Stanley Scott, *California Government and Politics* (Englewood Cliffs, New Jersey, 4th ed., 1967); Joseph Pratt Harris, *California Politics* (Stanford, 1961); William M. Leiter, *California Government: Issues and Institutions* (Pacific Palisades, 1971); John R. Owens, Edmond Constantini, and Louis F. Weschler, *Politics and Parties in California* (London, 1970). Colorado: Curtis Martin and Rudolph Gomez, *Colorado Government and Politics* (Boulder, 1964). Illinois: Austin Ranney, *Illinois Politics* (New York, 1960). Kentucky: Malcolm E. Jewell and Everette W. Cunningham, *Kentucky Politics* (Lexington, Kentucky, 1968). Louisiana: Allan P. Sindler, *Huey Long's Louisiana: State Politics, 1920-1952* (Baltimore, 1956). Maine: David B. Walker, *A Maine Profile: Some Conditioners of Her Political System* (Bureau for Research in Municipal Government, Bowdoin College, Brunswick, Maine, 1964). Massachusetts: Earl Latham and George Goodwin, Jr., *Massachusetts Politics* (Tufts Civic Education Center, Tufts University, Medford, Massachusetts, rev. ed., 1960); Edgar Litt, *The Political Cultures of Massachusetts* (Cambridge, Massachusetts, 1965). Michigan: Floyd C. Fischer, *The Government of Michigan* (Boston, 1965). Minnesota: G. Theodore Mitau, *Politics in Minnesota* (Minneapolis, 1960). New Mexico: Jack E. Holmes, *Politics in New Mexico* (Albuquerque, 1967). New York: Warren Moscow, *Politics in the Empire State* (New York, 1948); Ralph Straelz and Frank J. Munger, *New York Politics* (New York, 1960). North Carolina: Jack D. Fleer, *North Carolina Politics: An Introduction* (Chapel Hill, 1968). Pennsylvania: Edward F. Cooke and Edward G. Janosik, *Pennsylvania Politics* (New York, rev. ed., 1965). South Dakota: Alan L. Clem, *Prairie State Politics: Popular Democracy in South Dakota* (Public Affairs Press, Washington, D.C., 1967). Tennessee: Lee Seifert Greene and Robert Sterling Avery, *Government in Tennessee* (Knoxville, 2d ed., 1966). Texas: Clifton McCleskey, *The Gov-

ernment and Politics of Texas (Boston, 1969); Dan Nimmo and William E. Oden, *The Texas Political System* (Englewood Cliffs, New Jersey, 1971). Washington: Daniel M. Ogden, Jr. and Hugh A. Bone, *Washington Politics* (New York, 1960). Wisconsin: Leon D. Epstein, *Politics in Wisconsin* (Madison, 1958). Between 1954 and 1958 the Thomas Y. Crowell Company of New York published a series of books on various state governments emphasizing structure and administration. States covered were Delaware, Florida, Georgia, Illinois, Iowa, Mississippi, Montana, New Jersey, New York, North Carolina, Ohio, and Wyoming. For additional bibliographical information broken down state by state, see Charles R. Adrian, *State and Local Governments* (New York, 2d ed., 1967); and James W. Fesler, ed., *The 50 States and Their Local Governments* (New York, 1967).

The studies above focused on a single state's political system for the most part. There are also a number that are concerned with particular regions of the country. These works generally use the states within given regions as observations for the comparative analysis of broad theoretical constructs. The following are some of the better known books of this variety. In the East: Duane Lockard, *New England State Politics* (Princeton, 1959). In the South: Bernard Cosman, *Five States for Goldwater: Continuity and Change in Southern Presidential Voting Patterns* (University, Alabama, 1966); V. O. Key, Jr., *Southern Politics in State and Nation* (New York, 1949); and, more recently, William C. Havard, ed., *The Changing Politics of the South* (Baton Rouge, 1972). In the border states: John H. Fenton, *Politics in the Border States: A Study of the Patterns of Political Organization, and Political Change, Common to the Border States* (Hauser Press, New Orleans, 1957). In the Midwest: John H. Fenton, *Midwest Politics* (New York, 1966). In the West: Thomas C. Connelly, *Rocky Mountain Politics* (Albuquerque, 1959); and Frank H. Jonas, ed., *Western Politics* (Salt Lake City, 1961). As the pool of knowledge about state politics has grown, some scholars have begun to use the regional complex to observe more limited phenomena. See, for instance, Earl Black, "Southern Governors and Political Change: Campaign Stances on Racial Segregation and Economic Development, 1950–69," *Journal of Politics*, 33 (1971), 703-734; Eleanor Bushnell, ed., *Impact of Reapportionment on the Thirteen Western States*

(Salt Lake City, 1970); Robert Dishman and George Goodwin, Jr., *State Legislatures in New England Politics: Final Report* (New England Center for Continuing Education, Durham, New Hampshire, 1967); George Goodwin, Jr., and Victoria Schuck, eds., *Party Politics in the New England States* (New England Center for Continuing Education, Durham, New Hampshire, 1968); Malcolm E. Jewell, *Legislative Representation in the Contemporary South* (Durham, North Carolina, 1967); and Samuel C. Patterson, ed., *Midwest Legislative Politics* (Institute of Public Affairs, University of Iowa, Iowa City, 1967).

By expanding the number of observations to include all the American states, the field of comparative state politics has become fully horizontal and the major concern has shifted from description to prediction. The states themselves have become data points as scholars seek to test propositions about politics that transcend the limitations of individual or grouped state analysis. The development of this kind of effort seems to have sprung from two sources. In the early 1950's a lively interest in the concept of party responsibility stirred new concern in party competition in the states. Research began to appear designed to measure systematically intrastate party competition across a 48-state and then a 50-state spectrum. Some of these studies are Edward F. Cox, "The Measurement of Party Strength," *Western Political Quarterly*, 13 (1960), 1022-1042; Paul T. David, "How Can an Index of Competition Best Be Derived?" *Journal of Politics*, 34 (1972), 632-638; Robert T. Golembiewski, "A Taxonomic Approach to State Political Party Strength," *Western Political Quarterly*, 11 (1958), 494-513; Richard I. Hofferbert, "Classification of American State Party Systems," *Journal of Politics*, 26 (1964), 550-567; Malcolm E. Jewell, *The State Legislature: Politics and Practice* (New York, 1962); Austin Ranney and Willmoore Kendall, "The American Party Systems," *American Political Science Review*, 48 (1954), 477-485; David G. Pfeiffer, "The Measurement of Inter-Party Competition and Systemic Stability," *American Political Science Review*, 61 (1967), 457-467; Joseph A. Schlesinger, "A Two-Dimensional Scheme for Classifying the States According to Degree of Inter-Party Competition," *American Political Science Review*, 49 (1955), 1120-1128. For an evaluation of most of these articles see Richard E. Zody and Norman R. Luttbeg, "An Evaluation of Various Measures of State Party Competition," *Western Political Quarterly*, 21 (1968), 723-725. A second development that stimulated the growth of comparative state politics was the debate over reapportionment. It was first necessary to design indexes of malapportionment in the states. Accordingly, the following studies appeared: Alan L. Clem, "Measuring Legislative Malapportionment: In Search of a Better Yardstick," *Midwest Journal of Political Science*, 7 (1963), 125-144; Manning J. Dauer and Robert G. Kelsay, "Unrepresentative States," *National Municipal Review*, 44 (1955), 571-575, 587; Paul T. David and Ralph Eisenberg, *Devaluation of the Urban and Suburban Vote: A Statistical Investigation of Long-Term Trends in State Legislative Representation* (Bureau of Public Administration, University of Virginia, Charlottesville, 1961–62); National Municipal League, *Compendium on Legislative Apportionment: A Collection of Statistics and Appraisals from Local Non-Official Authorities in 50 States Relating to Inequalities in Legislative and Congressional Representation of Voters* (New York, 2d ed., 1962); Glendon Schubert and Charles Press, "Measuring Malapportionment," *American Political Science Review*, 58 (1964), 302-327; John P. White and Norman C. Thomas, "Urban and Rural Representation and State Legislative Apportionment," *Western Political Quarterly*, 17 (1964), 724-741. Studies matching these measures of malapportionment and party competition with various measures of public policy in the states include David Brady and Douglas Edmonds, "One Man, One Vote—So What?" *Transaction*, 4 (1967), 41-46; Thomas R. Dye, "Malapportionment and Public Policy in the States," *Journal of Politics*, 27 (1965), 586-601; Richard Hofferbert, "The Relation between Public Policy and Some Structural and Environmental Variables in the American States," *American Political Science Review*, 60 (1966), 73-82; Herbert Jacob, "The Consequences of Malapportionment: A Note of Caution," *Social Forces*, 43 (1964), 256-261; Allan G. Pulsipher and James L. Weatherby, Jr., "Malapportionment, Party Competition, and the Functional Distribution of Governmental Expenditures," *American Political Science Review*, 62 (1968), 1207-1219.

This vein of research soon exploded, as an array of independent variables were mustered to help explain fluctuations in the content of public policy outputs. Some of these are Charles F.

Cnudde and Donald J. McCrone, "Party Competition and Welfare Policies in the American States," *American Political Science Review,* 63 (1969), 858-866; Andrew T. Cowart, "Anti-Poverty Expenditures in the American States: A Comparative Analysis," *Midwest Journal of Political Science,* 13 (1969), 219-236; Richard E. Dawson, "Social Development, Party Competition and Policy," in *American Party Systems: Stages of Political Development,* ed. William Nisbet Chambers and Walter Dean Burnham (New York, 1967); Richard E. Dawson and James A. Robinson, "Inter-party Competition, Economic Variables, and Welfare Policies in the American States," *Journal of Politics,* 25 (1963), 265-289; Thomas R. Dye, "Inequality and Civil-Rights Policy in the States," *Journal of Politics,* 31 (1969), 1080-1097; Dye, "Executive Power and Public Policy in the States," *Western Political Quarterly,* 22 (1969), 926-939; Dye, "Income Inequality and American State Politics," *American Political Science Review,* 63 (1969), 157-162; Dye, *Politics, Economics, and the Public: Policy Outcomes in the American States* (Chicago, 1966); Robert S. Erikson, "The Relationship between Party Control and Civil Rights Legislation in the American States," *Western Political Quarterly,* 24 (1971), 178-182; Richard I. Hofferbert, "Ecological Development and Policy Change in the American States," *Midwest Journal of Political Science,* 10 (1966), 464-483; Hofferbert, "Elite Influence in State Policy Formation: A Model for Comparative Inquiry," *Polity,* 2 (1970), 316-344; Herbert Jacob and Michael Lipsky, "Outputs, Structure, and Power: An Assessment of Changes in the Study of State and Local Politics," *Journal of Politics,* 30 (1968), 510-538; Ira Sharkansky, "Economic and Political Correlates of State Government Expenditures: General Tendencies and Deviant Cases," *Midwest Journal of Political Science,* 11 (1967), 173-192; Sharkansky, "Economic Development, Representative Mechanisms, Administrative Professionalism and Public Policies: A Comparative Analysis of Within-State Distributions of Economic and Political Traits," *Journal of Politics,* 33 (1971), 112-132; Sharkansky, "Economic Theories of Public Policy: Resource-Policy and Need-Policy Linkages between Income and Welfare Benefits," *Midwest Journal of Political Science,* 15 (1971), 722-740; Sharkansky, "Government Expenditures and Public Services in the American States," *American Political Sci-*

ence Review, 61 (1967), 1066-1077; Sharkansky, "Regionalism, Economic Status and Public Policies of the American States," *Southwestern Social Science Quarterly,* 49 (1968), 9-26; Sharkansky, *Spending in the American States* (Chicago, 1968); Ira Sharkansky and Richard I. Hofferbert, "Dimensions of State Politics, Economics, and Public Policy," *American Political Science Review,* 63 (1969), 867-879; Jack L. Walker, "The Diffusion of Innovations among the American States," *American Political Science Review,* 63 (1969), 880-899.

As the field expands hypotheses other than output assessment are being explored, and there have been valuable attempts to firm up measures of both dependent and independent variables. See Charles M. Bonjean and Robert L. Lineberry, "The Urbanization-Party Competition Hypothesis: A Comparison of All United States Counties," *Journal of Politics,* 32 (1970), 305-321; John Crittenden, "Dimensions of Modernization in the American States," *American Political Science Review,* 61 (1967), 989-1001; Daniel J. Elazar, *American Federalism: A View from the States* (New York, 1966). Elazar's work on comparative political culture in the states is a landmark and provides rich insights that are especially provocative for building explanatory models for state policy making. See also Wayne L. Francis, "A Profile of Legislator Perceptions of Interest Group Behavior Relating to Legislative Issues in the States," *Western Political Quarterly,* 24 (1971), 702-712; Francis, *Legislative Issues in the Fifty States: A Comparative Analysis* (Chicago, 1967); Richard I. Hofferbert, "Socioeconomic Dimensions of the American States: 1890–1900," *Midwest Journal of Political Science,* 12 (1968), 401-418; Hugh L. LeBlanc, "Voting in State Senates: Party and Constituency Influences," *Midwest Journal of Political Science,* 13 (1969), 33-57. LeBlanc's study is a good example of how intrastate testing of an hypothesis (the massive literature on influences on legislative voting) has provided a stimulant for interstate comparative analysis. See also Norman R. Luttbeg, "Classifying the American States: An Empirical Attempt to Identify Internal Variations," *Midwest Journal of Political Science,* 15 (1971), 703-721; Ira Sharkansky, "Economic Development, Regionalism and State Political Systems," *Midwest Journal of Political Science,* 12 (1968), 41-61; Sharkansky, "Agency Requests, Gubernatorial Support and Budget

Success in State Legislatures," *American Political Science Review*, 62 (1968), 1220-1231; Gerald E. Sullivan, "Incremental Budget-Making in the American States: A Test of the Anton Model," *Journal of Politics*, 34 (1972), 639-647. Sullivan has demonstrated the great potential for the use of the comparative state method in the area of pure output analysis. J. Stephen Turett, "The Vulnerability of American Governors, 1900-1966," *Midwest Journal of Political Science*, 15 (1971), 108-132; this study compares the nineteen most competitive states.

Other Literature Consulted

Since the dominant pattern of population movement in America after closing of the rural land frontier was urbanization, anyone interested in understanding the nature of rural America will need to deal with the literature of urbanization as process and therefore (if we accept the "zero-sum" logic) the deruralization of America. Moreover, since this book argues that the isolation of "rural" and "urban" as constructs with analytical value is becoming disfunctional, it is also necessary to deal with both phenomena in their own right. In understanding urbanism as a dynamic in general, the following works are especially helpful: Nels Anderson and K. Ishwaran, *Urban Sociology* (New York, 1965); Paul K. Hatt and Albert J. Reiss, Jr., eds., *Cities and Society: The Revised Reader in Urban Sociology* (Glenco, Illinois, 2d ed., 1957); Kingsley Davis, "The Origin and Growth of Urbanization in the World," *American Journal of Sociology*, 60 (1955), 429-437; Lewis Mumford, *The City in History: Its Origins, Its Transformations, and Its Prospects* (New York, 1961); Louis Wirth, "Urbanism as a Way of Life," *American Journal of Sociology*, 44 (1938), 1-24. Studies that focus on urbanism as process in the United States are Donald J. Bogue, "Urbanism in the United States, 1950," *American Journal of Sociology*, 60 (1955), 471-486; William Edward Leuchtenburg, *The Perils of Prosperity, 1914–32* (Chicago, 1958); Blake McKelvey, *The Urbanization of America, 1860–1915* (New Brunswick, New Jersey, 1963); Joseph S. Vandiver, "Urbanization and Urbanism in the U.S.," *International Journal of Comparative Sociology*, 4 (1963), 259-273; William H. Whyte, *The Last Landscape* (Garden City, New York, 1968); Robert C. Wood, "Metropolitan Government, 1975: An Extrapolation of Trends—The New Metropolis: Green Belts, Grass Roots or Gargantua?" *American Political Science Review*, 52 (1958), 108-122.

In dealing with the other end of the rural-urban continuum, there is a paucity of up-to-date literature. One of the best methods to undertake to study rural society and politics is to consult the indexes for the *Journal of Rural Sociology*, the official journal of the Rural Sociological Society published at the University of Illinois, Urbana, in which will be found a wealth of scholarship, much of it dealing with politics and government. To supplement it there are many works in the field of rural sociology that are helpful. Among them are James H. Copp, ed., *Our Changing Rural Society: Perspectives and Trends* (Ames, Iowa, 1964); J. H. Kolb and Edmund deS. Brunner, *A Study of Rural Society: Its Organization and Changes* (Boston, 1935); Paul H. Landis, *Rural Life in Process* (New York, 1940); Everett M. Rogers, *Social Change in Rural Society: A Textbook in Rural Sociology* (New York, 1960); Walter L. Slocum, *Agricultural Sociology: A Study of Sociological Aspects of American Farm Life* (New York, 1962); Lee Taylor and Arthur R. Jones, Jr., *Rural Life and Urbanized Society* (New York, 1964). The most recent book dealing specifically with rural government is Lane W. Lancaster, *Government in Rural America* (New York, 1952). The only avenue open to study the traditional American rural political system in light of current model building and hypothesis construction is, of course, political history. A recent indication that this may be a rewarding area of scholarship is Don S. Kirschner, *City and Country: Rural Response to Urbanism in the 1920s* (Westport, Connecticut, 1970). More work of this kind is needed. Another way of dealing with rural politics is through the study of the small community. Representative examples of this approach are Charles Freeman and Selz C. Mayo, "Decision Makers in Rural Community Action," *Social Forces*, 35 (1957), 319-322; Granville Hicks, *Small Town* (New York, 1946); John H. Kolb, *Emerging Rural Communities: Group Relations in Rural Society—A Review of Wisconsin Research in Action* (Madison, 1959); Arthur J. Vidich and Joseph Bensman, *Small Town in Mass Society: Class, Power, and Religion in a Rural Community* (Princeton, rev. ed., 1968).

Spurred by the debate over reapportionment, much scholarship dealing with rural politics is presented in a way in which rural areas and urban areas are perceived to be at war with one another. See Gordon E. Baker, *Rural vs. Urban Political Power: The Nature and Consequences of Unbalanced Representation* (Garden City, New York, 1955); Harlan Hahn, *Urban-Rural Conflict: The Politics of Change* (Beverly Hills, California, 1971); Murray C. Havens, *City versus Farm: Urban-Rural Conflict in the Alabama Legislature* (University, Alabama, 1957). Hahn's study of Iowa does not seem to justify the title and tends to verify the observation that we are too quick to assume the conflict syndrome as a given in rural-urban politics. At any rate, there is a wide literature on the reapportionment revolution which is helpful in understanding rural politics. See Gordon E. Baker, *The Reapportionment Revolution: Representation, Political Power, and the Supreme Court* (New York, 1966); Howard D. Hamilton, ed., *Reapportioning Legislatures: A Consideration of Criteria and Computers* (Columbus, Ohio, 1966); Malcolm E. Jewell, ed., *The Politics of Reapportionment* (New York, 1962); Robert B. McKay, *Reapportionment Reappraised* (New York, 1968); Glendon Schubert, ed., *Reapportionment* (New York, 1965).

In dealing with the rural politics of the future I have tried to make the point that our traditional views of the rural-urban-rural continuum need revision. The following are sources that deal with this topic: Howard Becker, "Sacred and Secular Societies Considered with Reference to Folk-State and Similar Classifications," *Social Forces,* 28 (1950), 361-376; Howard W. Beers, "Rural-Urban Differences: Some Evidence from Public Opinion Polls," *Rural Sociology,* 18 (1953), 1-11; Charles M. Bonjean and Robert L. Lineberry, "Size-of-Place Analysis: Another Reconsideration," *Western Political Quarterly,* 24 (1971), 713-718; Richard Dewey, "The Rural-Urban Continuum: Real but Relatively Unimportant," *American Journal of Sociology,* 66 (1960), 60-66; Otis Dudley Duncan and Albert J. Reiss, Jr., *Social Characteristics of Urban and Rural Communities* (New York, 1956); Robert S. Friedman, "The Urban-Rural Conflict Revisited," *Western Political Quarterly,* 14 (1961), 481-495; Jane Jacobs, *The Economy of Cities* (New York, 1969); Herbert Kötler, "Changes in Urban-Rural Relationships in Industrial Society," *International Journal of Comparative Sociology*, 4 (1963), 121-129; Sidney W. Mintz, "The Folk-Urban Continuum and the Rural Proletarian Community," *American Journal of Sociology*, 59 (1953), 136-143; Deane E. Neubauer, "Some Conditions of Democracy," *American Political Science Review*, 61 (1967), 1002-1009; Irving A. Spaulding, "Serendipity and the Rural-Urban Continuum," *Rural Sociology*, 16 (1951), 29-36; Charles T. Stewart, Jr., "The Urban-Rural Dichotomy: Concepts and Uses," *American Journal of Sociology*, 64 (1958), 152-158. One of the best sources on this literature is chapter two of T. D. McDee's *The Urbanization Process in the Third World* (London, 1971). Our failure to understand the nature of politics in rural America is caused at least partially by the fact that we seem to have identified ruralism with peasantry. My views of American rural culture and its connection with the city have been influenced by the work of Robert Redfield. See Robert Redfield, *Peasant Society and Culture: An Anthropological Approach to Civilization* (Chicago, 1956); Redfield, *The Little Community: Viewpoints for the Study of a Human Whole* (Chicago, 1955); Redfield, *The Primitive World and Its Transformations* (Ithaca, New York, 1953). See also Jack M. Potter, May N. Diaz, and George M. Foster, eds., *Peasant Society: A Reader* (Boston, 1967).

Attempts to understand the linkages between the rural-urban dichotomy, technology, and government have been aided with the following sources: Nigel Calder, *Technopolis: Social Control of the Uses of Science* (New York, 1970); Harvey Cox, *The Secular City: Secularization and Urbanization in Theological Perspective* (New York, rev. ed., 1966); Karl W. Deutsch, *The Nerves of Government: Models of Political Communication and Control* (New York, 1963); John Diebold, *Automation: Its Impact on Business and Labor* (National Planning Association, Washington, D.C., 1959); Jacques Ellul, *The Technological Society* (New York, 1964); Victor C. Ferkiss, *Technological Man: The Myth and the Reality* (New York, 1969); Marvin Fisher, *Workshops in the Wilderness: The European Response to American Industrialization, 1830–1860* (New York, 1967); Friedrich Juenger, *The Failure of Technology: Perfection without Purpose* (Hinsdale, Illinois, 1949); Leo Marx, *The Machine in the Garden: Technology and the Pastoral Ideal in America* (New

York, 1964); Morris H. Philipson, ed., *Automation: Implications for the Future* (New York, 1962); Carl F. Stover, *The Technological Order* (Detroit, 1963); Alexis de Tocqueville, *Democracy in America* (London, 1900); E. A. Wilkening, "The Process of Acceptance of Technological Innovations in Rural Society," in A. L. Bertrand, ed., *Rural Sociology: An Analysis of Contemporary Rural Life* (New York, 1958).

Although this book does not precisely follow a system format, the methodological thrust has been influenced by the systems approach to functional analysis and by a faith in the comparative technique. The following literature speaks to these concerns: David Easton, *A Systems Analysis of Political Life* (New York, 1965); Easton, *The Political System: An Inquiry into the State of Political Science* (New York, 1953); A. James Gregor, "Political Science and the Uses of Functional Analysis," *American Political Science Review*, 62 (1968), 425-439; Theodore Lowi, "Toward Functionalism in Political Science: The Case of Innovation in Party Systems," *American Political Science Review*, 57 (1963), 570-583; Adam Przeworski and Henry Teune, *The Logic of Comparative Sociological Inquiry* (New York, 1970); Howard A. Scarrow, "The Function of Political Parties: A Critique of the Literature and the Approach," *Journal of Politics*, 29 (1967), 770-790; Frank Sorauf, *Party Politics in America* (Boston, 1968). More specific techniques of data analysis, especially cluster-bloc analysis, are covered in the following works: Lee F. Anderson, Meredith W. Watts, Jr., and Allen R. Wilcox, *Legislative Roll-Call Analysis* (Evanston, Illinois, 1966); Herman C. Beyle, *Identification and Analysis of Attribute-Cluster-Blocs: A Technique for Use in the Investigation of Behavior in Governance, Including Report on Identification and Analysis of Blocs in a Large Non-Partisan Legislative Body, the 1927 Session of the Minnesota State Senate* (Chicago, 1931); Aage R. Clausen, "The Measurement of Legislative Group Behavior," *Midwest Journal of Political Science*, 11 (1967), 212-224; John C. Grumm, "The Systematic Analysis of Blocs in the Study of Legislative Behavior," *Western Political Quarterly*, 18 (1965), 350-362; J. L. Hodges, Jr., and E. L. Lehmann, *Basic Concepts of Probability and Statistics* (San Francisco, 2d ed., 1970); Arend Lijphart, "The Analysis of Bloc Voting in the General Assembly: A Critique and a Proposal,"

American Political Science Review, 57 (1963), 902-917; Dennis
J. Palumbo, *Statistics in Political and Behavioral Science* (New
York, 1969); Stuart A. Rice, *Quantitative Methods in Politics*
(New York, 1928); Bruce M. Russett, "Discovering Voting
Groups in the United Nations," *American Political Science Re-
view*, 60 (1966), 327-339; Peter Willetts, "Cluster-Bloc Analysis
and Statistical Inference," *American Political Science Review*,
66 (1972), 569-582.

Vermont

The best general historical treatment of the events that shaped
Vermont's past is Earle Williams Newton's *The Vermont Story:
A History of the People of the Green Mountain State, 1749-
1949* (Vermont Historical Society, Montpelier, 1949). It is well
written, complete, offers an extensive bibliography, and contains a valuable section on government and politics. Other useful sources are Walter Hill Crockett, *Vermont, The Green Mountain State* (Century History Company, New York, 1921);
Hiland Hall, *The History of Vermont from Its Discovery to Its
Admission into the Union in 1791* (J. Munsell, Albany, New
York, 1868); Matt Bushnell Jones, *Vermont in the Making,
1750-1777* (Cambridge, Massachusetts, 1939); Miner C. Thompson, *Independent Vermont* (Boston, 1942); Zadock Thompson,
*History of the State of Vermont from Its Earliest Settlement to
the Close of the Year 1832* (Burlington, 1833); Frederic Frank-
lyn Van de Water, *Reluctant Republic: Vermont, 1724-1791*
(New York, 1941); Chilton Williamson, *Vermont in Quandary,
1763-1825* (Vermont Historical Society, Montpelier, 1949).

Other studies that treat particular periods of Vermont history by focusing on more isolated phenomena are (listed in
chronological order): David M. Ludlum, *Social Ferment in Vermont, 1791-1850* (New York, 1939); Neil Adams McNall,
"Anti-Slavery Sentiment in Vermont," (M.A. thesis, University
of Vermont, Burlington, 1938); Edward P. Brynn, "Vermont's
Political Vacuum of 1845-1856 and the Emergence of the Republican Party," *Vermont History*, 38 (1970), 113-123; George
A. Benedict, *Vermont in the Civil War: A History of the Part
Taken by the Vermont Soldiers and Sailors in the War for the*

Union, 1861–65 (Burlington, 1886–88); Bartley Costello, III, "Vermont in the Civil War," *Vermont History,* 29 (1961), 220-226; Alvin P. Stauffer, "Douglas in Vermont," *Vermont History,* 28 (1960), 256-267; Seymour T. Bassett, "Urban Penetration of Rural Vermont," (Ph.D. dissertation, Harvard University, Cambridge, 1952); John B. O'Brien, "Vermont Fathers of Wisconsin," *Vermont History,* 16 (1948), 74-82; Lewis D. Stilwell, *Migration from Vermont* (Vermont Historical Society, Montpelier, 1937); Mason A. Green, *Nineteen-Two in Vermont: The Fight for Local Option Ten Years After* (Rutland City Press, Rutland, 1912). Green's book covers the decision to allow Vermont towns to "go wet" (the local option on the sale of liquor). See also Winston Allen Flint, *The Progressive Movement in Vermont* (American Council on Public Affairs, Washington, D.C., 1941); Alon Jeffrey, "Vermont's Pastor-Politician: Fraser Metzger and the Bull Moose Campaign of 1912," *Vermont History,* 38 (1970), 58-69; and Richard Judd, "The History of the New Deal in Vermont" (Ph.D. dissertation, Harvard University, Cambridge, 1959).

There is a wealth of commentary on Vermont that combines socioeconomic, political, and cultural history and speaks generally to the nature of the state's political culture. A portion of it includes George D. Aiken, *Speaking from Vermont* (New York, 1938); Seymour T. Bassett, ed., *Outsiders inside Vermont* (Brattleboro, 1967); Ray Bearse, rev. and enlarged by, *Vermont: A Guide to the Green Mountain State* (Boston, 2d ed. rev., 1966); Charles Edward Crane, *Let Me Show You Vermont* (New York, 1937); Bernard DeVoto, "How to Live among the Vermonters," *Harper's Monthly Magazine,* 173 (1936), 333-336; Walter Hard, *The Connecticut* (New York, 1947); Ralph Nading Hill, *Contrary Country, A Chronicle of Vermont* (Brattleboro, 2d ed., 1961); Hill, *The Winooski—Heartway of Vermont* (New York, 1949); and Hill, *Yankee Kingdom: Vermont and New Hampshire* (New York, 1960). Hill's books are to my mind the most enjoyable and useful commentaries on Vermont historical lore and culture in print. See also William Storrs Lee, *The Green Mountains of Vermont* (New York, 1955); Bert McCord, "The Passing of the Hill Farmer," *The New England Guide* (annual, 1968–69); Noel Perrin, "The Two Faces of Vermont," in Bassett, pp. 123-130; Harris E. Thurber, "Some Values of the Vermont Community—Part I," *Vermont History*, 25 (1957), 194-214; Thurber, "Some Values of the Vermont Community—Part II," *Vermont History*, 25 (1957), 292-314; and Harold Fisher Wilson, *The Hill Country of Northern New England: Its Social and Economic History, 1790–1930* (New York, 1936).

The following are sources that deal more specifically with Vermont politics and government. First of all we are lucky in having the works of Andrew Nuquist. Although they are not concerned directly with matters of politics, Nuquist's two volumes on governmental structure in Vermont are profoundly thorough. See his *Town Government in Vermont* (Burlington, 1964); and Nuquist and Edith W. Nuquist, *Vermont State Government and Administration: An Historical and Descriptive Study of the Living Past* (Governmental Research Center, University of Vermont, Burlington, 1966). Another source that deals with Vermont's governmental system is a series of readings: Rolf N. B. Haugen and E. William Steele, eds., *Vermont—The 14th Original State: Background Papers and Final Report* (Burlington Clearing House, University of Vermont and State Agricultural College, Burlington, 1959). The most useful current source on governmental structure is the League of Women Voters of Vermont's Guide to Vermont Government; see Kathryn D. Wendling, ed., *Vermont Citizens' Guide* (Burlington, 3d ed., 1972).

Despite some difficulties with it, the best summary of Vermont politics prior to 1955 is Duane Lockard's *New England State Politics* (Princeton, 1959). Without this volume, Vermont would have gone substantially unnoticed by the cadres of scholars of comparative state politics developed since 1945. Another valuable source on Vermont, especially in terms of the recruitment function, is Joseph A. Schlesinger's *How They Became Governor: A Study of Comparative State Politics, 1870–1950* (Government Research Bureau, Michigan State University, East Lansing, 1957). Sociologist Frederick J. Maher, Jr., has provided a highly useful treatment of Vermont's electoral system which contains interesting commentary on certain hypotheses of V. O. Key and John Fenton. Frederick J. Maher, Jr., "Vermont Elections" (Ph.D. dissertation, Columbia University, New York, 1969). The era of breakthrough politics in Vermont (1948–54) is well treated in Douglas I. Hodgkin, "Breakthrough

Elections: Elements of Large and Durable Minority Gains in Selected States since 1944" (Ph.D. dissertation, Duke University, Durham, North Carolina, 1966).

Studies dealing with the party system are George Goodwin, Jr., and Victoria Schuck, eds., *Party Politics in the New England States* (New England Center for Continuing Education, Durham, New Hampshire, 1968); David R. Mayhew, *Two-Party Competition in the New England States* (Bureau of Government Research, University of Massachusetts, Amherst, 1967); George T. Mazuzan, "Vermont's Traditional Republicanism Vs. the New Deal: Warren R. Austin and the Election of 1934," *Vermont History*, 39 (1971), 128-141; Samuel L. Miller, "The Vermont Democratic Party and the Development of Intra-Party Responsibility" (M.A. thesis, University of Vermont, Burlington, 1960); and Sarah Q. Tompson, "The Formation of the Republican Party in Vermont" (M.A. thesis, University of Vermont, Burlington, 1952).

Studies dealing with the legislature are Henry P. Brubaker, "Fractional Behavior in the Vermont Senate" (Ph.D. dissertation, Syracuse University, 1970); Frank M. Bryan, "Who Is Legislating?" *National Civic Review*, 56 (1967), 627-633, 644; Bryan, "The Metamorphosis of a Rural Legislature," *Polity*, 1 (1968), 191-212; Daniel B. Carroll, *The Unicameral Legislature of Vermont* (Vermont Historical Society, Montpelier, 1933); Robert B. Dishman and George Goodwin, Jr., *State Legislatures in New England Politics: Final Report* (New England Center for Continuing Education, Durham, New Hampshire, 1967); Walter Hard, "King Reid," *Vermont Life*, 6 (1947), 28-29; Oliver Garceau and Corinne Silverman, "A Pressure Group and the Pressured: A Case Report," *American Political Science Review*, 48 (1954), 672-691; Vic Maerki, "A Vermont House Gets Remodeled," *Reporter*, 33 (October 7, 1965), 38-39; and William Jay Smith, "My Poetic Career in Vermont Politics," *Harper's Magazine*, 228 (January, 1964), 54-62.

Other sources on Vermont politics are Elin L. Anderson, *We Americans: A Study of Cleavage in an American City* (Cambridge, Massachusetts, 1937); Frank M. Bryan, "Reapportionment and the Vermont Town," *Rural Vermonter*, 2 (Spring, 1964), 6-10; Bryan, "Town Meeting Government Still Supported in Vermont," *National Civic Review*, 61 (1972), 348-

351; Robert V. Daniels, Robert H. Daniels, and Helen L. Daniels, "The Vermont Constitutional Referendum of 1969: An Analysis," *Vermont History*, 38 (1970), 152-156; William S. Ellis, "The Loneliest Governor," *Reporter*, 28 (April 25, 1963), 45; Lyman Jay Gould and Samuel B. Hand, "The Geography of Political Recruitment in Vermont: A View from the Mountains," in Reginald L. Cook, ed., *Growth and Development of Government in Vermont* (Vermont Academy of Arts and Sciences, Occasional Paper No. 5, Waitsfield, 1970); Louis Lisman, "The Direct Primary in Vermont" (M.A. thesis, University of Vermont, Burlington, 1932); Edmund C. Mower, "Administrative Reorganization in Vermont," in "Legislative Notes and Reviews" edited by Walter F. Dodd, *American Political Science Review*, 18 (1924), 96-102; John A. Neuenschwander, "An Engineer for Governor: James Hartness in 1920," *Vermont History*, 38 (1970), 139-149; Andrew Nuquist, "March Meeting," *Vermont Life*, 6 (1947), 4-7; Edwin C. Rozwenc, "Agriculture and Politics in the Vermont Tradition," *Vermont Quarterly*, 17 (1949), 81-96; Rozwenc, "The Group Basis of Vermont Farm Politics, 1870–1945," *Vermont History*, 25 (1957), 268-287; Roul Tunley, "The Democrat That Took Vermont," *Saturday Evening Post*, 236 (November 23, 1963), 82-84; and Melvin S. Wax, "Vermont's New Dealing Yankee," *Nation*, 168 (1949), 659-660.

In terms of political data sources, *The Vermont Yearbook* published annually by the National Survey in Chester, Vermont, provides one of the best town-by-town listings of SES indicators available. It also contains a storehouse of names and addresses for party, interest group, and bureaucratic leadership in Vermont. Political data of great variety and value are also found in State of Vermont, *Vermont House and Senate Journals* (Montpelier); and State of Vermont, Secretary of State, *Vermont Legislative Directory and State Manual* (Montpelier). These two sources alone cover the process of daily legislating, committee assignments, legislative voting results (including roll calls), voting results for all major statewide elected officers (primary and general elections), referenda results, and biographical sketches of all legislative, executive, judicial, and bureaucratic personnel.

Index

not easily attributed to a particular faction, 108; innovative policy changes enacted during era of, 109; *1964* and *1966* victories, 109; relation of town size to *1966* victory, 112; socioeconomic factors not related to *1966* victory, 112; relation of victory of to Humphrey vote, 112, 113; analysis of supporters of, 112-13; loses campaign for Prouty's U. S. Senate seat, 113-14; limitations of victory, 114; supports Robert Kennedy, 114; antiwar involvement, 115, 116; rejected in Winooski and by natives and large towns, 115; *1970* primary against Bove, 115; analysis of *1970* supporters of, 115-16; *1970* loss, 116; television impedes victory, 118-19; clusters of House Democrats in era of, 146-51; final term of, spawns regional alignments, 150-51; introduces first executive program since Civil War, 166; cohesion during era of, 166-67, 169; party competition during era of, 167; IPL during era of, 167; voting patterns after administration of, 188; issues emphasized, 189, 190; fewer education bills, 190; morality bills, 190
Hofferbert, Richard, 69
Holland, parkway vote in, 220
Homogeneity. *See* Cohesion, Party cohesion
Horse racing. *See* Morality bills
House of Representatives: description of average member, 31; committee chairmen compared with whole House, 32; Grangers in, 32; Masons in, 32, 144; effect of reapportionment on biographical characteristics of members, 51-54; members accept Senate appointments, 56; slow changes in nature of membership, 57; apprenticeship in, 62-63; Mountain Rule ineffective on selection of speaker, 65; biographical components, 66; malapportionment, 130-32; Burlington delegates increase after reapportionment, 133; clusters of Democrats in, 140, 144; absence of blocs at high cohesion levels, 145-46; farmer legislators from Champlain Valley, 145; blocs of native and freshmen legislators, 145; bloc structure, *1964–68*, 146-51; clusters of Republicans and Democrats in Hoff era, 146-51; effect of reapportionment on blocs, 147; break-up of blocs, 150; level of agreement, 154, 158; rural-urban alignments during Davis era, 154; Democratic cohesion, 159; clusters, 159-61; Index of Party Likeness, 164-65; conflict over fish and game, 183, 188; conflict over conservation,

forestry, and morality bills, 185, 188; conflict over highways, 185; conflict over taxes, 185, 189; kills parkway bill, 208; parkway vote analyzed, 209-15; characteristics of office holders before reapportionment, 209; Catholics vote on parkway, 209-10. *See also* Legislators, Representatives
Housing. *See* Fair housing bill
Hubbardton, Vermont regiment in rear guard action at, 10
Humphrey, Hubert, relation of *1968* vote to Hoff vote, 112, 113
Hunter, Floyd, power-elite theory of, 20

Idaho, party competition in, 72
Illinois: lawyer legislators in, 42; malapportioned legislature in, 180; cohesion in, 183
Immigration: escapees from Congregationalism and land speculators settle Vermont, 7; decreases, 13; encourage and discouraged, 252-53; discouraged, 254, 259, 260. *See also* Summer people
Income: state, farming prime source of, 12; state, relation to farm income, 38; farm, relation to farmer representation, 39; nonagricultural, relation to lawyer legislators, 41-42
Incumbency, power to ensure reelection, 62-63
Independent Party, formed by Crispe, 106
Index of Bloc Agreement, 138-39, 167, 274, 276. *See also* Agreement
Index of Cohesion, 195. *See also* Cohesion
Index of Likeness, 195
Index of Party Likeness (IPL), 196-97; in House, 164-65; variations as party strength changes, 164; of Democrats, drops in *1964*, 164, 166; variations after reapportionment, 166, 167, 171; during Hoff administration, 167; in *1960's* and *1970's*, 171
Indiana, lawyer legislators in, 42
Induction. *See* Analysis, inductive
Industrial revolution, skips Vermont, causing service-oriented agenda, 252-53, 255
Industry, skilled, importance in Vermont, 14
Innovative party concept, of Lowi, 196
Inputs, economic, relation to political outputs, 3
Iowa: relation of urbanism and lawyer legislators in, 36; Wiggins studies minority party, 198-99; executive inspiration in, 198-99; innovative minority in, 199
Iron law of oligarchy, 31